WEALTH WELL-GIVEN

The Enterprise and Benevolence
of
Lord Nuffield

William Morris, Viscount Nuffield, 1938

WEALTH WELL-GIVEN

The Enterprise and Benevolence of Lord Nuffield

Edited by

F. John Minns

ALAN SUTTON PUBLISHING LTD

First published in the United Kingdom in 1994 by
Alan Sutton Publishing Ltd
Phoenix Mill · Far Thrupp · Stroud · Gloucestershire

First published in the United States of America by
Alan Sutton Publishing Inc · 83 Washington Street · Dover NH 03820

A catalogue record for this book is available from the British Library.

ISBN 0-7509-0656-1

Typeset in 10/13 New Baskerville
Typesetting and origination by
Alan Sutton Publishing Ltd.
Printed in Great Britain by
The Bath Press, Avon.

Contents

Illustrations

Contributors

A.H. Burfoot, BS, FNA
Guy's Hospital, London

Robert B. Duthie, CBE, MAMB, Ch.M, FRCS, FACS (Hon), DSc (Hon)
Nuffield Professor of Orthopaedic Surgery, University of Oxford

Colin Hill, BSc (Econ)
Motor industry economist

B. Huntley
Curator-Hostess of Nuffield Place (1964–73)

Air Chief Marshal Sir David Lee, GBE, CB
Chairman of the Governing Trustees of the Nuffield Trust for the Forces of
the Crown

Tony Lewin, BA
Motoring journalist

J.W. McAnuff, MA, Ph.D
Nuffield Foundation, Deputy Director (1973-82)

F. John Minns, FCIOB

Peter Morris, PhD, FRCS, FRACS, FACS (Hon)
Nuffield Professor of Surgery and Fellow of Balliol College, Oxford (1974–)

T.J.S. Patterson MD, MChir, FRCS
Clinical Lecturer in Plastic Surgery, University of Oxford (retrd)

Ken Revis, MBE
President, Bullnosed Morris Car Club

A.H.T. Robb-Smith, MA, MD, FRCS, FRCP
Former Nuffield Reader in Pathology, University of Oxford whilst Director
of Pathology, Radcliffe Infirmary

C.E. Rutherford, BA
Great-niece of Lord Nuffield

Dorothy Silberston, MA
Curator-Hostess of Nuffield Place (1973–)

M.K. Sykes, MA, MB, BChir FFARCS, Hon FFARCS, Hon FFA (S.A.)
Nuffield Professor of Anaesthetics, University of Oxford

Sir John Thomson, KBE, TD, Hon. DCL
Chairman, Barclays Bank plc (1962–73); High Sheriff, Oxon. (1957); Lord
Lieutenant, Oxon (1963–79); Chairman, Nuffield Medical Trustees
(1951–82); Curator, Oxford University Chest (1949–74)

Dame Janet Vaughan, DBE, FRSM (Hon), FRS
Principal, Somerville College, Oxford (1945–67); Nuffield Trustee

Sir D.J. Weatherall, MD, FRCP, FRCPE, FRS
Nuffield Professor of Clinical Medicine, University of Oxford (1974–92)
Regius Professor of Medicine

E.F. Webb, MA, MBE
President of BUPA

INTERLOCUTORS (CHAPTER 33)

Sir Alex Jarratt, CB, Hon DSc, D. Univ, Hon LLD
Chancellor, University of Birmingham

A.L. Rowse MA, DLitt, FBA
Emeritus Fellow of All Souls College, Oxford

Sam Toy, MA
Chairman, Ford Motor Company Ltd (1980-86)

All royalties

from this commemorative volume

will be donated to

Multiple Sclerosis research

and to charities for the blind.

Preface

To ensure credibility as the initiating contributor to this book I must begin by correcting a recurring mistake made in the national press and by several authors of books on the life of Lord Nuffield, including the first good biography, that by P.W.S. Andrews and Elizabeth Brunner, (1955). On page 36 it states that 'William Richard was the eldest of a family of seven but five died at an early age'. Yet facing page 65 of the same book is a Morris family photograph (*c.*1900) of *five adults* – on the left Alice, standing beside William, with their younger sister, Emily, seated alongside parents Frederick and Emily Ann Morris (see p. 5) The simple error was in failing to notice that neither of William's two sisters, both seen in the photograph to be adults, had died 'at an early age'. Each sister had three children; Alice's eldest being me, christened Frederick John after my maternal and paternal grandfathers, respectively. The strength of will in the Morris family again being apparent in which Christian name was to be the first!

However, such a repeatedly published mistake did, in past years, have one considerable advantage for me; it began to diminish the considerable number of requests that I was subjected to by persons and charities wishing to gain an introduction to my Uncle William, particularly during the period of his most prolific benefactions, when begging letters reached him in hundreds each day. Only close relatives of very generous benefactors will have experienced this understandable pressure. Very sadly, the future Lord Nuffield had no children, no son to succeed him in his life's work. He is reported to have said 'I have more money than any man can possibly want, and for what it is worth I have a title, but all that I have been dies when I die. That is my personal tragedy'. He was aware of the growing families of his two sisters; aware, yet not very avuncular. I am sure that being childless was his greatest sadness which explains much of his way of life: a void that may even have contributed a lot to his very success.

These last few words may need explaining to many readers who have not personally experienced the enormous pressure of an intensely demanding business life. A life at the very top so totally absorbs a man's brain-power, energy, and causes absence from home to such an extent that he becomes almost unaware of, or disinterested in, his family's activities or anything other than what, to him, is his most enchanting work. His working environment takes preference above his domestic life unless he is jolted into the realisation that a devotion to his wife and children is of equal or greater importance, and a compromise is reached, halving the working time to perhaps only 50 hours a week!

Had he been blessed with children, William R. Morris would, I am sure, have been just as caring a parent as, be assured, were his sisters and his fond mother, but he was not, and this very difference may well have caused his uniquely intense concentration upon his industrial empire, rather than a normal sharing of allegiance between parenthood and just being an industrialist of lesser stature. Such sharing could have been constraining to him – no millions to hospitals or university? – Perhaps, no one will ever know.

What is known, however, is that he lived a very quiet, unostentatious personal life of almost total devotion to his life's work – his virtual obsession, sleeping much less than most people, thinking deeply during what was always a very long working day. He was a lone thinker, never a committee or boardroom man, taking decisions personally and preferring to talk to individuals in his small office rather than in troublesome groups. I doubt whether any industrialist has ever packed so many, such beneficially employed, hours of work, into so many years of self-employment. On his eightieth birthday in 1957 he was asked by a television newsman what he thought of the proposed 40 hour working week – a provoking question. Lord Nuffield replied 'I believe that a Nation that wants to be in semi-retirement in this competitive world must abandon all hope of progress.' This typical comment can now be judged 35 years later.

F. John Minns

Acknowledgements

I have only gathered here a bouquet of other mens flowers, having given of mine but the thread to bind them.

MONTAIGNE

Those who have so kindly contributed full chapters or statements, mostly written with first-hand knowledge, have given an authentic insight into the enterprise and effective benevolence of the man they still see to be worthy of commendation. From them I have gathered *a bouquet of flowers* that make this book unique. That they have given their time to write personally is a tribute in itself to his memory: my grateful thanks is given to all, for this was my first objective, and, secondly, for their consequential contribution to the charities which, hopefully, the publication of this book will achieve with 'Nuffield' abundance.

When Lord Nuffield began in 1936 to donate his well earned fortune for much wider public purposes than hitherto it was the highly regarded medical faculty of the University of Oxford that he first very substantially endowed. Half a century later it has been seen to be timely to gather authentic acknowledgement of the ongoing social benefits that have resulted from his proven foresight.

So firstly I am grateful to the University of Oxford for a grant of £1,000 towards the cost of publication of this book. This grant was made in the light of Lord Nuffield's remarkable munificence to the University and to Nuffield College. The University does not consider that chapter 28 represents a full picture of this particular piece of history, as indeed it is not intended to be; for another account the reader is referred to chapter 6 (and in particular pp. 63–70) of *Economics, Politics and Social Studies in Oxford, 1900–1985* by Sir Norman Chester (Macmillan, 1986).

It is to Sir John Thomson KBE that I am most especially grateful for his constant encouragement supported by a very generous grant towards publishing costs. His chapter – giving a unique insight into his relationship with Lord Nuffield as friend and banker is of great interest.

To Air Chief Marshal Sir David Lee, GBE, a Trustee and Chairman of the

Executive Committee of the Nuffield Trust for the Forces of the Crown who personally contributed chapter 14 and to Brigadier Richard Elliot, Secretary of the Trust which substantially sponsored publication I am most grateful.

Dr Michael Ashley-Miller, Secretary of the Nuffield Provincial Hospitals Trust kindly furnished Trust records enabling Dr A.H.T. Robb-Smith, who knew Lord Nuffield, to write chapter 15 which the Trust well supported with a substantial grant, so doing much to make the book an authentic record.

When work on this book commenced I was encouraged by the then Deputy Director of the Nuffield Foundation, Miss Patricia Thomas and Dr John McAnuff, a former Assistant Director, who kindly wrote chapter 24 to both I am very grateful for that early help.

To Sir Ashley Ponsonby, Bt., Lord Lieutenant of Oxfordshire, I am also grateful for his especial assistance.

During the recent economic recession sponsorship has of necessity had to be scaled down considerably by all well-wishers, however willing to be of such support. I also tender appreciation to the following sponsors who have financially assisted: The Rover Group, The British United Provident Association, Grant Thorton, Barclays Bank and Guy's Hospital.

Without the help of my wife Enid and my enthusiastic grandson Kevin Minns, BSc it would not have been possible during late retirement to cope with the more than anticipated correspondence and extensive paperwork that the compilation of writings from so many contributors necessitated, so it is to them and to all contributors that most of the credit is due for the completion of this book.

F. John Minns

Introduction

The Public Orator of Oxford University, speaking in Latin to Encaenia at the presentation of an honorary Doctorate of Civil Law to Sir William Morris in 1931 said (when translated):

> Among miracles, he is himself the chief miracle;
> among movement he is the source of motion

Why such very high praise from the great university?

The phenomenal advance of Morris the motor magnate who had prospered beneath the Spires of Oxford had inspired scholarly hyperbole reserved to honour those of only the greatest merit.

What else but a miracle could have transformed that very young bicycle-shop proprietor, who was first in business as a college tenant of 48, High Street, Oxford, into this internationally acclaimed industrial giant . . . was Sir William Morris the same courageous Oxonian who, way back in 1913, had risked prosecution by illegally employing motor buses on the streets of Oxford, forcing the dithering City Council to end the scandal of a monopoly of antiquated, horse-drawn trams? Indeed this was the first instance of Morris's ability as a bold, decisive organizer. The University Orator's memory and learned eloquence had expressed this significant factor of Sir William's character so succinctly in those witty words ending, 'he is the source of motion'.

Yet although being acclaimed as a genius in the middle period of his life, this first scholarly accolade is now seen as having been but a prestigious curtain-raiser to the extensive accomplishments and great honours yet to come.

Three years later, in 1934, having been raised to the peerage with the title Lord Nuffield, he was fast becoming a 'household word' for generous affluence as Britain's greatest philanthropist. In 1938 he was honoured greatly again and became Viscount Nuffield.

Many men have amassed great wealth, few have so zealously devoted themselves to worthily distributing *throughout their lifetime virtually all of their wealth* to causes so thoroughly approved by the general public.

After years of giving money to improve hospitals, he was able to reach greater heights through meeting many eminent men and women in medical research and the advancement of national health. They became his trustees to the furtherance of many agreed objectives. Five Nuffield Professors of Oxford University Medical Departments have kindly recorded in this commemorative book not only the purpose of each careful donation but the achievements resulting from the expert employment of the resources so funded. His Nuffield Foundation and several other trusts have been appreciated throughout the Commonwealth. How did he achieve so much? Was it only hard work? Could anyone have done it? As Thomas Edison said: 'Genius is one per cent inspiration and ninety-nine per cent perspiration.'

A *genius,* as many have held William Richard Morris to be, for he certainly epitomized Edison's cryptically expressed insight by starting at the early age of sixteen to show that extraordinary strength of will and enterprise. Having served only 9 months of his apprenticeship he resigned to become self-employed with a working capital of less than five pounds.

Perspiration came first, from the inevitable toil when so committed and determined to succeed without delay. Long hours of work immediately became an agreeable way of life to the young 'employer', so absorbed in his own creativeness, first with bicycles, then motor bicycles, then motor cars in ever increasing numbers.

Inspiration spurred him on. Nothing deterred him, whatever the magnitude of his vision. Each inspiration meriting action needed to be investigated promptly and, if good, turned into practical use as quickly as possible to satisfy his determination.

Factories producing Morris cars by the million, MG sports cars, beloved by enthusiasts, Wolseley and Riley, both retained in British ownership, all brought fame and fortune to Lord Nuffield.

Thirty years after his passing in 1963 the contributors to this book seek to interest readers in not only just how fascinating and valuable was his life but how this ennobled industrialist, starting from square one, justifed the place being accorded to him in British history among famous politicians, scholars, writers, and scientists of this century.

Beginning in the first chapter to answer the question, 'How did it all happen?' the story starts early in his life when strong motivation stimulated his latent talents. The story ends when his two-fold rise to fame reached a final climax of acclaim in the last words of this book, as so graciously expressed by Her Majesty, Queen Elizabeth the Queen Mother.

F. John Minns

PART ONE

The Unsought Wealth

Chapter 1

The road to success

F. John Minns

FIRST IT WAS MOTIVATION

Talent in young people often remains inert when they lack a strong motivation to find within themselves such a hitherto undetected capability. When motivation does awaken latent skill or any exceptional ability then this inborn talent fosters an absorbing, almost obsessive, activity.

Will Morris, as he was known at the age of sixteen, had a strong motivation. His father Frederick Morris, had been suffering ill-health for some years and it was only too obvious to William that he might very soon have to be the principal bread-winner of the family.[1] He needed to start work to help his father.

Having first been motivated into discovering the skills of his hands and his instinctive mechanical ability while serving as an apprentice to a local cycle dealer and repairer, William R. Morris soon became very anxious to make much faster progress and, after 9 months' employment, was convinced that he was underpaid. His urge to better himself just could not be restrained, and when refused a pay rise of one a shilling a week he promptly resigned. He once said that even if he had been granted a rise, it is doubtful whether his days as an employee would have continued much longer, for he considered that he had learned enough to see that doing the same jobs himself, working for himself, would be much better paid. He had 'only' to find his 'own customers'. WRM would be a better boss, giving him better pay.

So with a capital of only four golden sovereigns and such tremendous confidence in his own ability, so very mature for his age at sixteen, he set up his first workshop in a small brick shed in the garden of his parents' house, 16, James Street, Oxford. He soon needed more space and was granted the use of one of the two front rooms of this 'double-fronted' terrace house as a store and showroom. The disadvantage of this arrangement being the need to carry his bicycles through the house to the

3

workshop, and this led, when prospects so allowed, to the renting of his first shop at 48, High Street, Oxford, opposite the University Examination Schools, right amongst the Colleges.

Good fortune had stepped in at an early stage in the substantial shape of the good Rector of St Clements Church, the Reverend Francis Pilcher, who needed an abnormally large and very strong pedal cycle. This reverend gentleman's kindly interest could have been the most significant confidence-booster to a young man who was to become an industrial genius.

The rector was apparently so impressed with the supremely confident ambition of the youthful entrepreneur that he placed an order with him for the first Morris vehicle, a pedal cycle with a strong 27" frame. Morris mass production of later years had a one-off beginning blessed by the Church!

The daily sight of the large rector on his large new Morris bicycle in Oxford soon brought further orders to young Morris, and his very long working days had begun. Incidentally, this first bicycle was re-purchased 45 years later by its proud maker, then Lord Nuffield. It was found to be in sound condition and was re-plated for exhibition at the car factory.

In 1894, unable to afford assistance at his garden workshop bench or being too young to seek a bank loan for the purchasing of component parts to make or repair bicycles, he was known to have ridden on his cycle the 60 miles to Birmingham quite often to ensure getting the best choice of parts he needed at the lowest cash price; having to keep his stock very low, for he could not then afford to buy in bulk or even modest quantity.

A useful contract that he secured from the local head postmaster was to service and repair the bicycles used by the many boys employed in those days to deliver telegrams in the district.

Business in the bicycle trade – sales, hire, and repairs – has always prospered in Oxford, being a university town. Students found the new models of the late 'nineties' to be the cheapest and easiest form of transport to and from their 'digs' (lodgings, to the uninitiated) on the level town streets. Rough roads, especially outside the central areas, ensured a continuous demand for the quick repair of punctures. Few Oxonians, the locals, liked to walk from the distant suburbs to work or school, or use the slow horse-trams, so the 'bike' had rapidly become a household necessity. Young Mr Morris prospered. He found that riding his own make of racing cycle and winning at popular bicycle race meetings was the cheapest way to advertise the excellence of his products. He became a prolific winner of county trophies and medals until the long working hours at his workshop bench stiffened his leg muscles, so he had to use the time more profitably doing even more work.

The first bicycle shop, High Street, Oxford.
[Nuffield Place collection]

Morris family group. (L. to R.) Emily, Alice, Frederick, William, Emily.

My mother, his sister Alice, acted as his diary keeper during his early days as a rather preoccupied worker in his workshop, reminding him frequently of appointments and helping with his correspondence. In return for such help he gave her an elaborate ebonite clock, of a style fashionable at the time, which he had won at a bicycle race; I have this now as a family heirloom.

In 1899, having decided that he must widen his custom beyond the dons, undergraduates, and locals of Oxford, he booked space to display his machines at the annual cycle exhibition in London. However, his workshop continued to be overstretched with orders, so his few employees were fully engaged with completing cycles for waiting customers. Three days before the London show the exhibition models were still unmade and Morris had to set to himself to get them made for dispatch. For two days and nights he worked almost unceasingly to complete them to his satisfaction and on the very early morning of the show he set off to London to take the expected orders. Being so desperately tired, he fell asleep on the Inner Circle of London Underground Railway and was eventually awakened by a station porter who insisted that he had passed that station four times.

His entry into manhood, as the nineteenth century was coming to an end, must have given this very young businessman much thought about his future prospects in a world rapidly turning from horse and railway transport to mechanized personal conveyance and the ability to explore the countryside at leisure.

His progress thus far had been steady, and it must have given him satisfaction to have provided such security for his parents, sisters, and himself. By his modest standards he was a fairly well-to-do young bachelor but this so slender affluence did not last long.

INTO A NEW CENTURY

Entry into a new century must have been an exhilarating period for William R. Morris, aged 22, now well established as the most prominent Oxford trader in bicycles in High Street, 'the most beautiful street in the world', and able to advertise himself in the *Kelly's Directory of Oxford* as:

W.R. MORRIS
Practical Cycle Maker and Repairer
48 HIGH STREET and 16 JAMES STREET
Sole Maker of the Celebrated Morris Cycle

When paying hard-earned money for an advertisement, even though so very small at 2" × 2", he must have believed that false modesty was to be avoided.

When more premises were rented just around the corner in Queen's Lane, he was able to vacate his original workshop at 16, James Street, the family home, which must have greatly pleased my good-natured grandmother who had always encouraged him while he was working in the garden shed.

Further expansion of the business followed in 1902, when the old livery stables at the junction of Holywell and Longwall, off the High Street, were rented, eventually to become the first of several Morris Garages in Oxford. The use of the spacious yard in the front of the stables enabled Morris to purchase and offer for hire several second-hand tourist cars of the period to wealthy undergraduates of the university and the local residents, my father being one of the first staff drivers to give part-time help to his brother-in-law-to-be with his significant new sideline to the business. When his health allowed, Frederick Morris, William's father, was also able to assist his son at 48, High Street with the ever-growing clerical work of an expanding enterprise.

His ambition began to flourish then and never left him, but it was an ambition to make vehicles not money. This preoccupation with severely practical objectives rather than any urge to get rich can be seen as one of the causes of his two very casually entered partnerships which were soon to embarrass him financially. His single-minded aim was first to make the perfect cheap bicycle, then a good motor cycle, and, much later, a good reliable car at a price affordable to the working man. The product was his sole ambition, not the means of making a rich reward for himself. His charges and prices were always very low, relying on the volume sales to prosper. His outlook was to the workshop as the instinctive priority for his relentless energy, needing each day to achieve a better product than yesterday. Such a fixation gave scant attention to the growing need for financial backing and virtually none to his own personal gain.

Even as his enterprises prospered in later years, surplus funds were ploughed back into further expansion as they were created. Wealth came to him in later years almost as a surprise but did not alter him significantly or his way of life.

Many men of that period displayed Rudyard Kipling's famous 'IF' in their homes or offices, but visitors to Nuffield Place, near Henley, his last home,[2] will see in the ante-room of his modest bedroom, a card with the wording printed below. When did he buy it, early or late in his life? I do not know, but it is symptomatic of his outlook.

WHO AM I?
I am the foundation of business,
I am the source of prosperity,
I am the parent of genius,
I am the salt that gives life its pleasure.
I have laid the foundation of every fortune.
I can do more to advance any youth than his own
parents, be they ever so wealthy
I must be loved before I can bestow my great benefits.
Loved, I make life sweet, purposeful and fruitful.
All progress springs from me,
I am work.

BRIEF PARTNERSHIPS, THEN SOLO

Successful in assembling bicycles in modest numbers for several years, William Morris's interest turned in 1901 to the new and growing demand he could see for motor cycles, this time with great confidence, pitching straight into the market with his own product the Morris Motor Cycle, at first a motorized pedal-cycle.

This new enterprise needed even more workshop space and working capital to advance the business to the rank of small manufacturer. A workmate, Joseph Cooper, was willing to join the business and to add some modest additional capital. Cooper was a local man and a cycle-racing companion, so the two men had known each other for several years and were quite compatible workmates. It was not until they were in such close double harness that their wide differences in character began to be apparent, one being the confident risk-taker and the newcomer more cautious, striving to apply the brakes. Morris wanted to order three of the best new motor-cycle engines, being supremely confident that making three new motor cycles together would cut costs and be so easily sold. Cooper, believing in steady, safer progress only wanted to outlay the money for one engine to start with. Their capital was so very small and to commit so much without having the guarantee of selling even one motor cycle was more that Cooper had the nerve to do. Such an ill-matched business partnership could only result in the entrepreneur having to buy out the cautious man and to carry on alone. They remained on good terms and Cooper returned to work for Morris in the car factory many years later.

Of course, the repayment of Cooper's capital left Morris, having ordered the three engines, needing to borrow from a trusting friend and to work doubly hard to make up for the loss of his working partner. Hard work succeeded and Morris convinced himself that self-reliance was better than being held back by a partner.

However, his interest in making motor cycles did not last very long; he was distracted by the increasing number of rich motoring enthusiasts who brought their none-too-reliable motor cars of those early years to him for repair. He was also in demand to give driving lessons and to hire out the second-hand cars that he had bought.

Such local fame as a clever motor engineer and car agent for various makers made him the choice of a wealthy young undergraduate of Oxford University, who was anxious to invest in motor engineering. The undergraduate, together with an older man, F.G. Barton, a dealer in cars and cycles, chose Morris for his skills as their practical engineer, works manager, and partner.

The fairly substantial sum of money involved and the sales potential of these two men must have quelled Morris's severe resistance to partnership, being so short of capital himself. The older man, with his several shops, became general manager of the newly formed Oxford Automobile and Cycle Agency; but he was totally unable to restrain the young undergraduate, who had absolutely no business experience, from spending much too freely in premature publicity, with the result that this uneasy partnership of three strong-willed men in too small a business failed dismally within a year, leaving Morris with only his own tools and a pile of debts to his suppliers.

Recovery from such a disaster did convince Morris this time most emphatically to avoid partnerships like the plague. Undaunted, with the resilience of youth, he struggled back into his former modest trading activities with the goodwill of his landlords and suppliers, who had not lost faith in him as a brilliant practical man with an abundance of self-confidence.

NOW I WILL MAKE CARS

His marriage did not get off to a very comfortable start and much praise must be given to Elizabeth, his wife. She perforce had to manage to keep house on the utter minimum of income from her self-employed husband.

She practised economy in the first year of her marriage to such an extent that the habit never left her. Every pound hard-earned by her husband was urgently needed for that particularly difficult year to ensure recovery of the business. The newly wed Mr and Mrs William R. Morris had absolute confidence in their future and their determination was amply rewarded within a year or two as the business prospered once again.

Many wealthy undergraduates of Oxford University brought their motor cars to the garage in Longwall for repairs and services by Morris, and he became vitally interested in the obviously bright future of the motor industry. One such undergraduate was the young Earl of Macclesfield, who made an unsecured loan of £4,000 to Morris who was then anxious to start making cars himself. Armed with such a substantial cheque (for that time) Morris went to see his banker, Mr A.B. Gillett of Gilletts Bank, now Barclays Bank plc, in High Street, Oxford. I am grateful to Miss Audrey Taylor who, in her book *Gilletts, Bankers of Oxford and Banbury*, records Mr Gillett's account of the significant interview as follows:

'Morris was in the Bank asking to see me. He came with a scheme of his to assemble first class parts of a small car and was going to do the assembling. The money position came into it because I asked Morris what money he had got and he replied that Lord Macclesfield had lent him £4,000. I said to him "But how much have you got?" and he answered, "A shilling". Then I said "Well, I will lend you another £4,000", and he looked at me in utter astonishment and said, "Do you mean that?" I replied that, "My dear fellow, this thing you have told me about has got a fortune behind it". Then I asked "How many cars are you going to make this year?" He said, "Well Mr Gillett, it is all a question of finance but we now have £8,000. Even so that is not too much for what we are going to do. We are going to make 250 cars." And that is how we became customer and banker.'

Mr Gillett continued –

'Morris went up to the Motor Show about three weeks later and a week later when it was all over he walked into my office and put down on to the table a cheque from Stewart and Ardern, Motor Agents, for £1,250. I said "What is this?" He said "That is £5 for each car I promised to make." At that time, no-one had seen anything more than a blueprint. I just looked at him and said, "Now Morris what do you mean to do?" He said, "We shall make 250 cars; they will come gradually, perhaps five or six at a time – about five a week." I said, "Can you put a car together in five weeks?" He said, "We are hoping to do it quicker than that, in four, and probably in three weeks." He started off and did very well, and in the next year, 1913, much better. Then the war came.'

Thus began his spectacular rise to fame, a remarkable growth, not without its difficulties, but a success story that was to end with vast wealth carefully given to purposes best calculated to benefit his fellow countrymen and the British Commonwealth of Nations.

From becoming self-employed at the age of sixteen he began to display such an air of assurance that, with more personality than diction, he quickly gained the confidence of customers, inspired trust in lenders and convinced Gordon Stewart of Stewart and Ardern, major London car distributors, that he could produce 250 cars to justify his blueprints.

Having banked Mr Gordon Stewart's cheque, he had to turn on his other great capability. As he walked out of Mr Gillett's Bank into the High Street the real test was on. Hard work was now beginning to be the 'parent of genius'.

But to Mr A.B. Gillett, I am convinced, must be attributed the very great credit of putting one of the greatest industrialists and benefactors of this century firmly on his feet financially during that critical period of his career. I make no apology for stressing the vital help given to Morris by Mr Gillett, who later, following the take-over, became a Director of Barclays Bank, the Chairman of which, from 1962 to 1973, Sir John Thomson, has so kindly written a chapter for this book.

HORSE-DRAWN TRAMS, UNTIL MORRIS BUSES

A significant preamble to the story of W.R. Morris's astonishing growth as a motor manufacturer and industrialist would be to look back to the Oxford scene during the first 13 years of this century and to consider Morris's considerable impact upon it in November 1913.

The Oxford of those years still remained primarily a nineteenth-century university township in which the tradesmen served the colleges and the undergraduates ran up large bills with their tailors. The City Council, with some of its councillors undemocratically nominated by the University, was a very sluggish body, slow to promote any change in the status quo.

Symptomatic of this sleepy state of civic affairs were the out-dated horse-trams used by the disgruntled passengers on wet days or when not in any hurry! Oxonians regarded these antiquated vehicles as a rather sick joke until one citizen decided that if the Council could only dither year after year, he must act.

He was befriended and advised my a most eloquent Oxford solicitor, Frank Gray, who later became MP for Oxford. Whether Gray's inflammatory, crowd-inciting orations to eager listeners or the enormous instant popularity of that citizen's illegally operated motor buses finally forced the City Council to capitulate and withhold the imminent arrest of the two law-breakers is uncertain. The street 'battle' between the competing motor buses and the horse-drawn trams was perfectly ordered but so one-sided that the prestige of the City Council was severely deflated.

Such a farce did this controversy become that a local bookseller, H.G. Gadney, wrote a very amusing account 'Showing how many men were busy for 12 years and accomplished nothing and how one man was bus(s)y for one month and accomplished much'. A slightly condensed version of Mr Gadney's report is as follows:

Now it came to pass in the month of January, in the year one thousand nine hundred and two, that the people of a certain city, wherein dwelt many learned, but few wise, men began to say to themselves, 'Lo! our trams are rotten. They be drawn by horses, they jolt, they run not always on their lines, but often all over the road; they be very slow. Other cities are not like unto ours. There they have electric trams that run swiftly and smoothly and be bright to look upon.'

Then they that owned the horse-trams said unto the Councillors of that City, 'Such and such things will we do, so that we may have electric-trams, like unto other cities.' But the Councillors of that City said, 'Nay, these things that ye say be not good enough for us. We will have none of them.' Then said the owners of the horse-drawn trams unto that Council, 'Great is our sorrow that what we say is not pleasing. How say ye now? Will ye not buy from us the horse-trams and make them into electric, and have them for ever unto your own possession.'

And the Council said, 'That soudeth to us more like it, O owners of the horse-trams. Behold, we will go unto the great Council of the Kingdom, and beseech them that they give us the power to buy your horse-drawn trams and do as ye say with them, for without the great Council can we do nothing.' And they prepared to go unto the great Council and to beseech them as they said.

Then arose certain of the Citizens of that place and said on to another, 'Nay, we will not that the Council of this City own the trams. We do know this Council, for that they are no good to do such a thing, and if they have aught to do with it, we shall be in a worse state than before.' And so great was the outcry that the heads of the people were counted, and they that desired that the Council should not own the trams were in numbers very many times more than they that desired that they should. So the Council spoke no more of owning the trams.

Then the Council said, 'We must not be idle,' and they caused proclamation to be made unto all that owned electric trams, that they should say unto the Council how and for what price would they give electric-trams unto that City. And there was much holding of assemblies, and after many words the Council agreed with certain men that they should give electric-trams unto that City.

Then said they that owned the horse-trams, 'Lo, now, ye have made agreement with us that we should use the roads of the City for many years, and if we cease to use them, ye must pay us much money.' and many assemblies were held and many words we spoken, and the Council and the owners of the horse-trams agreed upon the price.

Now those men that had agreed to give electric-trams to the City had likewise agreed with the Councillors of other cities to give them electric-trams. So the Councillors of that City made many journeys unto those other cities, and they journeyed as journey Kings and the great ones of the earth, in great comfort, and with much smoking of tobacco and drinking of wine, as is the custom of that country. And since the Councillors paid not for these things themselves, but the Citizens paid, the Councillors delighted greatly in these journeys, but the Citizens not so much.

And after these journeys the Councillors aid, 'We have seen many cities, and the Councillors of other cities have told us, and we know that these electric-trams are not good, much money is spent upon them, and often these electric-trams stop when they should move, and we will have none of them.'

Now seven years had passed since first the Citizens had talked of electric-trams, and the Citizens began to be wroth with the Council and to say. 'These horse-trams are here still, when shall we see them depart?' But the time was not yet.

Then in the month of November in the year one thousand nine hundred and thirteen arose a Citizen of that place, very learned in the use of those carriages that run like lightning and without horses, whereof spoke the Prophet Daniel, and he sent word unto the Clerk of that Council and wrote, 'I will give this city something better than electric-trams, even the motor-bus, and I beseech the City that they give me leave to do so, for of a truth such shall be best for the citizens!' But the Clerk of that Council answered not at all, and whether he did this because he would not or because he was full of sleep is not told. Then the Citizen was angry and cried unto the Council, 'If ye give me not leave to give a motor-bus, I will give it without leave. Lo! on such and such a day will I give it.' And on that day, as he said it should be, did he give a motor-bus to the Citizens, even two motorbuses, and afterwards more. And the Citizens rejoiced greatly, and many of them rode upon the motor-buses with joy. Likewise were the horses that drew the horse-trams exceedingly glad and said one to another, 'Now is our lot easy and our burden lighter.'

Then the Council said one to another, 'Can this thing be? Shall this man give motor-buses without our leave? True he had taketh no money, but sells pieces of paper beforehand,' and they said unto their man of law, 'Can we not hale him to judgment? and the man of law took counsel with other men of law, more learned than himself, many times, yea even upon the Sabbath. And he came again unto the Council and said, 'Ye can hale him to judgment.' Then some of the Council and said, 'Let us do so,' and others said, 'Nay, give him leave to give his motor-bus unto the Citizens. We have played the fool, and know not what to do, and he showeth us a way.' And others cried again, 'Have we played the fool? speak for thyself, O presumptuous one.'

Then the Citizen again wrote unto the Clerk and said, 'I beseech the Council to give me leave'; and the Clerk answered and said 'It will be proper for thee, O Citizen, to give the motor-bus outside the Council Chamber at such and such an hour, so that the Council may see it! And at the appointed time that citizen bought his motor-bus to the Council Chamber, and after one hour it was said to him, 'Ye have not craved leave in proper form!' And he said, 'What is proper form?' And he said, 'What is proper form?' and they said, 'We know not'; and what the citizen said after that is not recorded, but he was exceeding wroth.

Then came others to the Council, even they that owned the horse-trams, and other from the great city of that kingdom, and said, 'We also will give motor-buses, if ye give us leave.' And certain of the Council spake together and said, 'If we say unto one, "Ye shall have leave," and unto other, "Ye shall not have leave," then will those other be angry. Therefore will we please all and say, "Ye shall all have leave, for each so many motor-buses."'

But the Citizens cried out upon this and said, 'This benefiteth us nothing, give one man only leave. Ye are fools, O Councillors.' and they said many things of the Council which it beseemeth not to write.

Then said they that owned the horse-trams, 'Lo, the Citizens are exceedingly pleased with their gift of a motor-bus. We have always loved the Citizens with exceeding great love, and, though we have no leave from the Council, yet will we likewise give motor-buses.' And they gave motor-buses. But the Citizens, most of them, looked on them with scorn, and made much of that Citizen who first gave them motor-buses, and held great assemblies in his honour and made feasts for him. For they said, 'He hath delivered us from the bondage of the horse-trams, and of the Council, and of those who own the horse-trams, and he is deserving of great honour.

The citizen was well satisfied, being able to return fully to making more, better, and cheaper motor cars, as is told in the following chapters.

Notes

1. Frederick Morris was born at Witney in 1849, the son of an Oxfordshire yeoman farmer. As a young man he travelled widely, seeking his fortune in America. He was a good horseman and while in Canada he drove a Royal Mail coach and six. At one time he became and lived as an honorary chief and 'bloodbrother' of a Red Indian

tribe. Returning to seek employment in England in his mid-twenties, he married Emily Ann Pether, daughter of an Oxfordshire farmer, on 9 November 1876. The *three* surviving children of this marriage were William Richard, born at Worcester on 10 October 1877, then Alice Gertrude, born 11 February 1879, and Emily Ann, born 1 January 1881. Sadly, four other children died at birth or when very young. When aged twenty-six William Richard married Elizabeth Maud Anstey of Oxford on 9 April 1904. Alice, the eldest of William's sisters, married my father, Percival John Minns of Oxford, on 29 October 1907, and Emily married Felix Arthur Yockney.

2. See Chapter 24.

Chapter 2
The Nuffield I knew

Sir John Thomson

As I used to visit Lord Nuffield frequently in his office at Cowley, I have been asked to jot down a few recollections that might throw some light on the personality of this great man. As a complete amateur in biographical writing. I must, please, be forgiven for using the first person.

He was scrupulously honest, kind, and generous in big ways and small ways, with wide vision and almost uncanny intuition, a picker of the right man for the right job, and with an overriding desire to use his wealth for the benefit of the community. He was cautious, but would occasionally take a big risk when the right opportunities occurred and then get back 'under cover' and restore rigid financial liquidity as soon as he could.

So, advisedly, I have described him as a great man. Many unpublished acts of generosity disclose how much he hated people to be unhappy and yet, sadly, I do not believe that he was himself a happy person. He was a restless perfectionist and too often felt that many of his numerous activities, whether business or charitable, were not being carried out as well as they should be. He would never cease to admit how much he owed to those who worked for him.

My first recollection of a connection with 'Morris' was before the First World War, when my father and my grandfather bought their first cars from him. They were Hupmobiles. I can still recall the thrill of being driven by a groom, converted into a chauffeur in a long white coat, along dusty roads at a great speed of around 15 mph. My grandfather notes in his diary in May 1914 how Morris's very nice man brought 'the motor', as he always called it, from Morris's garage.

The Morris team must have been persuasive as my grandfather hated cars, which he said frightened horses. In fact, an eminent Oxford butcher told me that he lost my grandfather's custom because he delivered the meat in a motor van into the stable yard. To persuade my grandfather to buy a car was quite an achievement!

But, of course, WRM's relationship with employees at all levels was a vital element of his success. Some readers will have heard the story of his going down to the works on the morning after his large donation of shares to all employees. 'Good morning, Bert', he greeted a long-serving employee, who was sweeping up filings off the floor. An immediate response came. 'Good morning guvnor, this is a fine job to give a shareholder to do.'

Naturally, in later days, Lord Nuffield needed the best secretarial advice and, indeed, protection from the host of people who sought access to present their individual pleas for financial aid or endowment. He was well served. I, personally, remember no sessions with his Lordship except those following a summons by Wilfred Hobbs or Carl Kingerlee, or my own request through one of them for an audience.

Hobbs was a man of outstanding charm and ability, a trained accountant, with his own brand of humour. He would ring you up and start saying 'forgive me for asking one of my usual sub-intelligent questions' and then bowl a really fast ball at you. Economy of time was one of Hobbs' traits and he had a most efficient lady assistant. For instance, he was a great fan of the *Daily Mirror*'s Jane cartoon and I remember the lady assistant coming smartly into his office with the paper folded to show only Jane's daily feature. Wilfred solemnly glanced at it, initialled it, whereupon she quickly walked out again.

Carl Kingerlee, too, was a devoted and most valuable guardian in Lord Nuffield's last days, and personally took a dedicated interest in all the workings of the benefactions, both public and private.

Morris's early financial difficulties, due to his partners' weakness, and his integrity in dealing with his creditors were indirectly a factor in setting him on the road to financial success. The support that he consequently received from Arthur Gillett, the banker, is described elsewhere in this book.

Tribute should also be paid to his other professional team. For instance, Andrew Walsh, his solicitor, played a vital role in the setting up of his complicated trusts and benefactions. As a young man I used to be sent to see Walsh and sat at his desk. I looked up at the text hanging over his head bearing the words 'when in doubt tell the truth'. The financial skill of the accountant R.W. Thornton cannot be overestimated. He became the founder of a large and important accountancy firm, which has now become Grant Thornton International, one of the world's largest accountancy and consultancy organizations. Thornton and Walsh were two most able Oxford professional men, whose capabilities Morris used to the full.

It was through the introduction of Arthur Gillett of Barclays Bank that Lord Nuffield enlisted the aid of Sir William Goodenough, who was to play such a major role in the setting up of the various trusts. A man of outstanding ability, who became Chairman of Barclays Bank, Sir William also had close connections with Oxfordshire County and the University. He was Chairman of the Oxfordshire County Council and a member of the University Chest, skilfully bringing the University's financial strategy up to date. Lord Nuffield's early dislike of universities had been overcome.

Sir William Goodenough was chairman of no less than five major Nuffield Trusts, including the Nuffield Foundation, which are described elsewhere in this book. He, alas, died in 1951 at an early age, having relentlessly overworked himself in charitable activities as well as his professional duties. Heredity does not play a big part in the Nuffield story but it is nice to record that Sir William's son, Roger Goodenough, is now the enthusiastic and most efficient Chairman of the Nuffield Medical Trustees and of the Nuffield Orthopaedic Trust.

Another person of high Oxfordshire repute in various fields, who gave Lord Nuffield great service, was Alderman William Hyde. He was Secretary of the Nuffield Provincial Hospitals Trust and the immense success and growth of BUPA owe much to Hyde's hard work and ability.

Much has been written about WRM's almost obsessive interest in health. It is said that he would have liked to have been a surgeon if a medical education had been possible for him, and that this interest was a motivation in his setting up so many benefactions for the advancement of medical treatment and research. When one went into his room for a talk he would offer you a cigarette, hand rolled, and assure you that the harmful constituents such as saltpetre had been removed from the tobacco. You would admire the wall case containing medals and other insignia recording his success as a racing cyclist, and, if asked how he trained, he would tell you jokingly that he trained on cigarettes, which must have been far from the truth! He had his back to a machine in a far corner of the room which monitored the air conditioning, and you wondered whether you should interrupt by drawing his attention when the red light suddenly came on.

He gave great personal attention to the innumerable begging letters he received, and he genuinely hated people being in want. He had an uncanny 'nose' for the imposter. I remember his sending for me one day when he had received a most plausible request for aid. He asked me to do some investigating for him and I said I would do my best but could not betray banking confidences. The letter turned out to be a most ingenious fraud, confirming WRM's intuition.

A close ally of WRM died and unwittingly left his widow in a bad financial plight, leaving her only a small income because of his over-generosity to a Nuffield Trust. WRM personally went most carefully into her affairs and kept her in comfort and free from worry for the rest of her life. The outside world, of course, never knew of such acts of personal kindness. There were many of them.

His own carefulness over money is well known and many have accused him of 'penny pinching'. One of my own experiences of this amused me. Before his death in August 1963 he drew up a list of people he would like to attend both the morning service at the crematorium and the afternoon interment of the ashes at Nuffield Church. The invitees were to be given luncheon at Cowley, but Lord Nuffield told Carl Kingerlee that there was no need to offer me a free meal because I lived close to the crematorium and could get lunch at home.

Incidentally, the Queen was officially represented by the Lord Lieutenant at the Memorial Service at the University Church in October 1963.

Lord Nuffield was not much interested in religion, but I remember being told that he hoped that, when he departed, the hymn 'Abide with me' would be sung at his funeral, because it moved him so much.

Lady Nuffield shared her husband's concern in saving every halfpenny. In the early days of the Elizabeth Nuffield Home, which was established in North Oxford for elderly people, the question of obtaining new carpets for the bedrooms came up at a committee meeting and estimates from furniture firms were produced. Lady Nuffield said she thought she could get better ones cheaper. She went up to the Works and haggled with the manager in charge of putting carpets into the top-class cars. The result was an excellent supply of carpets from Cowley at a cut rate.

Lady Nuffield's interest in the home named after her was one of the many example, of how close she and her husband were in later years, a matter that bought much pleasure to their friends.

After the Second World War, Lord Nuffield caused surprise by personally using a car which appeared to be very outdated. Its Wolseley body was certainly of pre-War vintage. He told me that people were constantly badgering him to help them obtain a new car. They were very scarce in that period. He was able to point to his own vehicle and say 'Well, look at mine, why do you want a new one?'

It was often asked whether W.R. Morris was a great engineer. I remember putting the question to A.A. Rowse, a distinguished engineer who had played a prominent part at Cowley in earlier days. He replied 'Morris was not an educated engineer but he possessed an uncanny instinct as to what it was possible to achieve. He would tell his designers what he wanted in the way of a new component which would perform a certain function in a new type of engine. They would come back and say "It's not possible" and he'd say "All right, forget about it." That particular requirement never was achieved by anyone, however hard they tried and experimented. But when he made some other request and received the same answer he would say "Go on trying" and they eventually did succeed. This happened far too often to be a series of coincidences.' An example of this flair was his early recognition of Cecil Kimber's skill in converting an ordinary model into a sports car, resulting eventually in the purchase of the factory at Abingdon and the great success of MG cars.

The records and achievements of the various charitable trusts and foundations are dealt with in this book. Many personal thoughts and memories come to mind, of which the following are just a few.

The story has often been recounted of Morris's first generous gift to G.R. Girdlestone to save his Oxford hospital when the wartime collection of huts was no longer financed by the government and 'GRG' kept it going for crippled children. One version, which differs from that which appears in Jackson's *Nuffield Story*, was told to me by a senior sister at the hospital, which, after being called the 'Wingfield', eventually became the Nuffield Orthopaedic Hospital of world renown. Girdlestone, son of a canon and a very religious man, was on his knees praying for the salvation of his hospital, which seemed doomed to collapse for lack of funds. The maid broke into Girdlestone's room and said that there was a man at the door who insisted on seeing him. Girdlestone was annoyed at being disturbed and said 'All right I'd better see what he wants.' The man at the door was W.R. Morris, who said 'I hear you could do with some money' and handed him a cheque. Thus began a long personal friendship between Morris and Girdlestone, and WRM provided generous finance for buildings and scholarships.

The Nuffield Orthopaedic Centre Trust was later set up through Lord Nuffield's donations to Professor Trueta and others. An approach was made to Nuffield late in his life to provide funds to build the new block, which was urgently needed. A rough estimate of £200,000 was obtained.

I was sent to see his Lordship who said we could have the money on one condition, that we should not employ an architect. When I asked why, he said 'Oh, there will be numerous plans, and the surgeons will say there is not enough room for their secretaries and so on. There will be endless delays and the building will never be up in my lifetime.'

We had no alternative but to accept the condition and were given a cheque for £200,000. An excellent builder, much admired by Lord Nuffield, was approached and the building was quickly erected at a cost of about £172,000. I went to tell Lord Nuffield and asked him to whom the balance of £28,000 should be refunded. He replied 'You can keep the change.' This was a most welcome donation to the Nuffield Orthopaedic Centre Trust.

There are often a few rumbles of discontent when great benefactions are made. When Lord Nuffield gave Oxford University his, in those pre-war days immense, gift of £2 million, for their Medical School, some local hospitals complained that they would be impoverished. So Lord Nuffield set up for them the Nuffield Hospitals Endowment Fund with an opening gift of £300,000. This money could have been grabbed by the state when the hospitals were nationalized but, thanks to the ingenuity of Sir William Goodenough and legal experts, the assets were retained and the fund was re-christened the Oxford and District Hospitals Improvement and Development Fund. Its investments grew in value and the benefaction continues to give valuable aid to local hospitals.

The wider public, who benefited so greatly from his generosity, were probably never aware of his intense interest in all things medical and surgical, and his desire to reduce pain and suffering. A well-recorded instance of this was his personal monitoring of the setting up of the Nuffield Professorships and their departments in the Oxford University Medical School. The most distinguished experts produced the plan but Lord Nuffield said they had left out the most important department, i.e. anaesthetics. He said 'No anaesthetics, no money for the school.' His stance was more than vindicated by the outstanding achievements of the Department of Anaesthetics under Professor Sir Robert Macintosh.

I once asked a Regius Professor of Medicine, alas no longer alive, about this story and he told that a very large number of lives had indeed been saved by the inventions of Sir Robert Macintosh and his teams in the Second World War.

Lord Nuffield's interests were interlocking. In 1938 he endowed the Nuffield Dominion Scholarships, bringing medical graduates from universities in Australia, New Zealand, and South Africa over to Oxford to further their education and experience in the Medical School. When asked 'Why no-one from Canada?' he replied 'They didn't buy my cars!'

I realize that the foregoing notes are no more than a random recollection of an octogenarian, who did have the privilege of serving no less than seven Nuffield Benefactions, as trustee or committee member, for many years before and after Lord Nuffield's death in 1963.

With the aid of inflation indices, one could calculate the current money value of the £30 million or so which he gave away, at about £500 million in today's money. It would be impossible to quantify the benefits he bestowed on the human race, especially his funding of medical research. Examples of the relief from suffering, which originated from Lord Nuffield's far vision and generosity, could be traced to even remote corners of the world.

Chapter 3
The Nuffield I worked for

Ken Revis[1]

In those early days, and we are now back in the first decade of the century, Morris was repairing cars and bikes for Oxford undergraduates who used to bring their machines to him. Sir John Conybeare, a wealthy undergraduate, who kept his car at Morris's place in Longwall St. said:

> I saw the original blueprints one night when I came into the garage at about 11 o'clock and Morris was still there working and we got talking and he invited me into his office where I saw a whole lot of blueprints of his proposed new car. I said it must be an expensive job to set up all the plant to make a car of this kind but he told me that he wasn't going to make any single part of it himself, as he was buying the engines from White and Poppe, the gearboxes from, I think Chater-Lea. All the electrical equipment would come from Lucas's and the tyres from Dunlop so he reckoned that it was only going to be a question of assembly and therefore only a very small amount of capital was required.

The car they were talking about was, of course, the first Bullnosed Morris Oxford. Morris, of course, thought big and was tireless in his efforts to make journey after journey to Coventry and Birmingham, talking to the experts who had experience of making parts of motor cars, Dunlop tyres, Lucas batteries and electrics, Rubery-Owen for chassis, Sankey for wheels, etc., and Rayworths Coachbuilders of Oxford made the original bodies.

Morris probably had his eye on Cowley in 1912. He had built a spanking new garage in Longwall St., Oxford, which became know locally as the Motor Palace and his business really did thrive in those days. His move to Cowley soon afterwards was not only an excellent business decision on his part, but also a sentimental one, because the building, which he first rented and then bought, was Hurst's Grammar School on the corner of Oxford Road, Cowley, and Holloway. It can be seen to this day with Morris Oxford Cars, written in a sort of ghost writing on the glass windows. It was the school where his father Frederick was educated. This scotches the rags to riches story of some journalists because Frederick was a quite well-educated man. The building had been used for a few years as a military academy for the sons of officers until Cowley Barracks was built in 1876. This building was where the first production Morris cars were built, although mass-production hadn't been heard of them, at least over here in Britain.

Ford, when they started their English factory at Trafford Park, Manchester, had some kind of flow production, but in the Morris building at Cowley the chassis was laid on the floor, the axle and wheels put on, then it was pushed forward to allow the engine (from White and Poppe) to be put in so that another chassis could be put down and assembled in the same way. Bill Anstey, Mrs Morris's brother, had the job of painting the wheels in the attic, and when they were called for by number or colour (there were only two colours, grey and green) he lowered them with a rope through the attic trapdoor to the assembly floor below.

Morris attempted to get his first car, the Bullnosed Morris Oxford, with a 1018 cc White and Poppe engine, to the Motor Show at Olympia, I think in 1912, but he had set-backs and went to the Motor Show without a car to put on the stand. However, he showed the blueprints and drawings of the car and was so persuasive, that Mr Gordon Stewart, of Stewart and Ardern, placed an order for 250 cars. This was a tremendous achievement. Gordon Stewart became Sir Gordon Stewart, and Stewart and Ardern the London distributors for Morris Cars. Mr Tobin, who later managed the Morris Garages with Alfred Keen, later a director, said:

The actual first car was assembled at Cowley. The engine arrived one afternoon from Coventry and we worked right the way through the night to put it together. In the morning it was ready and the Governor had a short trip up the road and said, 'We'll stop now and test it again on Monday.'

However, the first Morris Oxford didn't get far when Gordon Stewart came to collect it. A little way along the road the universal joint broke and had to be replaced. He then got as far as Dashwood Hill, near High Wycombe, when the universal joint broke again. So Morris then put in some very steamed up telephone calls to White and Poppe and spoke to Mr Poppe. He is reported to have said 'Are you all mad, you engineers in Coventry?' then he rang up Hans Landstad, White and Poppe's designer, who said Mr Poppe, his boss, was very pig-headed and had insisted on having the universal joints made in cast-iron not steel. Morris ordered an immediate change in the specification, from cast-iron to phosphor-bronze.

The first little Morris Oxford car, which became known as the Bullnosed

The old garage in Longwall St. Pre-war.

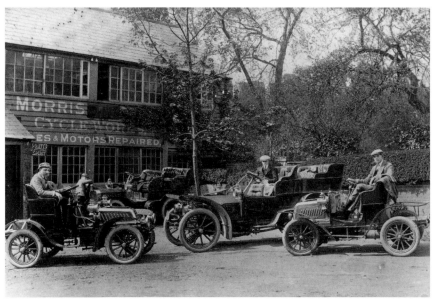

The Longwall St. garage from another angle.
[Nuffield Place collection]

25

Morris, was a sweet little car. It had an engine of 1018 cc, and was a two seater with a lift-up sort of box seat behind, called a dicky, and had brakes on the rear wheels only. The headlights were acetylene and the two sidelights and tail-lights burnt oil. It sold for £165.

Morris really wanted to beat Ford, who was making the Model T in Manchester, and he was already planning his next car, this time called a Morris Cowley, with an 11.9 horsepower engine, and, later still, a better version which he again called the Morris Oxford.

The First World War started as he and Landstadt, then his draughtsman, went to America to look for an engine manufacturer. They went to the Continental and Machining Company in Detroit, where they found mass production was very much more advanced than in Britain and they found that an engine similar to the White and Poppe one could be bought for about £17, as against the cost of £50 in this country. Morris bought some of these engines, but the ship on which they were loaded was torpedoed and none arrived in the United Kingdom. However, he did buy the American rights to produce a four-cylinder 11.9 hp engine and this was the engine used in the first Morris Cowley in 1916, but obviously, the war being on, very few cars were being made. The enlarged version of this engine, the 13.9 hp, 1803 cc was used in the second Morris Oxford. These two engines continued all through the twenties and even for the Flatnosed Morris of 1934, Bullnosed Morris production having ceased in August 1926.

Thinking of Morris's irresistibility when he was persuading parts manufacturers to supply large quantities at a low cost, here is comment from Arthur Rowse, who joined Morris in 1915 and became Director in 1926:

Morris had an extraordinary facility. His enthusiasm was such that he would make a proposition which was technically almost impossible and commercially somewhat doubtful and yet despite this at the end of it all you felt that if the right people got together the thing was not only possible but practical and could be done. Indeed there were a great number of instances in which it was done.

When Morris was able to start up again after the First World War, just as at the end of the Second World War, cars were not to be had for love nor money. Morris was selling cars as fast as they could be made and he was making money fast. So there was a car boom, with the only difference between then and after the Second World War being that after the Second World War the government insisted on a huge proportion going for export.

The French armament company, Hotchkiss, undertook to make engines for Morris, and by the Autumn of 1920 Morris was producing cars at a rate of 280 per month. However, a month later the car boom suddenly turned into a severe slump. People wanted cars but they were too dear, and the factory at Cowley and Morris's agents throughout the country were stuffed with unsold vehicles. Labour problems put up the costs and the idea was still abroad that cars were only for the rich.

In the spring of 1921, Morris took a tremendous decision to overcome the situation of the overstocked factory. This was really the most fateful decision of his life. These are his words:

I therefore sent for my manager and suggested to him that the price should be dropped by £100 per model and he said 'How can you do that with the small profit you are making today.' and I said 'Well you are making no profit at all. You are selling no cars and I therefore give you instructions to go and do exactly what I suggest and also to double up the supplies.' He went to the door, stood in the doorway and looked at me as much to say he'd gone at last. With that he slammed the door and went out.

There were bitter rumours in the motor industry, some said Morris was pushing his suppliers to ruin. This Morris denied:

Of course as soon as we started making cars in much larger quantities, we were then looking for lower prices on supplies and one of the men who came to see me, selling me a certain part of the car, and at that time I was doing the buying myself, said 'That's impossible. I cannot possibly reduce the price I have already given you. It'll ruin me.' I said 'Well, under those conditions you won't get the order because I'm not going to ruin any man, but I'm not going to pay your price anyway.' To cut a very long story short, the man took the order, which was a very large one and in twelve months came back and thanked me very much for cutting his price, because he said that he went back and put his own concern in order and for that reason for the first time in his life he hadn't an overdraft.

Morris also cut the agents' discount from 19 per cent to 17 per cent.

Soon after this, in 1924, Morris came in contact with a motoring journalist Miles Thomas. The year before, 1923, Morris had been driving his own car in the London–Edinburgh trial, and when a group of journalists went to Cowley to write about the new Morris Oxford, Morris noticed that Thomas, although he had been given a handout about this new model, took no notes at all, but although there were discrepancies in the handout, something to do with the weatherproofing or something quite minor, Thomas had written up a competent article while the others had followed the scripts. So Morris asked Thomas to come to work for him when his contract with his motoring journal could be ended, to take over the sales promotion and advertising, and he wanted him to produce a magazine called the *Morris Owner*.

Another thing Morris did at this time was to advertise that the car could be had at a particularly low price provided the order was put in before a certain date. All these things led to an enormous surge of Morris's output and as Thomas said 'orders came flooding in'. This was Morris's buying period. He bought the Hotchkiss company of Coventry in 1923, re-jigged it for higher production levels and it was called Morris Engines branch. He bought the Wolseley company in 1926 from Vickers. Just before the 1939–45 War he had bought the Riley company, which of course had been a world famous sports car manufacturer, originally called The Riley Engine company. The Riley engine in the early twentieth century was the first engine to have mechanically operated valves. He had bought Hollick and Pratt, the body-makers. He bought the SU carburettor company and a radiator company was started in an old roller-skating rink in Osberton Road, Oxford, by Harold Ryder and then moved to Bainton Road to become Morris Radiators Branch. This was really the big time for Morris. His company could be valued in millions and in 1936 it went public, quoted on the Stock exchange as Morris Motors Ltd.

In the great days of the 1920s, in about 1924, Cecil Kimber was the General Manager of the Morris Garages in Oxford, the company Morris kept to himself, in other words outside Morris Motors Ltd. Kimber was a sporting motorcyclist and bought for his garage the chassis of a Morris Oxford produced at Cowley with a 13.9 hp engine. Kimber tuned the engine, lowered the chassis, skimmed a rasher off the head, toughened up the springs, polished the ports, and put on a streamline body with pointed tail, and entered it very successfully in the London–Land's End trial. In fact, of course, it was a sporty Bullnosed Morris and it had a circular MG disc brazed onto the Bullnosed radiator: The Morris Garages, Supersports, Morris Oxford. In this car, known as 'old no.1, 1925', I have been driven round the circuit at Silverstone, pumping the petrol tank pressure up to 2 pounds per sq inch to keep the fuel supply going. Kimber asked the boss, Sir William, whether he could prepare more cars of this kind and, once he was given permission, other Morris Garages Supersports were made. It doesn't need too much imagination to realize that the initials MG came from Morris Garages. The car proved highly popular with the sporting boys and, as a result, a glove factory in Abingdon was bought in 1928 and the

Cecil Kimber with Sir William Morris, Bt, c. 1930.
[F.J. Minns]

MG Car Company Ltd was formed. In 1929 the M. Type Midget, fabric-covered wooden body, two-seater sports car with the overhead cam-shaft engine was made for MG by the Wolseley company. The engine was from the first Morris Minor of 1929. MG went on to produce many wonderful sports cars, the 1440, 1880, and the famous Tigress of 2468 cc of which only seven were made. In 1923 MGs won every class G World Record, that's up to 1100 cc, for standing starts from 1 to 5 km.

Sir William Morris was made Baron Nuffield in 1934, and from then on the various companies he owned, Morris, Wolseley, Riley, MG, Morris Engines, Morris Radiators, Morris Commercial, and many others, were called the Nuffield Organization. This was just a name for a group of companies, it was not a holding company, in other words not Nuffield Organizations Ltd.

My first contact with Morris Motors was in 1946 when I got an interview with Sir Miles Thomas, the Deputy to Lord Nuffield. My wife and I had just come back from India after looking after St. Dunstan's out there. Thomas said to me 'What can you do,' and I said 'Well, I can read brail and I can type.' At the end of the interview he said 'Well nose around until you find something interesting to do and we'll pay you £400 a year.' Sir Miles Thomas left the company soon after that, and I went to the new Deputy Managing Director, Reggie Hanks and said that I wanted to become a lawyer. He said 'Good God how do you expect to do that?' I returned a week later to say that I had become articled to a solicitor in Oxford. The company magnificently gave me a 5 year sabbatical leave and had me back to join the publicity department, where I finally became Public Relations executive for the group of factories in the Oxford area, that is MG, Morris, Pressed Steel, and Radiators. I helped to found the museum and did a period in the body plant, the old Pressed Steel, lecturing on factory law, etc.

Talking of Pressed Steel, this company, the Pressed Steel Company of Great Britain, was formed from Edward G. Budd, an American car-body company. Morris personally put a lot of money in 1926 into Pressed Steel so that they could press bodies and shoot them across the road, by overhead conveyor for the Morris company assembly.

My first contact with Lord Nuffield was in 1947 at the company sports ground when I was taken to meet him and given a plate on which was a bun and a cup of tea and so I was unable to shake hands with Lord Nuffield. He waved his hands to one of his aides and asked for a chair and I was told afterwards that it was amusing to see all the directors rushing around trying to find me a chair because all the chairs in the balcony were bolted together in fours. Finally, a chair was produced and placed behind Lord Nuffield who said 'I don't want it for myself, I want it for this young man Revis. He can't be expected to stand here and talk to me with a cup of tea and a plate in his hands.'

On the subject of William Morris ploughing back the profits into the business, I remember he used to say 'there will be no marble halls at Cowley'. This is true, I know, having worked there. The most splendid buildings at Cowley were the 'S' block where the four sales managers of Morris, Wolseley, Riley, and MG had their offices, and mine was alongside theirs. It certainly had a commissionaire's desk, a table in a small front foyer, and a rather magnificent heavy double door, but other than that nothing very special. In contrast, the Austin exhibition building at Longbridge was a huge building; one mounted twenty steps to get to it, it was as large as a cinema and the front foyer was carpeted. A large silver trophy, rather like the FA Cup, was on display there, for presentation to the person who had made the biggest contribution to the motoring industry. When I first knew of it, it had Alec Issigonis's name on it for his design of the Mini in 1959.

Lord Nuffield's concern with medicine is of course well known, and there was a department at Cowley known as the panel room with many disabled people, 50–60 including 7 or 8 blind people, all doing light assembly work, for example fixing instruments into facia panels. These were my special concern.

In the Bullnosed Morris Car Club, we borrowed £800 for the preparation of a very large volume called *The Morris Car*, in which all the catalogues from 1913 to 1930 were reproduced. The book sold for £25 and we repaid the interest-free loan to the Nuffield Foundation. At about that time, the head of the Nuffield Foundation was Sir Geoffrey Gibbs, who said of Lord Nuffield: 'The great thing about him was that if he trusted you he trusted you entirely'.

Notes

1. As is well known by members of the Bullnosed Morris Car Club, of which he succeeded Lord Nuffield as President, Captain Ken Revis MBE was blinded on war service whilst striving to render harmless an enemy mine. Highly commended by St Dunstan's to Lord Nuffield, he was given a staff appointment at Morris Motors and rose to become a public relations executive of the Oxford car factories.

PART TWO

The Making of Millions

BY

TONY LEWIN

Chapter 4

A keen ambition

As the very first, hastily lashed-together prototype Morris Oxford chugged unsteadily out of the Longwall Street garage where it had been built, few of the weary onlookers – not even William Morris himself – could have imagined that the car they were looking at would be the first of over 150,000 Oxfords and Cowleys to emerge from the Morris works, works which even then bore more resemblance to a disused military barrack-house than a serious production facility.

Even making generous allowance for his unflappable faith in his intuition and in the rightness of his ideas, not even William Morris could have comprehended the sheer scale of success that that car would unleash. At a time when Britain's roads were populated only by a few thousand cars, even an incurable optimist such as Morris could not have imagined that his car would sell in its tens of thousands every year – an unprecedented sales volume for that time – or that it would still be in demand 13 years later.

Still less could anyone have predicted that this inauspicious debutant from an Oxford backstreet would be the first of several million to carry the same emblem right round the world, or that the business it was instrumental in building up would eventually form the core of the world's third largest motor manufacturer.

Even Morris must have dismissed any such thoughts as wild and indulgent fantasies, confident though he was of the immediate prospects of selling his two-seater Oxfords. For him the pressing problem was a short-term one, and something of a luxury for a manufacturer with his first vehicle still not past the prototype stage. Morris's concern was to fulfill the firm order for 400 Oxfords that, in a remarkable coup of salesmanship, he had won at the previous autumn's Motor Show – despite the fact that the prototype Oxford had not been finished in time to go on to the stand, and that a set of blueprints and some very inventive performance figures had been the only information potential customers could go by.

That Morris Oxford, the first of the long line of Bullnoses that are every bit as much part of British inter-war culture as Ramsay MacDonald, Stanley Baldwin, or the General Strike, was rolled out in March 1913 – some 6 months after it was announced to the press and the public, and almost 3 years after 30-year-old Morris had formulated his first thoughts on the type of car that would, he hoped, bring about a massive expansion of car ownership and personal mobility, and dismiss once and for all the notion that motoring was only for the seriously rich.

Besides being cheap to buy, the car would have to offer a much higher standard of performance, comfort, and handling then the flimsy cyclecars that were all that was then available at an affordable price level. Just because the car was economically priced it did not have to be poorly made or unreliable in service – just the opposite, in fact, for customers on lower budgets who relied on their cars for their businesses or for their social engagements would be less able to tolerate the expense of repairs or the inconvenience of breakdowns than the affluent amateurs for whom expensive and powerful cars were more of a rich-man's hobby than a necessity of everyday life.

Not only were Morris's buyers' budgets likely to be restricted, his own was, too. With backing to the tune of just £8,000, his scope for original development work was not broad, even taking into account the way in which his intuitive ideas often led directly to a quick and convenient solution; not surprisingly, Morris elected, as has been well documented, to forsake creating his own car completely from scratch and instead to use as many proprietary bought-in components as possible. In that way Morris was likely to gain on two crucial counts: the bought-in components would not only work out cheaper than their in-house developed equivalents (in the medium term, at least) but their familiarity in motoring circles would provide the public with much greater assurance of reliability than the unknown quantity represented by new designs from a new producer just starting up in business.

As a result, the first Oxfords contained much more hardware bought in from outside suppliers than components designed and built by Morris's themselves: in particular, major assemblies such as the engine, clutch, gearbox, and rear axle were all bought in. Indeed, a contemporary magazine report on the car questioned teasingly whether there were any genuine Morris items on the Cowley at all. Morris did not differ from his contemporaries in this, however; most of the myriad fledgling producers faced similar difficulties, though rather than covering up the fact Morris turned it to his advantage by claiming the Oxford to be 'The only Light Car which embodies the joint Productions of the greatest British Experts.[1]

Ironically it was one of these outside suppliers – White and Poppe of Coventry – who were largely responsible for the delay in the launch of the Oxford. Problems in casting the block of the four-cylinder, 60 × 90 mm engine, besides preventing any car at all from being shown at the 1912 Motor Show, meant that the car shown at the North of England Show the following spring had to be displayed with a wooden dummy powerplant, though reports indicate that the unit was quite a convincing fake. Proper, fully operational engines began trickling through shortly afterwards, and Stewart and Ardern, whose order for 250 had rewarded them with the London franchise for Morris cars, accepted the first production vehicle in March 1913. Gordon Stewart's collection of the car from the Cowley works is another one of those well-documented episodes in the history of the Morris car enterprise.

That brief embarrassment proved to be the only real teething trouble with the Oxford, and production models were received with some considerable enthusiasm by press and public alike. Morris had done his background work well, and though his product was not a major technical leap forward over its contemporaries, it did at least represent an intelligent synthesis of most of the better ideas in current circulation.

Of some technical interest, however, were the all-steel wheels made by Sankey in Birmingham – Morris was the first manufacturer to exploit their greater strength, durability, and accuracy – and the torque tube which enclosed the propeller shaft. Described as a 'distinctive feature' in the original Oxford brochure, the torque tube was claimed to make the transmission—

. . . enclosed from starting handle to rear wheels and absolutely dust- and water-proof, the oil-retaining housing protecting it from undue wear, thus increasing the efficiency and providing greatly prolonged life and freedom from trouble.

It was perhaps no coincidence that the American Hupmobile car for which Morris held a franchise, shared that same feature. It was an expensive feature to include in a low-priced car, but can be seen as a clear demonstration of the priority Morris placed on quality and reliability rather than absolute reductions in cost. And as we shall see later, Morris preferred to keep the costs of his cars down by improvements in the production process and by increasing production volumes, rather than by paring equipment levels down to the bone or cutting back on quality.

The publicity material for the Oxford therefore made the equally important point that the car was unusually well-equipped for a light car and that its accessories and fitting constituted—

a record of completeness and quality on any small car sold at so reasonable a figure. Almost every requirement to make the Car absolutely complete and ready for the road has been included in the specification.

The 'reasonable figure' referred to was the sum of £165 – good value for a well-equipped and well-made two-seater, but some way above the £135 charged for the Ford Model T, at that stage already being built in Manchester from components imported from the United States. Plenty of other cars were cheaper, too, notably the £115 Humberette which, like the Oxford, showed the way in which the car market was moving, away from the flimsy cyclecars and three-wheelers and towards the genuine light car, laid out along big-car design principles but more modest in its dimensions, power, and performance.

The Oxford's welcome was enthusiastic, although at that stage there was little to mark it (or its ambitious creator) apart from the shoals of other fledgling British makes, of which J.S. Critchley's 1913 *Yearbook of British Motor Vehicles* listed no fewer than 64. The Oxford earned particular praise for its four-cylinder White and Poppe engine, an unusually high-revving unit for that time. *The Autocar* described it as the 'revviest small engine sold to the public', while the tester from *The Cyclecar* was more specific:

The engine is designed to attain a very high rate of revolution . . . and does not pull well at low speeds. Therefore, the revolutions have to be kept as high as possible and all changes down made early. Thus the change from top to second should be made whenever the speed drops much below 30 mph on a hill. As over 38 mph was actually attained in second gear, it will be seen that these changes do not necessitate a low average speed . . . at 38 mph the engine was doing over 3800 rpm, at which speed there was practically no vibration . . . It will be seen that the Morris Oxford is a speedy little machine.[2]

Also worthy of praise, according to contemporary press reports, were the comfortable suspension of the Bullnose (as the Oxford and later Cowley soon became affectionately nicknamed), presumably helped in no small measure by the springs which were exceptionally great in length by the standards of the day. The clutch and the steering did not emerge so glowingly, however. The former, an elaborate multiplate design, had a tendency to drag and to fail to free off from a cold start, and the latter was, by all accounts, excessively sensitive because of some of the more basic aspects of its geometry.

These faults swiftly corrected, the Oxford was quick to gain itself a good reputation – aided in no small measure by Morris's own competitive efforts in trials and reliability events across the country. Legend even has it that in some of the longer events other Morris drivers became tired before their cars did; they had to be forcibly revived with strong coffee by WRM in person, so that all five could earn their gold medals.

For the following model season Morris expanded Oxford production from a single model to a broader range, taking in commercial and van models priced between £175 and £230, while the more plushly equipped *de luxe*, sporting, and *coupé de luxe* models took the top price up to £255. The standard model, meanwhile, had risen to £180, an increase which the catalogue was at great pains to justify as being for 'improvements in the hundred-and-one details of a car and increased value'. The catalogue is also interesting in that its foreword neatly, albeit somewhat pompously, encapsulates the engineering and marketing philosophies that were to become central to Morris's strategies in decades to come:

Those who have been conversant with our car during 1913 will not find any radical changes in design in the following pages, not that we would discourage innovation, as every modification or change that promises for the better receives most careful consideration, but we will not make changes for the sake of coming into line with others, after having produced in the previous year a car which has proved so successful from every point of view.

Morris's plans for the 1914 model year called for a massive increase in production to 1500-plus, from the already impressive 400-odd he had sold in the 8 months the Oxford had been available in 1913. But here he came up against a serious hurdle, and ironically the hurdle was indirectly one of his own making. Besides the expansion of output for the already revealed Oxford derivatives, Morris was also determined to go ahead with a larger and longer version, capable of seating four passengers. This he would call the Cowley, and he expected it to sell in greater numbers still, even though it would inevitably be considerably more expensive. To keep that extra cost to a minimum, however, Morris hoped to achieve a reduction in the price of the proprietary parts he bought in, in particular the engine, which he wanted at the same time to be bigger and more powerful. White and Poppe were unable to quote either the price or, crucially, the large quantity Morris

Touring cars for hire outside the Morris Garage, Longwall St., Oxford.

New Morris cars impressively lined along Hollow Way, Cowley.
[Nuffield Place collection]

wanted. Nor could any other British or European engine supplier, so Morris took the dramatic step of travelling to America in search of a suitable source of low-priced powertrains.

Morris had long held a fascination and a respect for the mass-production methods then gaining ground in the USA; he was firmly convinced that the use of such methods, albeit on a less massive scale than at Ford's vast Model T plant in Dearborn, would give him the keen cost advantage that he was seeking – the key saving that would enable him to maintain or even lower his prices while still improving the quality of his output. But the purpose of this 1913 visit was a more immediate one: to secure supplies of a four-cylinder engine at a good price and at a suitable tempo. For a British producer the rate of 5,000 a year was unheard of: for the equivalent American firm Morris's order for 5,000 engines was an easy, routine transaction, one that could be slotted in between other, larger jobs.

Continental of Detroit agreed that they could adapt one of their existing engine designs to suit Morris's requirements: the cost, depending on whose account one goes by, was to be between £18 and £25 per engine/gearbox unit, a massive saving on the £50 which White and Poppe later quoted when presented with the Continental drawings and invited to counter-bid. Morris returned to the USA in 1914, accompanied by White and Poppe's chief draughtsman Hans Landstad who wished to discover the secret behind Continental's astonishing prices. Morris travelled first class, Landstad second class. The stores of how Landstad, a poor sailor, was persuaded by Morris to design and draw virtually the complete new Cowley chassis in his confined cabin in rough Atlantic seas are perhaps apocryphal, but the legend does illustrate important character traits of the two men – Morris's often ruthless determination to get enough detail finalized so that the maximum number of American parts could be specified, and Landstad's unswerving loyalty to, and faith in, William Morris.

Morris's visit was highly successful and a contract was signed with Continental for an initial batch of 1,500 engines. On his way home Morris came within hairsbreadth of death: the ship he had been due to sail on sank in the St. Lawrence Seaway with great loss of life but Morris, fortuitously, had missed the boat due to a late train connection. Transatlantic travel was little less hazardous when Landstad followed shortly before Christmas that year, after having seen the Continental engines into production: the First World War had just broken out. Typically, Morris had refused to go back on his order just because a war had flared up, and

Portrait photograph of a confident William Morris, 1910.
[F.J. Minns]

though the turning over of the Cowley factory to munitions work meant that car production work was officially halted, during the war years Morris's managed, as we shall see, to build almost 2000 Oxfords from components held in stock and from the few Continental engines that managed to make the perilous transatlantic trip.

This total meant that the war affected Morris much less than did the Second World War 30 years later; the transition to munitions production did, in fact, allow Morris to put many of his American mass production lessons into practice. And crucially, with plenty of time at his disposal to finalize the design details of his post-war Oxford and Cowley ranges, there can be no doubt that William Morris and WRM Motors Ltd were in a uniquely strong position to capitalize on the great boom that soon followed the ending of the war in November 1918.

Notes

1. From a Morris advertisement placed in *The Autocar* of 15 February 1913, quoted by Jarman and Barraclough in *The Bullnose Morris*, p. 23.
2. *The Cyclecar*, 6 August 1913. Quoted by Jarman and Barraclough, op. cit.
3. The fastidiousness with which Morris recorded every cost in the make-up of his cars is revealed in the detailed estimate for the 1915 Cowley which has been preserved. The most expensive item is the engine, complete, at £17.14.6d; front and rear axles come close at just under £17 complete, while the body, hood and screens are listed at £15. The cheapest items listed are various springs, washers, and clips, separately billed at 2d each; insulating tape valued at 1d and insulating staples at 2d go into each car, while the cost of fitting all five tyres is 8d and consumes 1d worth of French chalk. Each exhaust flange costs 4d, with 1d allowed for machining; overheads, advertising costs, WRM's American expenses, and the cost of experimental work and testing, boiled down to the effective cost per car, are all included, too, and a 10 per cent profit margin is applied to the total.

Chapter 5

Boom, slump, boom

The Great War had reduced car production to a trickle, yet during that war wages had been forced up by the pace of munitions work, leading to much greater spending potential among a much broader slice of society. That spending power was soon to find a ready outlet, fuelled by the widespread interest in, and familiarity with, motor vehicles created by that gruesome first mass-mechanized war.

Motorcycles, cyclecars, cars, and other means of personal mobility were suddenly the object of everyone's ambitions. And, thanks to the war, the wages, and the war gratuities, many more aspiring motorists actually had the means to fulfill their ambitions. In short, all was set for a boom in motor vehicle sales, and a vast proliferation of obscure makes and weird and wonderful vehicles appeared almost overnight.

William Morris had naturally foreseen this bull market, too, but he was infinitely better prepared than most. He had had the luxury of being able to keep production ticking over, albeit at a frustratingly low rate, during the war, thanks largely to the stocks of Continental engines which had found their way across the Atlantic during the early war years. Over 1,100 Continental-engined Cowleys had been built and sold before the Armistice; production of the Oxford, with a White and Poppe engine, had proceeded at an even slower pace because of still greater restrictions on supplies.

Morris knew, however, that Continental would be ceasing production of the Red Seal engine (at 1.5 litres it was considered too small for the American market); he had been looking for an alternative engine supplier for some time. The Continental-engined Cowley had built up a very good reputation during the war: it was very good to drive, it was exceptionally reliable, it was comfortable, and, remarkably, it was actually cheaper than the smaller, slower, and less well-equipped Oxford – the difference being, of course, due to the Cowley's almost completely American mechanical equipment coming in at rock-bottom prices.

Contemporary press reports gushes with praise for the model, and 'Runabout', writing in *The Autocar*,[1] was particularly smitten:

The car strikes me as inaugurating a new era. I speak in all soberness, but it has never before happened that I have sampled a new chassis without – secretly or explicitly – picking some holes in its road manners . . . Here was a car I could not criticise. Then I realised I was handling the first offspring of a wedlock between British ideals and American methods, begotten here – wholly; made there – partly.

Perhaps unfortunately for Morris's immediate prospects, that Anglo-American 'wedlock' was not to last long. Morris's cars sold very well at the tail end of 1918 but by the summer of the following year – the peak of the immediate post-war boom, as it turned out – production had to be trimmed because of a lack of components. Morris had by this time found an engine supplier willing to make a virtual copy of the Continental engine for less than his stipulated £50: that supplier was the Coventry branch of the French armaments manufacturer Hotchkiss. But even Hotchkiss became subject to development delays, and Morris's output of Oxfords and Cowleys was nowhere near in line with the tremendous pent-up demand for the vehicles, though by the middle of 1920 Morris models were freely available at last, and a total of almost 2000 were sold – despite a series of price rises since 1915, which had seen a virtual doubling of the cost of the Cowley as well as a threefold increase in the price of the Oxford, a model which in the intervening period had been re-launched as bigger and more luxurious version of the Cowley.

For 1920 Morris had planned to double output to some 4000 units, but he had encountered an unusual obstacle in a restrictive distribution arrangement he had entered into without the proper legal advice. Morris's solution was the seemingly drastic step of putting his thriving company, WRM Motors Ltd, into voluntary liquidation and found a new company, Morris Motors Ltd, with exactly the same assets but without the problematic distributors. That distribution bottleneck out of the way, Morris was set to expand his business still further.

Yet the last quarter of 1920 had seen an ominously marked falling-off in sales, with September's total at 276 but December's down to 92 and January's even lower at 74: the American market had crashed that year before and Europe was following suit. The presence of very cheap American contenders, such as the Ford Model T, did not help, and soon the Morris factory compounds were crammed with unsold cars.

Morris's reaction to the crisis – for that's what the situation was, and he recognized it as such – was to be the making of him as world-class motor

Morris Motors Ltd. Trim shop interior c. 1921.
[Courtesy of Oxfordshire County Libraries]

manufacturer. Resisting his colleagues' suggestions that he should reduce production to keep costs down ('How would that sell those cars out there?' he is said to have retorted) Morris determined instead to *increase* production and slash the prices of his cars.

Contemporaries were openly scathing about his idea, convinced Morris had hit upon a formula better suited to instant and total bankruptcy than recovery. But Morris remained true to his instincts, his belief in the so-called pyramid of demand where, to quote an article he later wrote in a business magazine:

Even a ten-pound reduction in price drops you into an entirely new market, a wider base of consumption power. If the man cannot pay the last £10 in the price, he cannot buy the car. When that £10 is knocked off, he very often can and will. The one object in life of many makers seems to be to make the thing the public *cannot* buy. The one object of my life was been to make the thing they *can* buy.[2]

And in response to his sales managers' suggestions that he was cutting the profit margin per car to paper-thin levels, Morris pointed to the yard, full of unsold cars, and reminded his colleagues that those cars were not making any profit whatsoever.

The price cut, of up to £100 or a full 20 per cent in the case of certain models, was a typically dramatic gesture from which Morris naturally extracted the maximum publicity value. But it was not as arbitrary a move as it looked, for Morris had looked very carefully at every aspect of his production processes and trimmed costs wherever possible. He saved most money by streamlining body production: even the dealers' profit margin was shaved to save a few pounds.

By all accounts it was a brave move, and Morris firmly expected not to show any profits for 2 years or more, his main priority being to keep the works going. Yet so spectacular was the leap in sales that the price cut unleashed a huge wave of demand: sales tripled from one month to the next, and soon stabilized at five times the slump figure. And, far from having losses to report, Morris's increased turnover gave him steadily increasing rates of profit, and it was soon clear that high production volumes were the key to keeping costs and prices below those of rival producers.

Morris himself is said to have been surprised at the sheer scale of the success this move unleashed, especially as the climate was still predominantly gloomy and Austin had had to call in the receiver not long before. Morris had clearly judged the public mood absolutely correctly, firm in his belief that people were failing to buy cars not because they did not want cars, but because those cars were offered at the wrong prices. Surprisingly, in view of the immediate boost to Morris sales that the February price cuts provided, Morris's rivals were slow to follow his lead, though by the time of the 1921 Motor Show most had trimmed their prices quite substantially.

What the other producers were not prepared for, however, was for Morris to cut his prices still further, again by a seemingly impossible £100 in some cases. Demand again shot up, and this time Morris was in a position to fulfill it. Output doubled and redoubled each year until by 1925 it had reached a peak of over 54,000, representing two out of every five cars produced in Britain. Morris was by now the market leader and dictated the pace when it came to price-setting and model specification; many competitors were driven to financial ruin slavishly trying to keep up with Morris's price moves, but with profits racing ahead to the million mark in 1925 Morris had already become a rich man.

His secret had been to keep his range as simple as possible: though at times there had been as many as two dozen different variants on offer, each had fundamentally the same chassis and engine, and each could be built in the then astonishing time of 41½ minutes. The cars themselves were straightforward, well presented, and reliable: Morris did not believe in cutting the specifications to the bone or aiming to be the cheapest of all, and his sales manager, later Vice-Chairman, Sir Miles Thomas once remarked that 'no-one wants to keep down with the Joneses'.

Other novel marketing initiatives added still further to the Cowley and Oxford's sales appeal. Morris was one of the pioneers of hire purchase, and for a while the cars were offered with a year's comprehensive insurance included in the purchase price. And there was no doubt, either, that the regular but mainly cosmetic annual changes to each model kept public interest running at a high level.

Yet for a proprietor who set so much store by efficiency and cost-saving, Morris's production processes at Cowley were surprisingly archaic. He had some grudging respect for Henry Ford and his vast Dearborn Model T plant but dismissed contemptuously the 'current notion that if you only make enough of given article, your price will come down romantically'.[3]

Morris did not see the point of installing a Ford-type moving conveyor belt system at Cowley, believing that such a device was only suitable for very large production volumes. Only once the chassis had their suspension and wheels fitted did Morris see fit to move the vehicles along mechanically:

they were pulled by a chain with hooks attached, and for many years that system suited Morris's output levels quite adequately.

Headlong expansion had meant that many of Morris's outside suppliers were unable to keep pace with his spiralling demands; the solution in many cases was for Morris to buy the businesses outright and make the necessary improvements himself. One such example was the Hotchkiss engine works, taken over in 1923 when the management had claimed it would be impossible to step up production from 300 to 500 engines a week as Morris had demanded. Within months Morris had the factory building 600 engines a week from exactly the same space, and shortly afterwards a massive new cylinder-block grinding machine was installed to take capacity up to 800 engines weekly. With other suppliers Morris was able to offer advice on the streamlining of production and the setting-up of machine tools, though there can be no doubt that he was an extremely demanding customer. As he himself stated:

Economy being our main principle, we frequently ask contractors to do work at prices they believe to be impossibly low. Usually they have not realised the savings which we can help them to effect by standardising operations, by giving a continual flow of work and by technical assistance.[4]

Yet there was one area in which Morris can be seen to have been fatally weak. Though he spent his every waking moment (which was generally the major proportion of each 24-hour day) in his office or at the Cowley works and ploughed all the profits directly back into the company's coffers, he sanctioned little or no investment in the design or improvement of his cars, let alone committing funds to research that might lead to radically improved vehicles in future years.

In consequence, the Bullnosed Cowley and Oxford underwent only very restricted development during their lifetime. The chassis and engines remained virtually unaltered (apart from the option, later standardized, or an 1.8 litre engine on the Oxford); the only major improvements over the years were the inclusion of four-wheel brakes and balloon tyres. By 1926, therefore, the Bullnoses were beginning to look just a little tired in comparison with the more youthful opposition, and, as if in confirmation of this observation, sales began to nosedive. The problem was not just confined to the old-fashioned image of the Bullnose: the vehicle itself was quite large and Austin's phenomenal success with the ingenious 'baby' Austin Seven had exposed Morris's lack of a suitable competitor.

The cure was a simple, but only partial one: a new range of cars of roughly the same size and still carrying the Cowley and Oxford names, but with new-style 'flat' radiators – cars which, although much more modern in their appearance and in some aspects of their construction, still made use of many Bullnose-era components.

Shortly before the announcement of the new models, William Morris had turned Morris Motors into a public company, issuing 3 million non-voting preference shares to a hysterical Stock Exchange and keeping the 2 million ordinary shares, and thus total control of the company, to himself. Morris had, however, always sought to keep away from any obligations to bankers, partners, or shareholders, so it was not without a few regrets that he brought the era of the Bullnose, the car that had shot him into the millionaire bracket and earned him a title, to a quiet close.

Notes

1. *The Autocar*, 23 October 1915.
2. *System*, February 1924, p. 74.
3. *System*, op. cit.
4. *System*, op. cit.

Chapter 6
The first crisis

The year of the General Strike and the aftermath of the first Labour government, 1926, was quite a momentous year for the nation. It was a year of some significance for Morris Motors, too, although the company's difficulties had little to do with what was going on outside the confines of Cowley and its expanding web of supply subsidiaries dotted around the Midlands.

Morris's central problem was one largely of his own making: after a long and highly successful production run with the Bullnosed Oxford and Cowley, his vision had become blinkered to any other type of vehicle, especially if that vehicle was smaller or cheaper. The nature of the market had changed: incomes were rising, bringing a whole new tranche of customers (in the main converts from motorcycle and sidecar outfits) into the lower end of the car net. Austin was successfully tapping this growing sector with the 'baby' Austin Seven, a car which, incidentally, the gifted Sir Herbert had designed on his own initiative and against the wishes of his board. No longer was a single-model policy good enough to maintain market position.

Yet Morris was strongly against the development of a small car, refusing to take the Austin Seven seriously and preferring instead to concentrate his resources on larger-engined cars which, he figured with a certain perceptiveness, would have much better export potential than small machines designed around peculiarly British driving and taxation conditions. Yet events were to prove that it would be the wrong time for the company to take such a long-term stand.

Swept along in the tide of Morris's single-mindedness, the company's reaction had therefore been to embark on the development, often hurried and invariably haphazard, of several bigger models, and to ignore the increasingly large share of the market then being taken by the Austin Seven. And despite repeated entreaties from his sales manager, Miles Thomas, it was only after 2 years, when the Austin Seven began perceptibly to nibble at the sales of the lower end of the Cowley range, that William

Morris woke up to the need for a small car to compete in the 7 hp class.[1] Morris's official biography glosses over this unfortunate phase, stating simply that Morris preferred 'first to try to educate the British public in favour of the bigger car, so that he [Morris] would develop a home market for cars which he could export.[2]

Development of what was to become the first Morris Minor could, however, only begin once the planned larger models had been successfully launched; those launches were made more complicated by Morris's acquisition of Wolseley in 1927 and his subsequent desire to incorporate Wolseley expertise, componentry, and manufacturing capacity in some of those vehicles.

It was an ironic twist that it had been Sir Herbert Austin who, 2 years previously, had proposed a three-way merger between his company (which was admittedly struggling for cash at the time), Morris, and Wolseley – the latter organization actually having been founded by Austin some 20 years earlier. Morris had rejected the idea, partly on the grounds that he did not want to relinquish the absolute control he enjoyed over his own organization, but also because he believed, prophetically as it later turned out, that 'the organisation would be so great that it would be difficult to control and might tend to strangle itself'.[3]

And, in the final twist of irony amid the tense atmosphere of the auction, it must have been especially galling to Austin, always hampered by a heavy burden of debt, to see Wolseley sold off to his bitterest rival, Morris, whose financial problems were non-existent. Morris's preliminary written bid of £600,000 had been exceed by Austin: at the receiver's office the rivals, and a mysterious third-party bidder who was later believed to have been a General Motors emissary, began to out-bid one another in £1000 steps. 'The bidding', reported Morris's sales manager Miles Thomas, present at the auction, 'went on, each leap-frogging the other, until I noticed a whispered conversation between a rather tense-looking Paton (Austin's finance director) and a very flushed and bright-eyed Mr Morris. I was able to hear the gist of the whispering which on Morris's part with his chin well stuck out, was to the effect that he was determined to out-bid Austin. He repeated that assertion out loud for all to hear. The Morris finances were very sound, and so at £730,000 Wolseley Motors was knocked down to Morris.'[4]

Morris now had an even more disparate collection of factories under his command, though Wolseley remained his own personal property and was not integrated into the main Morris empire until much later. Even so, it

Morris's first factory, Hollow Way, Cowley.
[Nuffield Place collection]

Chassis on the factory floor.
[Nuffield Place collection]

took some time to digest Wolseley, and this must have held back development work on the projects in hand.

The most important of these, ignoring for the moment the lack of a small-car project, was without doubt the Flatnosed replacement for the much-loved Bullnosed series. The Flatnose – not its official title, of course – was, in effect, an updated Bullnose with novel vibration-reducing rubber-mounted engine and a stronger chassis to handle the loads imposed by four-wheel braking. The bodywork was novel, too, not so much in its styling but in its construction, for the Flatnose was the first Morris to be planned with an all-steel body. Many figures in industry, including William Morris, had become convinced that the American technique of pressing the whole body from sheet steel was a much better way of building a car than stretching fabric over a wooden or metal frame. Morris had invested heavily in a joint venture with the US Budd Corporation and established the Pressed Steel Company near the Morris works at Cowley, but endless teething troubles meant that for some time the bodies produced were not of sufficient quality to be used in production vehicles. Miles Thomas documents in some detail the appalling standard of the early Oxford bodies out of the Pressed Steel plant:

> When the first Morris Oxford bodies were pushed through to my dispatch department for examination by the Morris management all hell was let loose. The panels were ripped, the aperture for the windscreen was awry . . . the doors only fitted where they touched. The whole thing was an impossible product.[5]

The upshot was that the bulk of early Flatnose production had to have coach-built bodywork instead of all-steel construction. The 1927 models were afforded a good reception by the press, with *The Autocar*'s critic viewing the changeover in surprisingly humanitarian terms:

> Though lots of enthusiasts will mourn the death of the Bullnosed Morris, a single glance at the 1927 coachwork justifies the change. The Morris policy is unquestionably right when human beings dislike being compressed into their cars and are being educated to appreciate coachwork.[6]

The new range imparted a certain additional momentum to Morris sales: the last years of the decade were some of Morris's best ever, buoying up profits to over £1.5 million into the 1930 trading year. But those benefits were to prove short-lived: the rosy figures concealed many serious underlying problems and may have been instrumental in reinforcing the atmosphere of complacency at Cowley, itself born out of the increasingly haphazard style of management put across by William Morris.

Ever since his acquisition of Wolseley in 1927, William Morris had, to quote Miles Thomas (who was possibly the closest anyone ever came to him) 'become increasingly preoccupied with minor technical details, besides showing a tendency to shun Board meetings, exhibiting a predilection for taking decisions without consultation, and apparently embarking on an undeclared policy of pitting the constituent companies against each other'.[7]

The muddled range of larger cars that emerged after 1927 was a testament to Morris's individualistic style of decision-making; even Morris's rival for the Austin Seven, the Minor, which came not a moment too early in 1928, bore the imprint of impulsive thinking and suffered a handicap in the marketplace as a result. Morris had been impressed by the then-advanced technology of Wolseley's six-cylinder overhead camshaft engines and decided that a four-cylinder derivative would be the ideal unit to power the new small car. But the engine proved troublesome in service as well as expensive to build, and sales were disappointing.

These results, combined with the collapse of Cowley sales in the early 1930s, led to a virtual halving of profits for 1931 and began to expose the weakness of the Morris management. All too often Morris, who was becoming increasingly fond of long annual sea voyages where he would remain incommunicado except for the occasional telegram of admonition or advice, would overturn decisions which had had to be made in his absence; the sprawling network of subsidiary plants were encouraged to drag each other down destructively rather than cooperate constructively,[8] and an unwieldy range of up to twenty separate models and twelve different engines compared unfavourably with Austin's four engines and four car types and Ford's reliance on just two of each.[9]

One after another, Morris's senior lieutenants departed in despair that their counsel was so rarely heeded: many of the great and loyal management talents that Morris had been keeping cooped up for so long departed at this time. In retrospect, this era can be seen as a critical turning point in the history of Morris, and it can also be said without causing too much offence that this was the time that, perhaps unbeknown to him, Morris began effectively to lose his constructive grip on the affairs of the company. Gone was the positive, guiding hand of a founder who knew the business inside out and who had his finger on the pulse of the car market;

Morris seated in the first £100 car.

MGs on display at the MG factory, c. 1930.
[Courtesy of Oxfordshire County Libraries]

in its place emerged a difficult and ultimately destructive form of non-management which saw the combine drift with little direction save that of downhill.

Even the diplomatically couched language of Morris's official biography reveals that there were serious difficulties:

There was some uncertainty in management at this difficult time . . . Mr Blake was under some difficulty in his relations with other managers when it was a question of developing a new model . . . There was some internal strife and, looking at the matter from our much later standpoint, Morris himself seems to have been too readily troubled with minor details. Be that as it may, he certainly got extremely annoyed with some of the faults which were uncovered in the details of the finished cars and was not at all satisfied that they were a necessary consequence of the speed at which the cars in question had been brought to the market.[10]

It had indeed been a daunting task for any manufacturer, even the market leader that Morris just about was, to launch half a dozen new models within the space of 4 years. And perhaps because of this, affairs at Cowley became steadily more and more muddled until Morris himself was forced in a dramatic move to go to Leonard Lord, who had been impressive in the way he had completely reorganized Wolseley, and say 'I want you at Cowley. Things are in a mess there.'[11]

To his great credit, Morris accorded with Lord's preconditions and handed over the complete control of Cowley. Lord was an abrasive but brilliant engineer: in particular he had won favour as the designer of the cheaper side-valve engine (which some say he copied closely from the Ford Model Y which had shot to success in 1932) for the Morris Minor, a move which brought the car's price down and its profitability up, and which ultimately allowed it to spawn Morris's historic £100 car. But Lord's real forte was in the new science of manufacturing technology: he was a production engineer *par excellence*. Lord had gone to Cowley in 1933 on the understanding that he would stay until Morris had once more gained ascendancy over Austin: he immediately set to on an emergency programme of capital investment on an unprecendented scale.

Lord rapidly brought Cowley into the twentieth century by abolishing old practices, ripping out antiquated tooling, and installing a proper moving production line, feeding components in by overhead conveyors. In 1934 alone some £300,000 was spent on the plant, three times what Morris had spent to date. By 1936 some half a million pounds had been invested, and Cowley was one of the most advanced plants in Europe, with an annual production capacity of 100,000. At the same time Lord set about rationalizing the other production facilities and reorganizing the Morris, Wolseley, MG, and Morris Commercial ranges on more rational lines, and by 1937 the catalogue had been reduced to fifteen basic models and eight basic engines, compared with a peak of twenty-three models and eighteen engines between 1933 and 1935.

Ford, in the meantime, had made a strong recovery on the strength of three or four models spearheaded by the do-or-die US-designed Model Y, launched in 1933; Austin, too, existed comfortably on seven or eight staple and successful lines. But Lord's changes were beginning to show positive effect: the Minor had been selling quite well in its cheaper side-valve form, but the first really important product of the Lord era was the Morris Eight, launched in 1934 and destined to be Britain's best-selling car of the inter-war period, surpassing even the 390,000 total of the Bullnosed Cowley and Oxford.

William Morris, or Lord Nuffield as he had just become, took the unusual step of absenting himself from the whole design process for the Eight, short of approving the original policy decision to market a car in that class. Lord's design bore an uncanny resemblance to the Ford Model Y – the very car that had jolted Morris so severely. The Morris was a better car, however, with hydraulic brakes and less primitive suspension, and soon helped to turn Nuffield's profits graph upwards again.

There was the slight diversion of the famous £100 car, said to be Nuffield's own idea. The long-suffering Landstad was commissioned to shave every possible shilling off the basic Minor until it could be sold for exactly £100: this achieved, the engineers went on to even greater feats of brilliance to produce two publicity-stunt versions of the £100 car – the first capable of 100 mph thanks to careful streamlining and absurdly high supercharging of its once-feeble engine; the second coaxed to give 100 mpg on a weird concoction of benzole while crawling along at an average of 15 mph the advertisements duly proclaimed the tiny two-seater to be the £100 car that does 100 mph and 100 mpg – no doubt the campaign would have fallen foul of today's strict controls over advertising licence.

The £100 car was a financial and emotional landmark but little else. By all accounts it sold poorly, surprising no-one but Nuffield who earlier, as William Morris, had boasted to *The Economist* that this was the 'first commercially successful British car to sell at the rough figure of £100'.[12] Miles Thomas, meanwhile, had the uncomfortable satisfaction of witnessing the proof of his theory that the last thing buyers wanted was something that

Chapter 7

Post-war: the slide begins

As far as appearances were concerned, the Morris organization had been the very embodiment of corporate health and dynamism in the immediate run-up to the Second World War; there was every reason to be extremely optimistic about the future.

The company had wrested market leadership back from transient upstarts Ford; it was turning in highly respectable profit figures, it was set to produce more cars than ever before in its history, and it controlled an unrivalled portfolio of famous marques which, correctly handled, promised almost unlimited expansion on the world's markets in years to come.

The Morris name spoke for itself, the down-to-earth people's car that had granted mobility to the whole nation over the preceding two decades: the name that spelt respectability as well as quality at an affordable price. Wolseley, too, had been turned round to become an important asset, in the public eye, at least. Wolseleys were bigger, sturdier, and more dignified than the Morris models with which they shared so many of their components; they incorporated cautious engineering innovations and enjoyed a classy, quality image similar to that of Rover, or perhaps even Audi or Mercedes today.

MG was thriving. Europe's biggest builder of sports cars, MG enjoyed an excellent rate of return on its assets, and the long-term export potential for the simple, honest, and appealing sports models – models which, according to an official from the factory at Abingdon, 'look a darned sight faster than they actually are' – was plain for all to see.

The fourth weapon in Nuffield's armoury was the recently acquired Riley company. Bought by Lord Nuffield privately for a knockdown sum in September 1938 (and even then there is the suspicion that he acquired the firm more as an act of compassion for the bankrupt Riley brothers than as part of a conscious policy of diversification), Riley appeared to provide Nuffield with no more than little-needed extra production capacity and managerial headaches. Yet, though there is little evidence to suggest that Lord Nuffield was conscious of it at the time, the Riley marque name also brought with it terrific marketing potential, this time in the form of quality sports saloons with strong style and high-grade engineering content – in other words the direct equivalent of today's highly successful BMWs.

On the industrial front, Nuffield was a heavyweight, too. Morris's Cowley works were not only just about the most modern in Europe but also close on the biggest, too; the Engines Branch in Coventry – on the site once used by White and Poppe – was, with an average weekly output of some 3250 engines, 'easily the largest producer of automobile power units in Europe'.[1]

In a special May 1939 supplement entitled 'Britain's Greatest Motor Business', *The Motor* had positively gushed with tributes to Viscount Nuffield, his business acumen, his huge organization, and his unrivalled philanthropy. 'The nation's greatest donor,' wrote *The Motor*'s managing editor, A.C. Armstrong, is a 'shrewd judge of man, himself an indomitable, untiring worker. All his life he has gathered round him brilliant executives. He has not been concerned with amassing wealth or wielding great power. He lives simply in a moderately sized home with a beautiful garden near Huntercombe.' In resounding tones, another writer in *The Motor* felt moved to compare the elaborate structure of Nuffield's organization and its many subsidiaries not with a mere car company but with no less an institution than the British Empire itself, the analogy being that of the many and disparate self-contained subsidiaries having a common head in Viscount Nuffield.

Yet much of the reality differed starkly from the rosy image so successfully engineered by Morris's public relations machinery. A large proportion of the 'brilliant executives' which *The Motor* proudly stated that Nuffield gathered around him all his life had left. His grip on the company was slackening: even his official biographers note that he was becoming 'increasingly remote from day-to-day management'.[2] His evident intransigence and intolerance led to a succession of departures and, to quote the words of a later commentator, Nuffield 'proved incapable of retaining his best men, and especially of fostering managerial cohesion in the face of rapid growth and of the complex industrial problems of a large organisation'.[3]

Those members of the management team who were still in place were clearly finding Lord Nuffield an increasingly difficult and erratic master; the relationships between head office and the dozen or more satellite plants were complex, to say the least, and the broad spread of brand names and models that looked so impressive on paper was riddled with costly duplication, overlap and anomaly. 'Morris did not try too hard to swim against the tide' wrote his long-standing (and, it is claimed, long-suffering) number two Miles (later Sir Miles) Thomas some 20 years later. 'He resigned himself to the inevitable, but drifted farther and farther away from the business that he had built up and now by interference, rather than by spoken or written opinion, still controlled.'[4]

As a consequence of these escalating management preoccupations, Morris had for many years been failing to plough back a sufficient proportion of his considerable profits into the all-important areas of research and development and product planning. Ford, Austin, and even Vauxhall (owned by General Motors) were investing much more, and the difference certainly showed in the deep-down disarray of the Morris group's ostensibly all-embracing model strategy. Where his rivals had relatively few model lines, produced in decent numbers and generally at a single central (and therefore easily managed) plant, Morris's seemingly less random selection of lower-volume products from his haphazard scattering of facilities must have cost proportionally much more to build; where his rivals were planning well ahead, Morris, having lost the important management momentum generated during those few short but dynamic years under Leonard Lord, was beginning to drift with little evidence of any long-term strategy.

To make matters worse, Lord parted with Nuffield in 1936 on terms which have been variously interpreted as cordial, cool, or even acrimonious. There had been tension between the two for some while: the dispute that finally forced the issue was over money. Lord demanded a substantial rise in remuneration as reward for his key part in turning the company round; with many millions now pouring into the company's coffers, there was perhaps some justification in Lord's wish to share a greater portion of the spoils, though the exact extent of his demands will never be known. Lord Nuffield, with equal stubbornness, turned down Lord's demands, though again Morris's official biographers gloss over the episode and state simply that the parting was Lord's 'personal decision'. Andrews and Brunner further state that 'he [Lord] and Nuffield retained their respect for one another' and Lord later commented:

. . . there was no row between us. A few minutes after we had decided to break our business relations we had a gin and French together, and we laughed over the fact that we could both sit drinking, although we had taken a step that grieved us both.'[5]

Robert Jackson in *The Nuffield Story* backs up the view that the break was not as bitter as had been reported:

> After the break came, Nuffield sent for Lord and showed how big his generosity was. They gossiped for a while about everything except the business in hand. Finally Nuffield said: 'Now that you're leaving me, Len. I want you to take this with you.'
>
> He handed over a cheque and it was for £50,000. [Quite a sum in those days]
>
> Part of the reason for the break was money and Lord said: 'But, WR, I can't take it. I'll take the usual compensation if you like, but I can't take £50,000 from you.'
>
> Morris's jaw jutted. 'Len,' he said quietly, waving the cheque back to Lord. 'If you don't take it, I'll never speak to you again. Our friendship will be over.'[6]

Yet the evidence for the equilibrium of the pair's later relationship is not unanimous in its support for such a rosy view: Miles Thomas, in particular, is critical of the way Morris is said to have handled Lord, though again there is an element of personal rivalry between the two aspiring second-in-commands that must have coloured certain judgments.

Lord was already on record as having said quite wittily of his relationship with his boss 'I am pig-headed and Lord Nuffield has his opinions'. Yet could there perhaps have been something slightly more than professional rivalry in his later and much-reported vow, referring to his former Cowley workplace, to 'take that place apart, brick by bloody brick'?

It must at times have seemed to Nuffield that Lord was indeed intent on going through with this half-jesting threat when, after less than 2 years administering Nuffield's Special Areas Trust (a position created and paid for by Nuffield himself, though it is still hard to avoid the suspicion that it was a delaying tactic on WRM's part), Lord was appointed managing director of arch-rival Austin's, with the clear implication that he was being groomed to step into the shoes of the increasingly fragile Sir Herbert.

In a sense, however, all that need not have mattered. For most motor manufacturers the war provided such a clean and complete break from their normal activities that what they were doing before the outbreak ought, to a large extent, to have been irrelevant to their post-war programmes. Whatever the rigours of wartime production and operation under strict government control, it certainly allowed hard-pressed managements a bit of a breathing space: the motor companies' prosperity was officially assured in a way that even the most bullish of peacetime markets could never have completely guaranteed. Wage and material bills were met, and a fixed and fair percentage return was automatically built into each contract.

Everything else being equal (which is not of course often the case, especially in wartime when attention is not supposed to be focused on peacetime pursuits), manufacturers ought by rights to have been able to devote significant attention over this six-year period to the shape of their post-war product line-up and to the design of the models within those ranges. Some did: Austin, for one, announced as early as 1941 that its post-war range would continue the themes set by the pre-war models.

Once the tide of the war had begun to turn and victory was no longer a far-off hope but had begun to be a foreseeable prospect, the War Cabinet began to apply its thoughts to the reconstruction of the shattered British economy in peacetime. Exports were to be vital to Britain's regeneration, and the motor industry was to lead the export drive. By early 1944 the Reconstruction Committee had completed a study of the motor industry and observed perceptively that the British manufacturers had grown under virtual monopoly conditions and that their 'wide variety of different models' would not be well suited to counter the Americans in the export markets. The answer, suggested the Committee, would be to concentrate production on fewer models but build them on a large scale, thus reducing unit costs. In particular, the Committee indicated that higher-powered cars would do better in export markets.

The industry itself would have nothing to do with this attempt at standardization and simplification and, to judge from the lack of enthusiasm with which it greeted the Committee's other suggestions, it appeared to want to tackle the harsh post-war world by muddling along just like it had done before the war.

For most this meant starting from where they had left off in 1939; Austin had enjoyed the advantage – which reputedly had Lord Nuffield seething with jealousy – of continuing to build a limited number of cars for the military throughout the war years while the Morris lines were wholly dedicated to military hardware. Leonard Lord, who had assumed control of Austin shortly after the founder's death in 1941, was determined to be the first back into production once the war ended, and had by April 1945 already sanctioned the expenditure of over £1 million on a new factory. Austin had the distinction of sending the first post-war British export to the United States (before the war with Japan was even over) and by the end of 1945 had built over 12,000 cars, only a minor portion of them sent abroad. Austin had been the first to come out with a new model, too, the '16' launching in August 1945, but the public were to have to wait two more years for the first genuine post-war models, the A40 Devon and Dorset, launched in 1947.

Morris, meanwhile, seemed to have been much less active on the design and planning front: the range announced for 1945/6 was extensive but entirely pre-war in design. But what passed for such apparent stagnation in the company's thinking gave little hint of the furious design and management struggles going on under the surface – struggles that centred on Lord Nuffield's lone insistence that pre-war models, and not advanced new designs, should constitute the post-war Morris, Wolseley, and MG ranges.

A design team under a particularly talented Morris engineer by the name of Issigonis – who was, of course, later to conceive the revolutionary Mini – had completed work on a highly advanced small car codenamed Mosquito, operating largely in secret and certainly without the knowledge of Nuffield. The Mosquito, which was later marketed as the Minor, was of then-radical unitary construction, meaning that there was no separate chassis but a light and rigid box-structure body in steel; the engine was to be an advanced flat four to provide a low centre of gravity, and it was to be mounted well forward to provide good straightline stability. Front suspension was to be independent, the wheels were to be much smaller than was customary, and a smooth, rounded four-door body with integrated front and rear wings was to provide a very modern appearance.

Lord Nuffield's deputy, Sir Miles Thomas, was a passionate supporter of the Mosquito project, believing that it had great worldwide sales potential; he favoured going into full-scale production as soon as the remaining stocks of parts for the pre-war models had been used up. Thomas continually urged the speeding up of Mosquito development, and in September 1945 the Board agreed to commit the company to a build rate of 500 a week. This would have accounted for over half of the total annual output allotted to the Morris marque for the immediate post-war years: the Nuffield group as a whole had been granted sufficient steel supplies for over 70,000 cars a year, and a board meeting in May 1945 had decided that 50,000 of those cars would be Morrises, 7,000 Wolseleys, 6,525 MGs, 7,000 Rileys and 9,000 Morris Commercials. That total, the board were informed by Thomas, represented 35 per cent of the normal peacetime production of the whole country.[7]

Lord Nuffield himself first saw the Mosquito at quite a late stage in its development (it was under test in early 1947) but immediately objected to its shape, which he likened to a 'poached egg on wheels', and attempted to place blocks on the car's inclusion in the Morris catalogue. Indeed, more than one commentator has suggested that if it had been left up to Lord

Nuffield, it is unlikely that the Minor would ever have entered production.[8]
Yet it was a measure of Lord Nuffield's gradually declining authority that,
despite his abundant protests and what Thomas called his 'right of
destructive criticism', the minutes of directors' meetings from 1946 on
include the Mosquito in future product strategies: the boss had effectively
been overruled and forward-looking management team held sway.

A confidential memo from Sir Miles Thomas dated 12 January 1946
shows a Nuffield Organization forward model programme that begins to
resemble a modern model strategy at last. Three main body sizes,
Mosquito, Intermediate (B), and Imperial (C), were to give a good spread
across the whole of the car market: Morris would be alone in marketing the
Mosquito, complete with flat-four engines of 800 and 1100 cc, with the first
variant scheduled to go on sale in January 1947.

The thinking surrounding the Mosquito's companion Wolseley was less
clear:

The (Wolseley) range will consist of the 'Wasp' – an A-type body with Wolseley
front, fitted with a 1-litre four-cylinder in-line engine. If it is impossible to fit a
steering column control for a four-speed gearbox, then a three-speed gearbox with
steering column control will be provided. The power–weight ratio should make
three speeds sufficient. This model will be launched in April 1947.[9]

Both Morris and Wolseley would market B-type intermediate four-door
saloons, the former with 1250 and 1500 cc flat-four engines, the latter using
1500 cc four-cylinder and two-litre six-cylinder in-line engines. Both were to
be introduced in June 1947.

Nuffield's contender in the bigger Imperial class was rather less clearly
pictured, even though the projected September 1947 launch date was only
18 months away:

The other car in the Morris range will be the 'Imperial' and will be the C-series
body fitted with a six-cylinder in-line engine as large as possible bearing in mind
that its four-cylinder version is of 1½ litres.
There will also be a large Wolseley car with the 'C' series body – a four-door six-
light saloon fitted with a six-cylinder engine as large as possible (similar to the big
Morris).[10]

MG were also to market a 'B' series saloon, but this time with the big six-
cylinder engine; the current 1250 cc saloon was already scheduled to be
replaced (in January 1948) by a 'B'-bodied model with independent front

suspension and an MG front, the combination having initially been slated for 1941 launch under Nuffield's pre-war model plan. Sports cars, already seen as potential high earners, would see the then-current Midget 'succeeded by a new open Midget fitted with a 1-litre four cylinder in-line engine, to be introduced in June 1947'.[11]

In the event, few of these models reached the streets in line with this somewhat ambitious development calendar, but the plan did provide evidence of some longer-term strategic thinking, even if many of the permutations were to be achieved by the type of badge-engineering which became BMC's hallmark in the late fifties and throughout the sixties.

The most important of these cars was unquestionably the Minor/Mosquito, and it is interesting to trace the changing decisions of the board in relation to the model. The January 1947 launch date was foreseen as early as 1944, and the September 1945 production target of 500 a week was upped to 1,500 a week in February 1946, with a total production run of over a quarter of a million envisaged. The minutes of the Board meeting held on 3 March 1946 show the importance Sir Miles Thomas instinctively attached to the car:

It was emphasised by the (Vice) Chairman [Thomas] that the introduction of the Mosquito marked the beginning of a new era in the activities of the Nuffield Organisation.

By the end of that year the Mosquito schedules had begun to slip slightly and it was decided to abandon the relatively costly flat-four engines and use the existing pre-war side-valve in-line unit instead. Remarkably, Board members decided on 14 April 1947 that the Mosquito would be marketed as an MG: just when and where this surprising decision was overturned is not recorded, but overturned it was and the Mosquito appeared in a blaze of glory as the Morris Minor at the 1948 Earls Court Motor Show.

As an aside, it has been suggested – perhaps with some considerable foundation – that the evident stupidity of some of these decisions was proof positive of how overblown and unwieldy Morris's Board of Directors had become. The overcrowded directorate was in itself the legacy of Nuffield's practice of taking on as main board directors the senior executives of firms he had personally taken over – executives whose own firms, it must be remembered, had generally been failures prior to Nuffield's rescue. A possible line of thought is that Nuffield's deliberate detachment from the day-to-day running of the company eventually afforded him a sufficiently clear perspective on the capabilities of his directors that he was able to see many of them for what they were – ageing, indecisive, and unimaginative men whose own businesses had failed. It is entirely plausible that the Board's series of muddled decisions relating to the launch of the Minor provided the final straw for Nuffield, and that this was what set him on the course of firm and decisive action which was to lead to the dramatic wholesale purge of dead wood from the Morris boardroom later that year.

Little of this behind-the-scenes wrangling was allowed to reach public ears, and nothing could detract from the obvious sensation of the Minor's introduction. There was a new Oxford, too, showing very definite signs of Minor influence, and the Morris Six, a version of the Oxford with a much longer bonnet and the type of upright grille Lord Nuffield favoured, also made its debut. All Austin could muster against these glittering debutantes was a new A70 and the way-out American-styled A90 Atlantic convertible: the A40 Devon and Dorset had been selling well, but it looked at last as if things could begin to go Nuffield's way.

The Nuffield Organization certainly needed a tonic, for although it had been turning in strong profit figures ever since the war, there was the widespread feeling that all was not well within the group. The Second World War had not been followed by a huge boom like that following the 1914–18 conflict: cars had not been as easy to sell in the early post-war years as many had expected (purchase licences, fuel rationing, and a flood of used MoD vehicles on the second-hand market being the principal depressing factors), and the American market, which had been the salvation of British producers in the early years, was beginning to prove unpredictable.

Nor were these exports a mere profit-enhancing luxury: they were essential for Britain's recovery in the post-war world and were an integral part of the new and far-sighted Attlee government's economic strategy. Labour President of the Board of Trade (equivalent to today's Secretary of State for Industry), Sir Stafford Cripps, had assembled Britain's motor barons at a dinner in November 1945 and torn them off a strip. Senior industry figures booed and cat-called Cripps' sensible suggestions that Britain could not succeed in the export market if its efforts were dispersed across numberless types and makes, and they were taken aback by the cabinet minister's assertion that the *minimum* export figure that could be contemplated was 50 per cent. Enraged, Cripps retorted:

I have often wondered whether you thought that Great Britain was here to support the motor industry or the industry was here to support Great Britain. I gather from your cries that you think it is the former.[12]

The Government was, in any case, in the unprecedented position of having a threefold hold over the motor industry. Allocations of steel, a vital commodity still very short in supply despite the nationalization of the steel industry, were conditional on each manufacturer fulfilling his export quota (though in practice there was little retrospective sanction the Board of Trade could apply if one make happened at the end of year to have sold a few thousand more units at home than were sent abroad); later the export targets were made tougher still, with Minister of Supply, George Strauss, requiring first 60 per cent and, as from 1949, 75 per cent of output to be exported. The Government's second built-in control over the industry was in the granting of planning consents for new factory capacity. Labour's planners stubbornly resisted pressure to allow factory extensions or extra capacity on existing sites where unemployment was generally very low; instead, firms were directed much against their wishes to areas of high unemployment such as Merseyside, Scotland, and Wales.

Labour's third hold over the motor industry was the most feared of all: the threat of nationalization. Though it never became official Labour policy to take the motor industry into state ownership, top motor magnates lived in constant fear that should they step the slightest bit out of line, public ownership would instantly follow. Labour intellectuals such as Ian Mikardo and even Roy Jenkins had published papers suggesting full-scale nationalization for the complete industry, and there was every reason to believe that they might be adopted into the party's strategy. The nation's motor plants could, Mr Mikardo reasoned, be directed to produce not only the cheap and effective car for the masses along the lines of the German Volkswagen 'people's car' that the politicians wanted, but also to make bigger and more powerful models which would be much more successful in export markets than existing British products had proved.

Other figures, more centre than left-wing, suggested varying degrees of nationalization, and with hindsight it could be said that such a policy might have been of long-term benefit to the industry. With the Government stepping in during an already prosperous phase and providing a high degree of financial continuity and long-term investment planning by the participating firms, we could have had a blossoming Volkswagen or Renault instead of a beleaguered British Leyland.

Notes

1. *The Motor*, 2 May 1939.
2. P.W.S. Andrews and E. Brunner, *The Life of Lord Nuffield* (1955), p. 216.
3. R. Church and M. Miller, 'The Big Three: Competition, Management and Marketing in the British Motor Industry, 1922–1939', in *Essays in British Business History*, ed. B. Supple, p. 179.
4. Sir Miles Thomas, *The First Viscount Nuffield Memorial Paper*, Institute of Production Engineers, 18 November 1964.
5. J. Leason, *Wheels to Fortune*, p. 69.
6. R. Jackson, *The Nuffield Story*, p. 111.
7. Minutes of Directors' meeting, 14 May 1945.
8. J. Wood, *Wheels of Misfortune*, p. 106.
9. Minutes of Board Meeting, 12 January 1946.
10. Board Meeting, ibid.
11. Board Meeting, ibid.
12. W. Plowden, *The Motor Car in Politics*, quoted in J. Wood, op. cit., p. 98.

Chapter 8

Export – at all costs?

For Morris the export road had been a relatively rocky one. The seller's market that existed just after the war had begun to collapse as the Americans came in with the '49 and '50 models and the pound slipped against the dollar; Lord Nuffield's response had been to send cables from Australia advising of the need for a six-cylinder car.

That advice was certainly well-founded in relation to the Australasian territories, and history was later to prove Nuffield right, but as far as the key export markets of the United States and Europe were concerned, Nuffield, by now approaching his fifth decade at the helm of his company, appeared unable to see that there was something more fundamentally wrong than just the prices set by his export departments.

Nor had it been a happy time within the Nuffield Organization. Lord Nuffield bitterly resented the high costs of tooling up for new models, perhaps understandably as he was more perceptive than many of his colleagues in recognizing the end of the era of unquestioned largesse and easy sales that had marked Morris's affairs for several decades. Nuffield was no longer suggesting, as he had done in the early post-war years, that basically pre-war models would be adequate for the marketplace, but even so, his insistence on the strict minimum of technical change can now be seen as a short-sighted policy adopted at precisely the time when heavy, long-term investment in new models, new technologies, and new manufacturing techniques was most necessary.

This unwillingness to come up with a clear forward vision of the company's medium- to long-term future course had an inevitably demoralizing influence on Nuffield's staff, although it must also be said that the Board of Management did not appear to provide much in the way of inspiring leadership – perhaps, again understandably, in view of the constantly changing steel quotas and export requirements imposed on the automotive industry throughout the period, changing strictures which did their best to make long-term planning impossible or at least very hazardous.

Nuffield tended to take a deliberate back seat in the running of the organization, remaining incommunicado for long periods on end, especially during his frequent and lengthy sea voyages. His management involvement generally took an indirect form: rather than attend Board or plant meetings in person, Nuffield preferred to deal with individuals on a one-to-one basis. Records of Board meetings show that one of his favourite techniques was to intervene via a chosen and loyal go-between, a hapless director whose main role in life appeared to be to take Board decisions to Nuffield, obtain his comments and responses, and return with the chairman's decision – which would invariably be adopted, even though in several recorded instances it might have run counter to the advice of the bulk of the Board.

One such example was over the issue of radiator grilles. Nuffield always felt passionately about this aspect of car design, insisting that the radiator gave the car its face and its personality and that the only proper radiator was a large, upright central one. It followed, therefore, that different 'personalities' could be imposed on a given car by the straightforward tactic of grafting on a different radiator grille or 'face'. This conviction led Nuffield to press for the Group to save on investment and tooling costs by creating a broad model range, and enough of a spread of marque names to keep all of each make's loyal supporters happy, by the simple expedient of providing what was fundamentally the same car with different radiator grilles. In becoming so instrumental in forcing through this cost-saving engineering philosophy on the organization – a philosophy which later became known, somewhat disparagingly, as badge engineering – Nuffield also succeeded in alienating some of his technical staff who advised strongly against many of the cost-saving engine/chassis juxtapositions he was proposing. Against the recommendations of engineers who insisted that not all the chassis were suitable for all the engines, more than a few combinations were rushed into production, only to be withdrawn again shortly afterwards. Yet perhaps more importantly from a longer-term viewpoint, the knowledge that the boss did not really want to see serious engineering changes made led to an understandable decline in morale and motivation among sections of the Morris design and research staff.

Lord Nuffield was active on the commercial front, too: partly in response to feedback from world markets that Nuffield car prices were too high, and partly in response to his own instincts of prudent housekeeping, he began providing his Board with what may have been rather too much old-fashioned advice – counsel which his directors naturally felt compelled to go along with. In October 1947, at one of his rare appearances at a Board meeting, he suggested that a return to pre-war values would be the solution to the organization's difficulties; he even urged his directors to—

leave the room with the idea of starting all over again . . . the organisation is fortunate in enjoying all possible advantages such as brains and up to date plant, and there is no reason at all why we cannot soon restore ourselves to the leading place we once occupied.

The consequences of this schoolmaster-like dressing-down were immediate. Instead of the organization gelling together to cut overheads, reduce prices, and speed up the development of new models, it began to lose its top management and with it, as some see the situation, its drive and dynamism. Sir Miles Thomas, perhaps the ablest manager in the British motor industry at the time and Nuffield's most faithful supporter for over 25 years, was tipped into resignation less than 3 weeks later, saying afterwards that he would have been 'deaf as well as blind not to have seen that all was not well between the Chairman and myself'.

One of the reasons later given for Sir Miles' departure was his acceptance of outside appointments, in this case the honorary appointment as chairman of the Colonial Development Corporation. Nuffield did not believe that the responsibilities of the office of vice-chairman of his organization could be anything other than full-time, and that it certainly should not allow enough free time for outside activities, even those which did not conflict with the work in connection with the motor business.

A matter of weeks after this, following the appointment of Reginald Hanks to replace Thomas, seven further members of the board were asked to depart, leaving only small central core of nine directors. Morale reached an all-time low, and many commentators have pointed to this wholesale clear-out of senior management as the beginning of Morris's downturn as a serious world-class manufacturer.

It could equally well be argued, however, that although Lord Nuffield's manner of presentation was both unfortunate and old-fashioned in its appeal to a return to the moral values of a bygone era, he was one of the few who had the vision and the perspective of experience to realize the poor calibre of many of the directors he had gathered around him; again, it must not be forgotten that many of these directors were there principally because their own businesses had been failures and Nuffield had had to rescue them. So the abrupt sacking of so many top-level managers need not necessarily be seen as an indication of major disagreements concerning the running of the company; more likely, such a clear-out should be interpreted as Lord Nuffield's recognition of the ineptitude of many of his senior staff, and he should instead deserve respect for the decisive manner in which he axed a whole generation of dead wood.

It was around this time, with Hanks more concerned with sorting out the organization of the various Nuffield plants around Oxford, Birmingham, and Coventry, that Lord Nuffield began once again to think on a broader scale. Without the knowledge of his Board, he approached his former colleague and now direct rival, Leonard Lord, at Austin's, with a view to pooling certain aspects of parts supply and component design, and coordinating future model plans. It was a brave idea and was trumpeted in the press with great excitement, with commentators forecasting significant costs savings on many major components and the likely benefit of lower selling prices, increased competitiveness in the market place and, ultimately, a detectable improvement in exports. But the reality of the arrangement saw both participants defensive about their own costing methods and even more reluctant to give away any real secrets, especially those concerning future model plans. Although some useful rationalization was achieved in reducing the numbers of parts, such as dynamos, the agreement was dissolved less than a year after it had started.

But, even so, the avenues towards later collaboration had at least been mapped out; the two opposing barons, who 10 years earlier had parted on what Miles Thomas perhaps overdramatically described as a 'note of heated disagreement'[2] had now indicated the need for a truce in the war, if not quite a desire to join forces; Nuffield had lost much of his will to direct and manage and must have seen in Lord an energy that would assure the prosperity of his precious organization in years to come.

Yet once that fusion had finally taken place, Nuffield was again to be a disappointed man as he witnessed his old rival, the man he had recently forced himself to trust, slowly dismembering the Morris side of the business, making sure that major decisions were swung Austin's way and making it pretty plain that the old rivalries had not been buried after all.

Many of those moves seemed more prudent at the time than, with the benefit of hindsight, they seem to us now: if the finger of blame for the ultimate failure of BMC, BL, and Leyland has to be pointed at the complacent management style of sixties, then the seeds of failure were certainly sown in the internal arguments that wrecked those critical first few years of union.

Notes

1. Sir Miles Thomas, *Out on a Wing* (1964).
2. Sir Miles Thomas, *First Viscount Nuffield Memorial Paper*, p. 11.

Chapter 9
Merger: dropping the reins of power

No businessman who has built up an organization employing tens of thousands of wage-earners can suddenly drop the reins without a thought for the vast family associated with his labours.

The words are Lord Nuffield's, in response to one of an endless stream of questions asking him why he refused to retire.[1] It is not recorded precisely when this particular reply was given, but such was Lord Nuffield's tenacity and determination that the remarks could have dated from almost any time between 1935 and 1950. Indeed, it appears to be the received wisdom that one of the principal causes of the difficulties faced by the Nuffield Organization after the Second World War and in the run-up to the merger with Austin in 1951 was the stubborn refusal of its founder and Chairman, Lord Nuffield himself, to reliquish the power and control he had enjoyed for almost half a century.

The reality is perhaps rather different. The decision-making structure Nuffield set up in the 1930s was designed to allow the day-to-day running of Morris Motors to be undertaken by a board of directors under a deputy governing director placed immediately below Nuffield himself; Nuffield was, however, still directly responsible for MG, Wolseley, and Morris Commercial, which he owned personally. When a later reorganization transferred these personally owned firms into the ownership of the group, Nuffield's role as a management decision-maker had become largely superfluous; later still, after Nuffield had sold off further huge blocks of his personally held shares in order to finance his charitable foundations, he even ceased to be the majority shareholder in the organization and could, in theory, have been out-voted at a shareholders' meeting.

It can thus be seen that Nuffield did, in a sense, enter a form of retirement in that he had relinquished the ultimate control of his organization. Yet despite this theoretical clipping of his wings, the influence he continued to exert was considerable, as Sir Miles Thomas points out with some force:

> Insofar as the actual business of designing and making motor cars and trucks was concerned Sir William Morris played little or no creative part. He could give vent to a considerable amount of negative criticism, but that was all.[2]

Thomas's accounts, not always the most reliable, certainly serve to stoke up the image of Nuffield the ruthless, interfering autocrat, desperately clinging the power. Other commentators take a more charitable view, however:

> It was a necessary precondition for success that the individualistic small-firm manager should step down when it no longer became possible for him to run the business himself. Despite the surviving myths of Morris as a dictator, he accepted the usurpation of his throne for the sake of the survival of the enterprise.[3]

Yet, even having accepted this usurpation of his throne, Nuffield still found it hard in practice to relinquish the control he had recognized that he must in theory concede, and his interventions continued, made all the more difficult by the fact that as the financial and technical affairs of the organization grew more and more complicated, so his grip on the issues in hand grew less secure.

However, this 'destructive interference' of which Thomas so frequently complains did have its more positive side, especially after the Second World War, when Nuffield was purportedly even more securely in the background as far as everyday decision-making was concerned. His was a unique position, standing back from the petty squabbles of company politics, a respected figurehead of a hugely respected organization, yet able to see matters with the broad perspective that was denied to those in the thick of the struggle. Nuffield made himself awkward on many well-recorded occasions, and there must have been many more unrecorded instances where the Board had cause to regret the Chairman's intervention on an issue. Yet there were periods when his broad, experienced and unhampered overview of matters gave him a much clearer picture than that seen by the key executives at the sharp end; there were times, too, when a clear-thinking outsider was able to break a deadlock or intervene dramatically in order to avert a crisis.

There could be no clearer example than the management crisis of 1947 which culminated in Sir Miles Thomas crossing swords with Nuffield and resigning from the vice-chairmanship of the organization. Lord Nuffield's swift, decisive, and dramatic action of asking seven of his directors to leave was something no-one else could have contemplated, yet it is unlikely that anyone closer to the scene could have so clearly recognized the hopeless lack of direction shown by the Board, composed as it had been largely of aged and rigidly minded divisional directors.

This long-due overhaul of top management soon produced the required results, and there was a 'sharp revival in the company's fortunes, confirming the significance of factors of personality in determining the performance of the large and expanding corporation'.[4] Nuffield once again returned to the background to allow his new directors free rein within the 'loosely drawn limits' he had established, limits defined only by Nuffield's intuition and experience in anticipating future market developments.[5]

At the heart of it, however, Nuffield had clearly recognized that the organization he had created had long since outgrown the managerial skills he possessed. Having no heir – his constant and most bitter regret – made it impossible to consider the organization as a family firm in the old sense of the term. He could not, like his biographical parallel Henry Ford on the other side of the Atlantic, hand control over to the next generation: instead, the organization achieved (more by good fortune than careful planning) a surprisingly smooth transformation into a major international corporation, guided not by a central individual but by a network of self-regulating boards and committees.

The broad overview was still Nuffield's privilege and this, as we have seen, allowed him to recognize the wood where others could only see trees. Though the post-war Labour Government was most definitely not of Nuffield's preferred colour and he differed fundamentally in how to set about achieving the objectives, he shared with Clement Attlee and the Cabinet the strong conviction that exports were vital to Britain's future prosperity in the world and that the motor industry was the force to lead the export drive. The Government's tactic was to ration supplies of steel and set specific margins by which exports had to exceed domestic consumption: Nuffield, true to his political persuasions as an extreme free-market thinker, reasoned that unrestricted steel supplies would allow much greater production volumes which would, resurrecting his old Cowley argument, result in greater economies of scale, lower unit costs, and, finally, an ultimately greater volume of exports gained through increased price competitiveness.[6]

Yet even within the confines of the rationing system, Nuffield's international perspective made him realize the importance of worldwide price competitiveness, and it was this more than any other factor which convinced him, first, that costs had to come down and that, secondly, when seen on an international scale in comparison with General Motors and Ford, Morris Motors was small fry indeed. There was also the important consideration of the two American-owned multinationals in Britain, Ford and Vauxhall, who were beginning to make serious inroads into Morris and Austin's combined market share, which had once stood at almost 50 per cent but which now threatened to drop below 40.

Thus were born the twin ideas of commonizing and standardizing component parts so as to reduce unit costs and, on a much grander scale, the merging of Morris and Austin to create an industrial combine of significant international weight.

Lord Nuffield was the catalyst who finally allowed this momentous move to take place, in the first instance by exploring the concept of the components standardization scheme to which we have already referred, and secondly in making the main overtures to Leonard Lord at Austin's for the merger proper.

It was Leonard Lord of Austin who, in fact, made the very first move, telephoning Lord Nuffield in October 1947 to wish him a happy seventieth birthday. In their subsequent meeting Lord broached the subject of an entente, or even a merger, and was not surprised to find Nuffield still enthusiastic despite the setback of the failed Standardisation Committee moves. However, under the chairmanship of Reginald Hanks, the Morris Board turned the proposal down.

Merger with Austin was something that William Morris, as he then was, had stubbornly resisted when proposed by Herbert Austin in the 1920s; the proposed combine (which was also to take in Wolseley) would, according to Morris, have become too large and too unwieldy and would have suffocated under its own weight. Now, however, Nuffield could see that merger with Austin was the only way in which he could guarantee the survival of his organization on a broader international level; he could see, too, that beyond the expected savings as components and designs were shared, production runs were lengthened and unit costs were trimmed, considerable savings and efficiencies in management could be made, especially as the merger provided the opportunity to put into place a whole new and, hopefully, well-streamlined administrative structure.

The Nuffield Organization was by now once again the dominant force in the British motor industry, having, largely thanks to the success of the Morris Minor and the fading appeal of Austin's immediate post-war models, wrested back market leadership after the inglorious low-point of 1947 when, accustomed to a pre-war market share of some 33 per cent, Morris's slice of British production had slumped to a nadir of just 50,000 out of 280,000 vehicles turned out.

By the autumn of the following year, Lord Nuffield had judged the time to be right: the trough was safely passed, the company's management restructuring had been internally digested and the organization was back on a sound financial footing. He approached Lord, initially without the knowledge of the Nuffield Board, and an agreement was announced at the end of November, with integrated operations commencing in February 1952.

There was much excitement in the press about the advent of the British Motor Corporation and, with Lord Nuffield appointed as its titular Chairman, there was much to be proud of. The new combine was to rate as the world's third-largest car builder and possibly the world's biggest car exporter; BMC would employ more car workers than the whole of the rest of the UK motor industry put together, and its share of the UK market would be of the order of 40 per cent.

Yet once all the celebrations had died down and the two organizations had begun to work together, it became increasingly plain that for all the good intentions, the liaison was not to be an easy one. Critically, it was, in particular, clear that the old antipathy between Leonard Lord and Lord Nuffield's Cowley operation had not been forgotten. The reality was that the companies continued to operate more or less as they had done before the merger, selling their own models through their own dealer networks and with the vast array of overlapping models competing just as before.

The headquarters of the BMC combine was located at Austin's so-called 'Kremlin' in Longbridge, and to all intents and purposes the merger amounted to a takeover of Morris by Austin. Those present at the time confirm that Leonard Lord spared little in his efforts to run Morris and everything Nuffield down, and even Reginald Hanks, previously Managing Director of Morris and now Lord's number two, was quoted as saying 'We have been in competition with Austin's for some time and we shall remain in competition.'[7]

Divisions were being deliberately fostered, according to those caught in the middle, and no opportunity was wasted to sour the relationship. Even ostensibly objective interdivisional cost comparisons were blatantly fixed: a production engineer at Longbridge recalls Lord disregarding carefully calculated cost figures for components and simply stating 'Let's put it at ten pounds under what Bill Morris does it for on the Oxford and the Cowley.'[8] John Thornley, soon to take over the running of MG, was one of the few who enjoyed excellent relations with the 'reputedly impossible' Lord. Yet even he was shocked at the bending of the rules by which BMC were supposed to be judging which were the best components to install in their production cars.

The dreadful thing that happened at the time of the merger was a result of Austin's accounting, which was based on the theory of 'kidology' – self-deception, or kidding yourself.

To assemble an axle there was a piece price, and that was the price that went into the costing. What actually happened was that on the line the charge-hand issued pink tickets which represented charging over and above the piece rates – and the pink tickets were ignored by Austin's accountants. But someone had to pick up the tab at the end of the year.

When BMC was formed, a great exhibition was created in the dungeons below the 'Kremlin' administration block at Longbridge. The equivalent Nuffield and Austin components were laid out side by side, with their production prices. Of course the Austin price beat the Nuffield price all the way down the line, and the Austin parts were chosen.

The engineering of a lot of the Nuffield stuff was superior, *and* the prices included every damn thing. If you costed that into every Austin part, you really were in the gravy. This to a very large extent contributed to the downfall of BMC.[9]

Thornley stops short of stating that Lord deliberately poisoned the long-term prospects of the merged organization: instead, he points the finger of blame at George Harriman, the BMC supremo who took over from Lord:

I hold Harriman responsible for running BMC into the ground. He tried to administer it as Lord had done – which was largely by guesswork. But Len had the habit of being rather more right than he was wrong. Even if it was only 51 per cent to 49 per cent, if you pursue that line for long enough it begins to show. Harriman wasn't that lucky, or that clever.[10]

By the time Harriman took over from Lord, Nuffield had long since departed from the scene. Having seen his precious organization safely, or as safely as could be expected, given the sourness of the merger atmosphere, united with the other major industrial force in the country, Nuffield served less than a year in his largely honorary capacity as

Chairman of BMC before handing over the reins to Leonard Lord. The hand-over when it came was unexpected but also surprisingly undramatic, considering Nuffield had been at the helm of his company for an uninterrupted half-century or more. It must have been a moving moment indeed, when in front of a small group of shareholders at the December 1951 AGM the frail, 75-year-old Nuffield announced his retirement from the chairmanship of BMC and stated that, as honorary president, he would continue to monitor the company's affairs and would be available for consultation should he be needed.

It was a measure of the modesty and shyness of William Morris, Viscount Nuffield, that it was his adopted title that was destined to become a household word, whereas his surname was merely a make of car – eventually to sink without trace in the Rover empire 30 years later. And, more cruelly still for the man through whose enterprise and intuition a whole nation had woken up to the age of personal mobility, William Morris was set to be perpetually overshadowed by his Victorian namesake, mentor of the Arts and Crafts Movement and, in an intense irony, the bitterest opponent of the very mass production techniques that William Morris the younger turned to such good effect.

Notes

1. R. Jackson, *The Nuffield Story* (1964), p. 240.
2. Sir Miles Thomas, *Out on a Wing* (1964), p. 159.
3. R.J. Overy, *William Morris, Viscount Nuffield*, p. 96.
4. *Overy*, op. cit., p. 62.
5. P.W.S. Andrews and E. Brunner, *The Life of Lord Nuffield* (1955), p. 251.
6. *Motor Trader*, CLXXV (1949), p. 44; speech by Lord Nuffield. Quoted in Overy, op. cit., p. 70.
7. R.J. Wyatt, *The Austin*. Quoted by Adeney, op. cit., p. 201.
8. Adeney, op. cit., p. 201.
9. *Classic and Sportscar* magazine interview with John Thornley, October 1989.
10. *Classic and Sportscar*, op. cit.

Chapter 10

Some conclusions: the perspective of half a century

Considering that he granted mobility to so many millions; considering that his products made such a great contribution to Britain's exports; and considering the vast amounts of his personal fortune that he gave away in the form of charitable benefactions; it is a major injustice that William Morris is not better remembered.

It says something about the priorities of this nation that whenever the name William Morris is mentioned it is invariably assumed that it is our subject's Victorian Arts and Crafts Movement namesake that is intended. William Morris the elder was undoubtedly a fine artist, craftsman, and writer, but one does not have to be a complete philistine to appreciate that on the graph of human culture, communication, and social development, William Morris the car-maker of Oxford deserves to rate more of a blip of recognition than William Morris the printer of Kelmscott.

Eccentric, odd, and difficult the car-maker Morris may well have been, and obscure he may still be to the great mass of people either too young to have known Morris as a living make of motor car, or old enough to have forgotten their school history lessons and the few brief flashes of fame that Morris's bigger benefactions bestowed upon him; none of this must be allowed to detract from the greatness of his achievements.

For Morris is a man who must be judged by what he did rather than what he was, by the immensity of the empire he built up rather than by the private, unapproachable conflicts of his character or the unmentioned preoccupations that saw his personal insecurity escalate in direct proportion to his fortune and his financial security. For here was a great man, survived by no heir save his massive Nuffield Foundation, and commemorated in a rough country churchyard by nothing more than a modest horizontal marble slab bearing the inscription 'William Richard Morris – Viscount Nuffield'.

Yet his was the satisfaction of mobilizing an entire generation; his was the intuition that provided the people with what they wanted at precisely the time they wanted it; his was the initiative that time after time in the face of adversity chose the most daring of solutions, profited from that daring, and went on to scale further heights. And, no less significantly, once those heights had been scaled and Morris had become an exceedingly rich and powerful man, he had the flexibility to break away from the formal Victorian model of the self-made, unbending, and power-hungry proprietor and accept, albeit reluctantly, that some of his control had to be conceded to others. His blend of the old-fashioned ethics of hard work and good housekeeping kept his organization securely out of debt and more able than its rivals to exploit the latest in engineering innovation in order to build better and cheaper, yet all the while he never abandoned the 'quality *and* quantity' maxim which had guided him in his early business life.

With the perspective of 50 years we can see Morris as a much more successful innovator than his immediate rivals. Not in the domains of vehicle design or company management structure, perhaps, but in the way in which his instinctive nose for where the demand lay prompted him to advertise heavily and in a trend-setting manner; the way in which he was prepared to shoulder the considerable risk of being first into hire purchase, which soon doubled his market and saw over half his sales take place on credit; innovation in selling and marketing, with the *Morris Owner* magazine cleverly reinforcing the brand's standing among owners and potential customers; innovation in customer support, with dealers quoting standardized prices for servicing; innovation not in any technical sense but in the rapid adoption of ideas borrowed from bigger and more desirable models.

Perhaps most important of all, only Ford and, to a lesser extent Austin, possessed that instinctive vision that Morris displayed in deciding what to sell and where. In an industry dominated by small-scale producers and conservative selling attitudes Morris provided an inspiration and reaped the benefits. Only after Morris had already come to take almost half of the market for cars did the rest of the motor industry move away from a high dependence on clever engineering to a greater dependence on good selling.[1]

It was only when the issue began to concern the control of the enterprise that Morris's commitment to innovation began to falter, and it was in this trait that the seeds of the organization's undoing lay. Morris's vision after the First World War began to fade in direct proportion to the decline in sales of the Cowley and Oxford models that had launched him to fame, and

Lord Nuffield assisting at the 1932 Morris Motors sports day. The cycle races must have evoked memories from his youth.
[Courtesy of Oxfordshire County Libraries]

as Morris the individualist began to lose his direction so, too, did Morris the company – with the result that revenue fell, senior management had to be brought in, and the company had to be kick-started back into action.

Twice more the company suffered a serious loss of momentum after that initial shock, yet on each occasion the solution was a bold one – to invest in the very latest production technology in order further to reduce production costs and restore Morris's customary advantage as price and quality leaders.

That was enough to take the organization through to the 1950s in good health for the merger with Austin, though it is tempting to speculate that had a younger generation of managers been aboard in that crucial post-war period, the company that emerged at the end of the era of rationing could have been much more internationally minded, more commercially adventurous, and more technically innovative still. And if that hands-on management had not had its hands partially tied by the shadowy figure on the sidelines, perhaps the company would have emerged healthier still, perhaps even with far-sighted schemes such as the graduate trainee programmes which gave rivals Ford and Vauxhall such a key advantage in later years. The man who stood on the sidelines still had his part to play, though increasingly his concerns were becoming those of broader matters than just his core business.

Broader public recognition steadily became a more important consideration in Morris's life; as is documented elsewhere in this book, his record as a public benefactor is second to none. At heart a shy and self-effacing man, he nevertheless sought to gain influence in public life, if not outright power. He was never persuaded to stand for Parliament, but, if he had done so, he would certainly have stood on the right of the Conservative party. In the 1930s he even subscribed £50,000 to Oswald Mosley's New Party, though he was careful to avoid other direct links with this extreme grouping; in 1932 he became president of the League of Industry, an organization of committed capitalists which some unkind contemporary commentator likened in colour to Mosley's black shirts.

Like many of the industry and press barons of his day, Morris took it upon himself to help ensure the defence of his country against what he correctly perceived was the growing military threat from Nazi Germany. Yet Morris's involvement in military matters was not to be a particularly happy one, and two serious clashes, the first with the Air Ministry and the second with no less a figure than Air Minister Lord Beaverbrook, the Canadian-born proprietor of the huge-selling *Daily Express*, left Lord Nuffield – as he had some time earlier become – with his pride seriously injured and his distrust of Civil Service bureaucracy reinforced. The first incident concerned the Air Ministry's unwillingness to accept aero engines from the Wolseley factory Nuffield had specially built for the purpose; Nuffield suspected, perhaps with some reason, that a cartel of the three or four established aero-engine makers was out to protect its members' interests and guaranteed profits. In a fit of pique, Nuffield closed the brand-new, never-used plant down.

Perhaps as a result, Nuffield was disposed to distrust the shadow factory scheme for wartime aircraft production, suggesting what he believed to be a more efficient system of horizontally integrated production which demanded less in the way of tools and equipment. To cut a long story short, Nuffield did, in the end, build a special factory at Castle Bromwich for large-scale Spitfire production and began to tool up for aircraft manufacture in much the same way as he would have done for a new and complex car. Tooling up for what amounted to mass production of aircraft, which elsewhere were virtually hand-built, inevitably took far longer than expected, and the Ministry understandably became more and more impatient waiting for the first Spitfire off the line. To add to Nuffield's difficulties, combat experience in the Battle of Britain led to running changes in the Spitfire's design; changes that his inflexible system of production found hard to accommodate. Matters came to a head when Beaverbrook rang Nuffield personally and angrily demanded to know when he could expect supplies. Dissatisfied with Nuffield's reply, the newly appointed Beaverbrook levelled accusations of poor organization at Nuffield, who in turn retorted 'Right, you try and run this place.' Much to Nuffield's astonishment and horror, Beaverbrook agreed on the spot, and under Ministry control Castle Bromwich went on to become Britain's biggest producer of Spitfires, with over 70 per cent of all aircraft built.

Nuffield's other foray into defence was in the field of tanks and fighting vehicles. This time the designs put forward by Nuffield Mechanisations Ltd were more successful, and the Crusader tank was ordered by the army. However, in its earlier forms it proved embarrassingly unreliable in the Western Desert, and Morris had to undertake expensive modifications in the field. Other Nuffield Mechanisations projects were ingenious, such as the Nautilus landing barge, propelled by the lorry's own wheels which drove rollers connected to the craft's propellers, and the Salamander, a small floating tank. The Argosy large landing-craft was more conventional, as was the Firefly Tank Hunter, a large, self-propelled gun.[2]

Many, many more areas of activity were charted by Nuffield, either personally, through his Organization or through subsidiary companies set up specifically for the purpose. It has clearly been impossible to go into more than a tiny fraction of these, and in concentrating our attention on the core Morris business we are, of course, guilty of the comparative neglect of the smaller marques of Wolseley and Riley and doubly culpable in not devoting more space to the most successful string of all – MG.

It is clearly impossible to sum up in a single chapter – or for that matter even in a single volume – so substantial an achievement by so modestly born a man. Comparisons with Henry Ford and Louis Renault come naturally: all three were intensely private men, devoted to the success of their businesses and little else; all three frowned on the kind of extravagance and excess that was to be the undoing of that other great automotive genius, André Citroen, and each found it hard to let go their solo hold of the reins of their organizations. Yet of the three, Nuffield, despite his equal reluctance to relinquish power, was perhaps the most flexible in the long run and was certainly endowed with the greatest insight into the car-buyer, the car market, and the means to stay one step ahead of his competitors without spending significant sums on research.

Yet, above all, above his entrepreneurship, his flair for the dramatic gesture, his willingness to invest when all others were holding back, was Nuffield's intuition as to what the future would bring. It rarely let him down, and even several years after he had gone into retirement he forecast in a speech to the motor trade that the Japanese (who at that stage had only built a handful of primitive cars) and the Germans would soon be threatening Britain's export markets.[3]

History does not record whether he suggested that our home markets would come to be threatened, too. Perhaps even he could not have anticipated quite such a squandering of the domestic industry he did so much to build up.

Notes

1. R.J. Overy, *William Morris, Viscount Naffield*, p. 79.
2. Nuffield Mechanisations Ltd submission to Army Combined Operations. In collection of Nuffield College Library, Oxford.
3. Quoted in *Motor Trader*, 10 October 1956.

PART THREE

The Giving of Millions

Chapter 11
The background to the giving

Colin Hill

It is sad that the name 'Morris' no longer appears on new cars, vans or trucks. Only the MG marque survives from all of the once-famous motor vehicle names associated with Lord Nuffield. Within one or two decades the name William Morris will be known only to a few motoring enthusiasts, or perhaps associated with a designer of fabrics and wallpapers rather than of motor vehicles. But the name Nuffield will endure, if only because of his outstanding generosity to Oxford University in particular and to medicine in general. Even then, many of the gifts which do not bear his name (such as the purchase of the Observatory site for the Radcliffe Infirmary in Oxford – now part of the University as Green College) will continue to further the causes that were so close to his heart.

Like most of us, Lord Nuffield's personality was a complex mixture of attributes. He was excellent at selecting people, yet poor at delegation. He was suspicious of his fellow directors, yet commanded great loyalty. He was a person of great vision, yet he disliked change. he could be astonishingly mean in some things, yet outstandingly generous in others. He made millions, yet he lived simply. His benefactions may well have been approved by the shade of John Wesley, one of whose aphorisms – earn all you can, have all you can, give all you can – if applied with equal determination by the acquisitive society of the post-war decades would have left us with a more prosperous and compassionate society than we have so far achieved.

It is difficult now to determine what initially prompted his philanthropy. It may well have been his interest in medicine and his close friendship with Sir William Osler. The earliest record of a substantial charitable donation is a response in 1917 to an appeal by the latter to establish a rehabilitation workshop for wounded servicemen – an enterprise which, largely through continuing interest and financial support from Nuffield, developed into what is now the Nuffield Orthopaedic Centre.

His philanthrophy was not, however, confined to medicine or even to what might be called 'popular' causes. For example, in 1926 he gave a donation of £10,000 (about £200,000 in today's money) to enable parents of children in Borstal Institutions to visit them – a much more difficult journey to make in those days. This suggests a social compassion for groups of people thought by society in general to bring about their own troubles rather than being victims of external circumstances not entirely within their own control.

On the whole, Nuffield's gifts tended to be to institutions rather than to individuals. This seems to be confirmed by the contents of his will. Perhaps this was because most people he knew were capable of standing on their own two feet, and those whom he didn't know, who almost daily appealed for his help, he regarded with an often justified suspicion. We know little about these matters; how a man chooses to help one cause or one individual rather than another is a matter for his own conscience. What we can reasonably assume is that the catalyst for the gifts of such prodigious sums from the second half of the 1920s onwards was the tax man. His generosity prior to this is not in question, but it must have appealed to his sense of business efficiency that he could, through the tax system, make his charitable giving even more effective. John Major's Budget in 1990 recognized more fully the extent to which private generosity can widen the horizons of social concern, and made it easier for people today than it was for Nuffield to increase the value of charitable giving.

The tax problem arose because companies were not liable to higher rates of tax (supertax as it was then called), whereas individuals and closed companies were. In such a company there was obviously a temptation to build up its capital value by ploughing back reserves rather than declaring dividends to individual shareholders. If the Inland Revenue considered that a company was unreasonably exploiting this position, it could direct that the whole income of the company could be treated as if it had been distributed to shareholders and hence would be liable to supertax, thereby drastically reducing the accumulation of reserves. It may be helpful to the understanding of the position briefly to outline the development of the corporate structure of the Morris enterprises.

WRM Motors was formed in 1912 to separate the manufacturing side of the business from Morris Garages Ltd. In 1919 the name of the Company was changed to Morris Motors Ltd. Morris was the sole ordinary shareholder. To tidy up the administrative and financial control of the whole of his interests, Morris later formed a holding company called The Morris Company to which he transferred 98 per cent of Morris Motors

The quiet Morris: his office in Hollow Way where ideas formed in isolation.
[Courtesy of Oxfordshire County Libraries]

The exciting Morris: the Dragonfly Racer.
[Nuffield Place collection]

shares (overwhelmingly the most important company in the group) and the entire share capital of three other companies owned by Morris Motors. The new Morris Company was owned and controlled by William Morris. The main purpose of this restructuring was to allow funds to be moved freely between the various Morris enterprises. This could be done either by inter-company loans or by inter-company dividends (on which supertax was not payable).

William Morris drew comparatively little in the way of salary from his enterprises. During the First World War, for example, he drew a salary of only £1,500 p.a. (about £50,000 in today's terms) from the business. Until 1923, with one minor exception in 1915, Morris Motors never paid a dividend – all of the profits after tax, aggregating to nearly £1 million, had been ploughed back into the business. Nearly three-quarters of this profit was generated in the two years 1922 and 1923. No dividend was paid in 1922, but for 1923 a dividend of £230,000 was declared, of which 98 per cent went to the Morris Company.

The Inland Revenue challenged the immunity of this dividend to supertax and made a direction that distributions to shareholders had been unreasonably withheld – hence the company was liable to supertax on the whole of the assessed profits. Morris Motors appealed and won the case, as they did a subsequent case for the years 1927 and 1928.

Expert independent testimony convinced the Special Commissioners that the reserves of Morris Motors were, if anything, low rather than high, given the economic climate and the extent of competition. Morris won both of these cases, but by then he had decided that the risk of some future supertax liability for Morris Motors was too great so long as such a high proportion of the equity continued to be his personal property. Henceforth he would devote more of his time to considering how best to give money away rather than to making more of it.

His solution was to turn Morris Motors into a public company. The poor trading results in the slump of 1931–34, coupled with the need to consolidate the various companies in the Morris empire delayed the public flotation until 1936, by which time he was confident that the company was again showing an adequate return and was financially secure. One-quarter of the shares were placed in the 1936 flotation which produced for Morris a capital sum of over £1 million (about £20 million in 1992 money). The remaining 75 per cent of the ordinary shares he was free to retain, sell or donate directly to the trusts which he had already started to set up in 1935. Most of his trusts from 1937 onwards were financed by gifts of shares in Morris Motors.

It should not be thought that the interest of Lord Nuffield – as he became in 1938 – in charitable causes began in 1935, nor that he took no interest in how the money was used. So far as can be ascertained from the inadequate existing records, he had certainly given away somewhere approaching £1 million before that date to a whole range of causes. By 1933 he had, for example, given over £80,000 to what is now the Nuffield Orthopaedic Hospital and had seen that one of his most senior directors, Sir Miles Thomas, was appointed to the Hospital Management Committee.

But from 1936 onwards the steady flow of giving became a flood. Of the 8 million 5 shilling ordinary shares in Morris Motors which Nuffield had retained at the 1936 flotation he had given away virtually all by 1943 in forming four major trusts – the Nuffield Benefaction for Employees (1937), the Nuffield Trust for the Forces of the Crown (1939), the Nuffield Provincial Hospitals Trust (1939), and the Nuffield Foundation (1943). The value of shares given to these four trusts was £15 million (over £300 million in 1992 money). Even so, his giving had still not finished. In 1961 he gave to the Nuffield Foundation all of his shares in Morris Garages Ltd, his original company, all of which shares he had until then retained. These had a book value of £240,000 but, in so far as a market value could be estimated for them, was probably nearer to £500,000.

That was the last major gift during his lifetime. He died in 1963 aged 85. It was generally assumed that by then he had given away virtually all of his money, but in fact there was a further £3 million for charities, most of which, together with his home at Nuffield Place went to Nuffield College. This brought the total of his gifts to charities to over £30 million at the time of the gifts.

In so far as it is possible to recalculate in 1992 money the value of these gifts and legacies, his total distributions can be estimated at about £578 million at current values. The range of his interests and the extent of his generosity is shown in Table 11.1.

Sources

P.W.S. Andrews and E. Bruner, *The Life of Lord Nuffield* (1955).
R. Jackson, *The Nuffield Story* (1964).
Sir Miles Thomas, *Out on a Wing* (1964).

Table 11.1   Summary of major benefactions of Lord Nuffield at historic and approximate 1992 equivalent values

Benefaction	Dates	£000's value at:	
		Time of Gift	1992
Oxford University	1926–1951	3,966	94,405
Other universities	1938	120	3,025
Medical and allied	1927–1954	2,071	47,795
War charities	1939–1940	557	11,795
Major trusts	1935–1943	17,572	375,100
Other	1926–1952	509	11,193
Lifetime benefactions	1926–1954	24,795	546,315
Legacies	1963	3,150	31,765
Total benefactions	1926–1963	27,945	578,080

NOTE: The calculation of the 1992 value of benefactions is necessarily approximate. Precise details of the timing of each individual gift is not available.

Taking the value of the £ in 1926 (the first year for which records of Lord Nuffield's giving are available) as 100, by 1936/7, after Morris Motors became a public company and when the first of the very substantial gifts were made, it had risen to 125. In 1943, the year of the forming of Nuffield Foundation, it had fallen to 89. At the end of 1989 it was estimated at 5.7. Thus, a gift of £1 million in 1936 was then worth just over twenty-two times as much, i.e. about £22 million.

The majority of the legacies were for the benefit of Nuffield College.

Chapter 12
The Nuffield Foundation

Colin Hill

Nuffield structured all of his major benefactions with certain safeguards for the business that he had created. First, it should survive as an independent British organization. Second, the Inland Revenue should not jeopardize that survival by claims on his personal holdings in that business. He was not seeking to avoid paying personal taxes in order to increase his own wealth, for his style of living was modest, nor had he any close relatives to whom he wished to pass on his estate. His 'child' was his business and, come what may, he was going to see that his child survived.

In 1943 Nuffield, aged 65, was very much aware that if he took no preventative action his personal holdings in Morris Motors would be valued at their market value at time of death. To pay the duties these shares would have to be sold, thereby risking a collapse in their price and opening the way for predators to gain control of the Nuffield Organization. Furthermore, a fall in the share price would severely depress the value of the endowments which he had already made by gifting his shares to various charities.

Simply giving away the money (in the form of shares) would not, in his judgement, be a sufficient protection for the share price, in which he now had no personal financial interest. He could not imagine any circumstances in which any of his trusts might want to sell their Morris Motors shares, but if they did their holdings were large enough to affect the price. He therefore wrote provisions in the Nuffield Trust deed that these shares could be disposed of during his lifetime only with his written consent or, in the event of his death, to pay death duties. Since most of his estate was willed to charities, the death duties would have been small in any case, so this second proviso, if implemented, would not have had any serious effect on the share price.

These restrictions on the freedom of action of the ordinary trustees were made against warnings of the dangers of being highly committed to a single share, and in 1955, some 8 years before Nuffield died, a Charity Commission Scheme removed the proviso about death duties.

THE TRUSTEES

The Nuffield Foundation is unusual in having a two-tier structure of trustees. The ordinary trustees, responsible for maintaining the value of the endowment, and managing trustees who were responsible for the charitable disbursements. Unfortunately, there was little harmony between these two groups during the decade following Nuffield's death.

During the critical period in the second half of the 1960s the ordinary trustees were retired Morris Motors people and therefore emotionally involved, loyal to the memory of Lord Nuffield and optimistic for the future of BMC (and later of BMH and British Leyland) in spite of all the internal and external evidence which should have given them pause. The latter, with a more detached and academic background, were much more sceptical about the future of the British motor industry and urged the ordinary trustees to diversify their investments.

The motor industry remained profitable until the early 1960s, even though it was lagging behind major parts of British industry in terms of both share price and earnings per share. Even though the Chief Charity Commissioner and the managing trustees had urged them to do so, the ordinary trustees did not use their powers to diversify their shareholdings until 1971, some 3 years after BMC had been absorbed by British Leyland and several months after British Leyland had substantially cut its dividend.

There can be no doubt that this failure to respond was a serious error of judgement. First, because no prudent investor keeps all his eggs in one basket, particularly when what is at risk is not his personal fortune but assets held in trust for others. Second, because the writing on the wall for the motor industry was apparent within a year or two of Nuffield's death.

While the first reason makes it difficult to justify the lack of action on the part of the trustees (since loyalty to their original benefactor was obviously not furthering the cause for which he provided the money), at least there was some case, however tenuous, for believing that the motor industry could recover from its steadily deteriorating position and, in their defence, it is worthwhile considering how the situation may have looked to them in the second half of the 1960s.

BACKGROUND TO THE MOTOR INDUSTRY 1945–75

For nearly 30 years after the end of the war successive British governments, Labour and Conservative alike, had tried to maintain the value of sterling and to minimize deficits in the balance of payments by acting almost exclusively on consumer demand. Politically, it was easier to restrict demand for durable consumer goods than for consumption goods such as food and clothing. Government expenditure, the largest single element of gross national product was held to be sacrosanct, or at least more beneficial than unrestricted consumerism. Expenditure on durable consumer goods (excluding housing) was, and indeed still is, only a relatively small part of national expenditure. To use this as the major weapon in controlling the national economy necessitated frequent and dramatic intervention in the terms on which these goods could be supplied. Since the largest total outlay on durable consumer goods is cars, the effect of these changes on the motor industry, and indeed on all durable consumer industries where steady production is a major key to profitability, was catastrophic.

The two major instruments to control this demand were purchase tax and hire-purchase restrictions, the latter having the greater effect. In the 12 years between 1950 and 1962, just before Nuffield's death, these conditions changed eighteen times (see Table F), usually being progressively relaxed shortly before general elections and progressively tightened shortly afterwards.

This policy caused fluctuations in demand between one year and the next in the order of 30 per cent and sometimes more. Even so, the protected home market continued to show overall growth and a high, but diminishing, proportion of output was exported, albeit at much lower profits than home-market sales. Not surprisingly Britain's share of world production and exports steadily diminished. From 1965 onwards, however, the decline of the industry accelerated, as did the rate of Government intervention in demand management. In the second half of the 1960s the UK was the only major motor-manufacturing country where the home market progressively declined. In the 3 years between 1965 and 1968 there were eleven government interventions to affect demand for cars, of which nine were designed to reduce it.

The effects of these policies on the profits of BMC and its successor companies were dramatic. BMC's profits fell from £20 million in the early 1960s to zero in the financial year 1965/6 and to a loss of 7.5 million in the first half of 1966/7. The scale of these losses was greater than that of any other British motor manufacturer which suggests that although the primary cause may have been Government incompetence BMC's management was far from being blameless.

In 1968 BMC was saved from immediate disaster only by the shotgun marriage to Leyland Motors. At the time of the merger the BMH – as it then was – profit forecast for 1967/8 was virtually zero and its overdraft some £60 million. Leyland were not exactly enthusiastic about the merger and but for Government pressure and the promise of a £25m loan on favourable terms to the new corporation it is unlikely that the marriage would have been consummated. While the detailed confidential figures leading to the merger were not available to the trustees it is inconceivable that they were unaware of the general position of BMH, since both the annual reports and public discussion would have made it obvious that all was not well.

Initially, however, the merger appeared to be successful. In the first two years of operation profits averaged over £38m, the share price rose and at the end of 1968 the value of the Foundations endowment rose to a peak of £40 million. But in 1969/70 BL profits fell to £4m although the dividend (the major source of the Trust's income) was maintained. Still the trustees took no action to dispose of any BL shares.

DIVERSIFICATION OF THE ENDOWMENT

Action to diversify the endowment, when it came, was too little and too late. Not until 1971, the year in which British Leyland drastically cut its dividend, did the ordinary trustees move. If, as the Latin playwright has it, 'True wisdom consists not only in seeing what is before you eyes but in foreseeing what is to come', then the wisdom appears to have been lacking just when it was most needed. Between 1945 and 1965, although the market value of the portfolio had doubled, in real terms the increase was negligible, being roughly in line with inflation over the 20 years, even though these were the boom years of the motor industry. Indeed it could be argued that the main factor in keeping the share price up was the relatively generous dividend policy adopted by both Morris Motors and BMC, and continued by BL until 1971 when the dividend was drastically cut.

The managing trustees were acutely aware of the dangers of the investment strategy of the ordinary trustees. In 1968, as a result of advice which they had taken, they formally requested a review of that strategy, but no action was taken. In 1970 the Chief Charity Commissioner wrote to the ordinary trustees encouraging them to follow this advice but still no action was taken.

The trustees made their first move in 1971 following the dividend cut by selling one third of their BL shares. The remaining two thirds were acquired by the Government in 1975 (on what was effectively the nationalization of BL) at a unit price only 37 per cent of what it was some 30 years earlier. This incurred a book loss of £4.2 million. In real terms the end of 1975 value of the endowment was only 40 per cent of what it had been 30 years earlier. By end 1992, even though its book value had multiplied over seven times since the final disposal of the BL shares it had regained only 68 per cent of the real value of the original Nuffield gifts 50 years earlier. The results of the trustees' decisions are illustrated in Table 12.1.

Table 12.1   Value of Foundation portfolio 1945–92

		(Millions of £s)	
	Actual	1992 £s	Index 1945=100
1945	10	196	100
1955	13	173	87
1965	20	198	100
1975	17	80	40
1985	66	104	52
1992	128	128	68

Table 2 illustrates what might have happened had the ordinary trustees followed a more orthodox investment policy in which maintenance of both the capital and income were primary objectives. The unit trust figures are those of an actual but typical high return trust calculated on an offer to bid basis.

Table 12.2   Indexed value of portfolios 1965 – 1992
(Historic values in £s – 1965=100)

	Nuffield Trust	Unit Trust
1965	100	100
1975	42	187
1985	52	593
1992	68	782

For the greater part of this period – i.e. until end 1979 – the Ordinary Trustees were responsible for the Trust's portfolio. They then handed over £29m of assests for which they were responsible to the managing trustees which enabled the latter to form a Common Investment Fund. From then onwards the trustees always sought professional advice in the construction of the portfolio. Following their take-over the value of the portfolio confortably bettered inflation.

THE FOUNDATION'S INCOME

The primary purpose of the investment portfolio was and is to generate income for distribution in accordance with the Trust's objectives. Table 12.3 shows the development of this income over the same period as the portfolio valuation in Table 12.1.

Table 12.3   Average Annual Income 1945–1922
(£s million)

	Actual	1992 £s	Index (1965=100)4
1945–54	0.66	8.78	45
1955–64	1.95	19.31	100
1965–74	1.54	7.24	37
1975–84	2.60	4.09	21
1992	5.74	5.74	30

The prosperity of the motor industry in general and the generous dividend policy followed by Morris Motors and its successors in the decade from the mid 50s to mid 60s is clearly indicated by these figures, as is the collapse of both of these factors in the 1970s.

Table 12.4 compares the relative performance of the Foundation's portfolio income with that of the Unit Trust featured in Table 12.2

Table 12.4   Indexed average value of portfolio incomes 1965–1992
(Historic values in £s, 1965=100)

	Nuffield Trust	Unit Trust
1965–74	100	100
1975–84	79	235
1992	133	788

In general terms, and bearing in mind that these comparisons are not strictly comparable owing to some changes in the data bases for each trust, it is obvious that had the ordinary trustees followed a more conventional investment strategy the value of the portfolio would now be worth over ten times as much as it is today and its income about six times as great.

The managing trustees since 1980 have brought about a remarkable change considering that during the various stock market crises since 1980 they have had to balance the needs of income (which means a high proportion of fixed interest stocks the nominal value of which declined with the high inflation of the 1980's) against the longer term objective of rebuilding the capital base.

Since the managing trustees took over in 1980 the value of the portfolio has increased from £29m to £128m (about 4.5 times) and the income has averaged slightly over 5 per cent of the value of the portfolio.

THE FUTURE

The Nuffield Foundation reached it's fiftieth anniverasary in 1993. Within a few years of its inception it was the largest foundation in the UK. Its research budget for scientific projects, most of which were large scale, exceeded that of the Governement's own Department of Scientific and Industrial Research. The financial debacle of the 1970s outlined above has however caused a total re-think of how the founder's wishes have to be interpreted.

While substantial grants are still made for scientific research projects there has been a major switch in many areas from research to action. While much of this can be attributed to the straightened circumstances of the Foundation, the change in public perception of how both Government and private funding should be used in the areas of interest of the Foundation has also had an impact on the trustees' thinking. In the third quarter of this century it was a widely held view that any problem, social, scientific, medical, educational or industrial could be solved by throwing enough money at it. This view was not confined to the UK nor even to the industrialised world.

The cost-effectiveness of this approach is now being strongly challenged. Centralisation and the infinitude of costly and often self-perpetuating research projects are slowly yielding the high ground to smaller scale undertakings which are action rather than research based. Of course both approaches are necessary, but more and more they are being seen as interdependent and complementary rather than exclusive and competitive. The trustees have demonstrated this, as a comparison of their grants in

1993 compared with those of the 1950s and 60s shows. For example, in 1956 a grant of £200,000 (over £2.5m in 1992 £s) was made to Nuffield College for buildings. The largest grant in 1992 was for less than one tenth of that in real terms.

The trustees have also recognised that large one-off grants are often not the best way of achieving long term results for new initiatives. Many of their grants now guarantee funding for three or more years which, among other advantages, allows the beneficiaries to concentrate on the job in hand rather than spend time every year in seeking new sources of funding to carry on their work.

In many ways Lord Nuffield would almost certainly have approved of this approach. In the first place it is realistic rather than grandiose, and Nuffield was a very practical man. Second, his interests included schemes for the benefit of underprivileged groups, as one of his early projects to help with the costs of relatives paying visits to family members in prison showed.

The task facing the trustees is much the same as that which faces governments – the classic economic question of how best to allocate scarce resources. While this is easily stated as a simple proposition its application is far more difficult once it is recognised that there are no scientific criteria either for estimating the cost or the value of any of the competing alternatives. In the end it is a matter of judgement and of accepting the responsibility for the outcome of one's choice. In this at least the trustees have some advantages over the politicians in that they can take a longer and more dispassionate view of their onerous tasks and that they are freer to follow their consciences rather than the whims of a fickle electorate.

The Foundation has changed from being the largest endowment in the UK to one that does not even figure in the top ten. But its long term financial future is probably more secure than at any time in its fifty years of history, largely due to the dedication and ability of the trustees since 1968.

Appendix

INFORMATION RELEVANT TO THE ACTIVITIES OF THE NUFFIELD FOUNDATION FROM INCEPTION UNTIL 1988

Table A Total benefactions received from Lord Nuffield or his estate

Date received	Amount (£ million)	How provided
1943	10.00	Morris Motors shares
1961	0.24	Morris Garages shares

Table B Disposals by trust of shares in Nuffield enterprises

Disposal year	Type of shares	Value at time of: Gift	Disposal	Gain/loss
1971	BL Ordinary	£3.3 M	£6.0 M	£2.7 M
1975	BL Ordinary	£6.7 M	£2.5 M	(£4.2 M)
1983	Morris Garages	£0.2 M	£0.7 M	£0.5 M
Total		£10.2 M	£9.2 M	(£1.0 M)

Table C Market value of net assets of trust at year end (£ million)

Year	Amount	Year	Amount
1945	10	1975	17
1955	13	1985	66
1965	20	1989	115

Table D Income, distributions and administrative costs for periods shown

Period Year end	Income (£000s)	Administration costs amount (£ million)	% of income	Distributions amount (£ million)	% Income
1946–1955	6.6	0.35	5.4	5.2	79.3
1956–1966	19.5	0.77	3.9	17.3	88.9
1966–1975	15.4	1.48	9.6	12.0	78.0
1976–1985	26.1	3.07	11.8	19.1	73.1
1986–1988	12.7	1.27	9.9	9.7	76.3
1992	6.2*	0.7	14.0	5.7	92.0

Source of Tables A–D: Nuffield Foundation.
*Total Foundation income.

Table E Purchasing power of £1 (1925 = 100)

Read across

1926	100	1935	126	1945	89	1955	61
1965	45	1970	37	1975	21	1976	17
1977	15	1978	14	1979	12	1980	11
1981	9.3	1982	8.3	1983	7.9	1984	7.5
1985	7.1	1986	6.9	1987	6.6	1988	6.2
		1990	5.5	1991	5.1	1992	4.9

Sources: Central Statistical Office and others. Owing to changes in source data and method of compiling the index over the period, this should not be regarded as a continuous series, but the relativities are sufficiently accurate to illustrate the orders of magnitude of changes referred to in the text.

Table F Purchase to tax and hire-purchase conditions for cars 1050–73

Year	Month	Purchase tax changes	Hire purchase restrictions		
			Details	Min. deposit (%)	Max. repayment time (months)
1950	April	Reduced to 33⅓%			
1951	April	Increased to 66⅔%			
1952	Feb.		Introduced	33⅓	18
1953	April	Reduced to 50%			
1954	July		Removed		
1955	Feb.		Re-introduced	15	24
1955	July		Increased	33⅓	24
1955	Oct.	Increased to 60%			
1956	Feb.		Increased	50	24
1956	Dec.		Eased	20	24
1957	May		Increased	33⅓	24
1958	Oct.		Removed		
1959	April	Reduced to 50%			
1960	April		Re-introduced	20	24
1961	Jan.		Eased	20	36
1961	July	Increased to 55%			
1962	April	Reduced to 45%			
1962	Nov.	Reduced to 25%			
1965	June		Increased	25	36
1965	July		Increased	25	30
1966	Feb.		Increased	25	27
1966	July		Increased	40	24
1966	July	Increased to 27½%			
1967	June		Eased	30	30
1967	Aug.		Eased	25	36
1967	Nov.		Increased	33⅓	27
1968	March	Increased to 33⅓%			
1968	Nov.	Increased to 36⅔%			
1968	Nov.		Increased	40	24
1971	July		Removed		
1971	July	Reduced to 30%			
1972	March	Reduced to 25%			
1973	March		Re-introduced	33⅓	24
1973	April	Replaced by car tax and VAT (equivalent 20 23% purchase tax)			

Chapter 13

Concern for unemployed and employed

F. John Minns

As Britain began in the 1930s to recover from the severe depression of that period, public and government alike began to be deeply concerned that merely to dish out money – the dole – to men long unemployed through no fault of their own in parts of the country unhappily described as 'the depressed areas', although vitally necessary, was only a partial solution, just a stand-offish cash subsistence to meet the basic consequence of this human hardship.

Lord Nuffield, answerable only to himself, with his constant concern for working men, saw the Government's difficulty and stepped in with a gift of £2 million, quite a lot for the purpose in those days, to be used by a Nuffield Trust for Special Areas. This Trust he empowered to grant *large unsecured* loans to be made available for financing the re-employment of workers in the hard-hit areas, so reviving these areas from within. The capital so provided was to rehabilitate bankrupt industries, such as the then dormant collieries, and start new businesses, often small at first, to revive enterprise at a truly local level.

To ensure that such loans were wisely used he persuaded his former chief assistant, Leonard Lord, then unemployed, to manage the Trust and give continuing advice to the recipients of the loans granted by the trustees.

These loans, if or when repaid to the Trust, were then to be donated to the King Edward Hospital Fund for London. In this way Lord Nuffield not only enabled unemployed workers to regain the dignity of working, thus reviving distressed areas, but, having done so, he was also able to donate to London Hospitals through the King's Fund while his Nuffield Provincial Hospitals Trust was helping hospitals outside the London area, as described in Chapter 22.

Lord Nuffield was very agreeably surprised at the great success of this

Special Areas Trust and also enjoyed much pleasure in hearing from year to year of the total repayments of the various loans by businesses prospering again. He had previously given £30,000 to finance another self-help scheme called the Upholland Unemployment Settlement, in Lancashire.

Of the many towns and districts helped by the Trust — on the Wear, Tees and Tyne, in Wales, and in the north-west of England — Whitehaven, the seaport and colliery district where 2,000 miners, a large majority of the local workforce, had long been on the dole, perhaps achieved the most spectacular revival. Within 2 years these men were all back at work again and the colliery was operating successfully. The Borough Council offered to confer its honorary freedom upon Lord Nuffield, but he did not accept this honour until 1953. Travelling to Whitehaven then by train, a rare form of conveyance to so confirmed a motorist, he arrived to a great welcome and was much impressed by the visible change from severe depression to prosperity in the few years since the end of the war.

The trustees appointed by Lord Nuffield to administer this Special Areas Trust fund in 1936 were Sir Nigel Campbell, Viscount Portal GCMG, DSO, MVO, and Sir Seebohm Rowntree CH. They and their successors in office must also have been well satisfied with having achieved the secondary objective of securing the total repayment of high-risk loans and investments. Guy's Hospital was an ultimate beneficiary, commended by Lord Nuffield, of a large grant from the King Edward Hospital Trust Fund for London, and an account of how this and other grants were used by Guy's is given by Mr A.H. Burfoot in Chapter 16.

A year later he gave one million of his own £1 ordinary shares in Morris Motors, which then had a market value of £2,150,000, to his hourly paid employees, so enabling them all to share in the prosperity of the company. Dividends from this Trust paid to employees in the first year totalled £111,799. The response of one new shareholder to such a welcome windfall is told in Chapter 6. I am sure that his humour was enjoyed by all within hearing, particularly 'Guvnor' himself. Those were the days!

Chapter 14

The Nuffield Trust for the Forces of the Crown

Air Chief Marshal Sir David Lee

Nobody can be more grateful for the generosity of Lord Nuffield than the men and women of the Armed Forces. They still benefit from that generosity today, 50 years after his creation of the Trust.

The shadows of war were creeping across Europe during the early summer of 1939. The Conscription Act had been passed and young Territorials were being called to the Colours. Lord Nuffield greatly admired the universal willingness of these men and women to accept the Act and decided to make life more comfortable and agreeable for them. War broke out and he immediately set aside one million ordinary Morris Motors stock units, a gift which was then worth £1,650,000, to create the Trust for the Forces of the Crown on 14 October 1939. At the same time he made an additional gift of £50,000 to cover the first year's expenditure until a return on the investment of the capital sum began to come available.

With the actual coming of the war and the mobilization of reservists, the larger intake of men and women and the deployment of the Forces produced a bigger and much more widespread need for the facilities the Trust intended to provide, particularly in isolated situations where the paucity of amenities was acute. The trustees wished to get on with their work quickly, but one difficulty stood in their way; it would take at least a year for the initial income for the original gift to materialize. The Trust had not, and never has had, any source of income beyond the interest on its stock and it could not draw on its capital sources since those funds were to be a permanent memorial to the spirit which animated Lord Nuffield's benefaction. Once again, Lord Nuffield did not hesitate to support the provision of a further loan of £50,000 to add to the £50,000 already donated to help the Trust during the first few months of the war.

From that day, the Trust has never looked back. Year by year the capital value of the trust fund has grown, the income has increased, and the disbursements of grants to the Forces has raised accordingly. During the war years, however, the income accruing was only about £87,000 pa, but this level has escalated in recent years to reach over £800,000 in 1988.

The object of the Trust was, and still is, to make grants for the provision of facilities and equipment of a recreational, or welfare nature for the benefit of all three services. Certain strict principles were laid down, and it is useful to record the most important of these, as they have never been discarded or changed to any great extent.

Perhaps the first, and overriding principle is that the Trust should not contribute towards anything that should more properly be provided by public funds. Thus, for example, you will never find basic amenities such as football, cricket, and hockey pitches being subsidized by the Trust. The trustees have to keep a very close eye upon all requests for grants to ensure that they are in strict conformity with this principle, and that Lord Nuffield's gift is not used for grants that should be funded from other sources.

The second principle, of almost equal importance, is that the grants should provide for the maximum number of men and women in the services. For this reason, sports such as polo, are not looked on with favour by the trustees because they are clearly played by relatively few people. On the other hand, other minority sports and recreations, such as golf, sailing, and sub-aqua diving have increased so much in popularity that they now fall into a category acceptable to the trustees. This shift in emphasis is very much in accord with the trustees' overall aim of ensuring that the views of Lord Nuffield, as expressed in his lifetime, are given full weight with the changing pattern of life.

Another principle is that the grants should be classified as major or minor, the former presently being of £10,000 or less, and the later of not more than £1,000. Wherever possible, the recipient of the grant is expected to contribute as much as it can afford to the cost of the project. There is an exception to these categories, which will be described later.

At this point, it seems appropriate to acknowledge the fact that Lord Nuffield's gifts promoted the development of a modern system of welfare support for the Armed Forces. Previously, in the relatively small pre-war services, the well-being of the men could be left to the individual care of officers, but that arrangement was inadequate for the much larger forces that war necessitated and which continued during the Cold War that followed the Armistice. There is no doubt that the formation of the

Nuffield Trust bought home to service chiefs the realization that some scheme over and above the mere provision of basic recreational and welfare facilities would have to be developed. Lord Nuffield's vision, in other words, provided the foundation stone for today's comprehensive 'welfare' system, covering all those serving in any of the three services worldwide.

Since its inception, the Trust has maintained two bodies of trustees. These include three ordinary trustees, who are experienced business men and bankers, responsible for the investment policy of the trust that produces the annual income, which is then available for distribution; and three governing trustees, who are retired senior officers, one from each service. Through the secretary, who is the only full-time employee of the Trust, they consider the detailed recommendations for the expenditure of the individual service's annual share of the available income, which are approved at the executive committee meeting which is held in March each year. This executive committee is well qualified to decide on the order of priority of the many bids received because it consists of the three serving Principal Personnel Officers, namely the Second Sea Lord, the Adjutant General, and the Air Member for Personnel. The bids that are tabled at this meeting have already been carefully filtered by the secretary of the Trust and representatives from the various service departments of the Ministry of Defence.

The first secretary of the Trust was Mrs Margaret Robinson MBE. For many years she kept an eagle eye on the administration of the Trust and ensured strict adherence to the basic principles. She was eventually succeeded in 1970 by Captain T.P. Gillespie, Royal Navy (retired) who was equally strict and administered the Trust with remarkable economy. Rarely, if ever, can a charity have been run with such low administrative costs throughout its first 50 years of existence. In 1988 Captain Gillespie retired and Brigadier R.G. Elliot OBE became the new secretary; continuity being such that he is only the third person to hold the appointment in 50 years!

The facilities provided by the Trust cover an immense range and it would be impossible to describe all of them in a short chapter. In war-time, one of the first things the Trust did was to distribute thousands of radio sets to the British Expeditionary Force. Later, thousands more were sent to ships at sea and isolated anti-aircraft sites and barrage balloon units at home. Its Leave Schemes were another unique feature of the Trust's work in the early days. By far the biggest and most valuable scheme was the Nuffield Air Leave Scheme which started in 1943. It was principally for bomber crews who were under great strain at the time. They could spend their leave at a hotel, chosen from a list of some thirty located all over Great Britain, at little or no cost to themselves. They could take a relative or friend with them, and these were put up at special rates. This scheme, of course, ended with the war.

In more recent years, the Trust has been anxious to help particularly those who help themselves or are required to live in isolated conditions that lack proper amenities. Minibuses have traditionally been one of the main items requested. The Trustees have tried hard to maintain the link with Morris Motors of Cowley by subsequently buying British Leyland and, more recently, Freight Rover vehicles supplied by Messrs Hartwells of Oxford, who have always been most understanding of the particular requirements of the services and deliver the vehicles, immaculately prepared, wherever in the world the recipients might be stationed. Among the other very popular types of sporting equipment are yachts; sailing dinghies and surfboards, together with motor boats for water-skiing and sub-aqua diving. Fitness training equipment such as 'multigyms' and weight-lifting equipment have also gained favour, particularly in isolated stations. Other grants have been made for gliders, golf-course machinery, riding equipment, theatre lighting, and instruments for voluntary bands. So much for examples of sporting equipment, but these by no means exhaust the list. Grants for television sets and video equipment for use in HM ships at sea, troops serving in Northern Ireland, the Falkland Islands and with the United Nations Force in Namibia, RAF detachments in isolated locations, and for patients in military hospitals have been especially welcome. The women's services, including the nursing services, have not been neglected, since, as specifically directed by Lord Nuffield, special grants are made to them to be spent on small items of equipment that are not available from other sources and which improve their quality of life. At the other end of the spectrum has been the support of those taking part in a wide variety of expeditions and other adventurous pursuits. These have included NORPED, the annual services' expedition to Norway; the British services' expedition to Everest; sponsorship of the services' yacht during the Whitbread Round the World Race, and adventure training expeditions Drake and Raleigh.

Over the years the Trust has also invested in a variety of 'fixed assets'. Nuffield's name is best known through a number of well-known clubs which were sponsored and managed by the Trust. The largest, and probably the most famous, was the Nuffield Centre, a recreational club for all servicemen and women below commissioned rank. It was originally situated in Wardour Street, near Piccadilly Circus. After the adjoining Café de Paris had been bombed, it was found that by pulling down a wall the two premises could be connected, so the club obtained permission to take over the Café de Paris and rebuild. After the war, it had to move, and in July 1948 reopened in what was formerly Gatti's Restaurant in Adelaide Street, near Charing Cross.

Lord Nuffield is understood to have taken a keen interest in the Nuffield Centre because he wished members of the Forces to be able, while on leave, to enjoy the amenities of London life without 'going broke' in the process. The Centre therefore provided subsidized rates and first-class entertainment free. The regular programme included two variety shows a week and an orchestra on Sundays; the artists gave their services free, though, of course all expenses were paid by the Trust. During the war these all-star shows were broadcast on the radio and subsequently the 'Centre Show' became a regular feature on television. Very large numbers were catered for during the war; on moving in 1948 the average numbers showed a temporary drop but soon rose to 15,000 per week. At the end of 1954 the eight-millionth guest visited the Centre. A further move in 1974 to Villiers House, John Adam Street was prompted by the termination of the lease and development of the Adelaide Street site. After temporary closure, the centre reopened at the new location in June 1974. The Centre quickly regained it popularity but by 1978 actual usage had begun to fall and it soon became obvious that it would be uneconomic to extend the lease beyond the current one. The Trustees subsequently decided with deep regret that the Centre should finally close for business at the end of March 1980.

Junior officers and their wives were also not forgotten, as the Trust established the Nuffield Club for junior officers, where rates were fixed according to ability to pay rather than actual costs. During the war the Club was in Halkin Street and was known as Nuffield House; but in 1947 it had to move, and it reopened in Lord Bessborough's former house in Eaton Square. However, with a falling membership that reflected the dwindling welfare requirement for the Club in peace-time and consequent increasing subsidy, the Club was closed in 1976.

In the post-war years, the biggest new venture was the building of the Nuffield United Services Officers' Club at Portsmouth, at a cost of some £170,000, with further financial assistance in the running of the Club in its initial stages. The Club was officially opened by HRH Princess Elizabeth in

July 1951. The Club proved to be a great success for over 25 years but, with a reduction in the welfare need for such a club and following upon a decision by the Ministry of Defence to sell the freehold of the land on which the Club Buildings stood, the Club was closed in 1979.

The Trust also experienced some problems with 'fixed assets' abroad in the days when the services were deployed in many overseas theatres. More substantial facilities, such as swimming pools and squash courts, could not be transferred when the services left the theatre. As an example, great difficulty was encountered in obtaining adequate compensation when the British Forces left Singapore, the Gulf, Aden, and Malta, and had to abandon many of these assets. In the course of time most of the problems were solved, but not without lengthy negotiations; the money received in compensation for these lost assets was, of course, returned to the Trust for future redistribution. With the benefit of hindsight, the trustees decided that no further 'fixed assets' would be provided in the overseas theatres that remained, and even at home stations these were limited to those where a proper length of tenure could be guaranteed. The secretary of the Trust was very closely involved with the disposal of such facilities and it is interesting to note that, in 1959, when I was commanding the Royal Air Force in Aden, the then secretary, Margaret Robinson, was given a free trip round the world in RAF transport aircraft to inspect the Trust's gifts. She stayed with me while in Aden and her visit happened to coincide with Lord Nuffield's arrival in a P & O liner on passage to Australia. I said that I would like to go on board to meet him, which I did. Margaret Robinson briefed me not to mention his generosity or to describe the many facilities that he had been instrumental in providing. 'He does not like to be thanked, and he does not know the detail of the Trust's gifts', she told me. I spent an hour with Lord Nuffield and we discussed the situation in Aden, in which he was extremely interested but, before leaving, I felt that I must, out of courtesy, thank him for making the Nuffield Trust possible. He acknowledged my thanks but did not comment and passed on his way to Australia.

During the 1960s and 1970s the services withdrew from the overseas theatres that I have mentioned above and were also reduced considerably in size. At the same time the Trust's funds were growing steadily and more money was therefore available for distribution. The trustees felt that there was a danger of frittering away these large sums on sporting equipment and relatively small projects. Consequently, it was decided to initiate a scheme whereby a 'super grant' would be allocated each year to the individual services in rotation and in addition to the normal major and minor grants. It was intended that the super grant would be spent on large and worthwhile projects in the United Kingdom, where security of tenure was assured. The sum allocated had been increased in line with inflation, and now stands at £150,000.

This scheme has been a resounding success and the trustees feel that it would undoubtedly have met with Lord Nuffield's approval as it conforms closely with his principles as we understand them. These super grants have been spent in a variety of ways. The Royal Navy has taken the opportunity to help fund improvements to The Naval Home Club at Portsmouth and the Royal Fleet Club at Devonport. Many of the other projects to date have been adventure and recreational centres. These is a joint-service centre at Rothiemurchus Lodge and another for the Royal Air Force at Feshiebridge, both near Aviemore in Scotland. The Royal Air Force also has one near Brecon in Wales and the Royal Navy are currently building one on the edge of Dartmoor. A Naval sports complex at Southwick Park and a water-sports centre on the River Thames belonging to the Royal Air Force complete the list of such centres. The Army has developed swimming pools on Salisbury Plain and sponsored improvements to the Union Jack Club in London. These are all valuable and popular centres which, in particular, satisfy the principle of providing for large numbers of men and women in all three services.

It can thus be seen that the Trust has prospered over the years. Thanks to the dedicated work of successive secretaries and the profitable investment policy so ably handled by the ordinary trustees, both the income and the capital derived from Lord Nuffield's original gift in 1939 have increased most satisfactorily, the capital sum invested having risen to some £16 million. In 1989, at the 50 year point, the total allocations by the Trust exceeded £15 million and the dispensation for that particular year reached some £830,000, a huge increase on the distribution from the first year of the Trust's life which stood at £87,000. Bearing in mind that there is no income from donations or any other source other than the Trust's own investments, this must reflect excellent and economical management.

The Royal Navy, the Army, and the Royal Air Force are deeply grateful for the many and varied ways in which they continue to benefit from Lord Nuffield's generous and imaginative benevolence, which has so successfully filled the gap between those things that are provided from official sources and those extras which make living conditions more comfortable or recreation more enjoyable. In this context, at no time can this have been more appreciated than by those serving in the arduous conditions of the Second World War or the numerous operational deployments that have followed, including Malaya, Korea, Borneo, Aden, Cyprus, Belize, Northern Ireland, and the Falkland Islands.

Chapter 15

Early gifts to medicine, later munificence to medical science

A.H.T. Robb-Smith

It is interesting, although often difficult, to determine the influences that caused a philanthropist to devote his riches to one cause rather than another.

It was reading Sir William Osler's *Textbook of Medicine*, revealing how little was known of the causes and therefore the cures of so many diseases, that led that other medical philanthropist, J.D. Rockefeller, to establish the great medical research institutes that bear his name. There is good circumstantial and anecdotal evidence that Osler also directed Lord Nuffield towards his medical benefactions.

When Professor Osler was appointed Regius Professor of Medicine at the University of Oxford in 1905, the Oslers came to live at 13, Norham Gardens, to which a 'Motor House' was added as they had acquired a motor car and a chauffeur. But motors were not very reliable in those days and Professor Osler soon learnt that there was a very skilled motor mechanic not far away. So when the chauffeur reported that the car would not start there would be a cry, 'send for Willy', and in no time William Morris would arrive on his bicycle with his tools and the defect would be quickly remedied.

But the relationship was far from one-sided. Osler had a great admiration for skilled craftsmen and enjoyed talking with Morris, while Morris had a respect for Osler's kindness and medical knowledge and would often talk of his symptoms and worries. Many of these were emotional rather than physical, but on one occasion when Morris was talking about his indigestion, Osler took him into his consulting room, gave him a thorough examination; then told Morris that he believed he had a duodenal ulcer, which could be serious and advised him how he should modify his lifestyle and have proper treatment. At that time the clinical features of duodenal ulcer were not well known but Osler had already recognized and studied the condition.

Nuffield, in later years, liked to talk about his duodenal ulcer and maintained that it was a peculiar type which could not be detected by ordinary means. But a few years before his death when he was being treated by Professor Leslie Witts, the Nuffield Professor of Medicine at the Radcliffe Infirmary, an X-ray showed the scar of a healed duodenal ulcer which had caused some narrowing, but surgical treatment was not needed.

Nuffield never wavered in his gratitude and admiration for Osler and on several occasions insisted that a medical building that he had provided should bear Osler's name. In 1957, shortly after his eightieth birthday, he was the principal guest at the jubilee dinner of the Royal Society of Medicine. It was, he said, due to the skill of Sir William Osler nearly 50 years before that it was possible for him to be dining with them that night.

Osler had a gift for suggesting to those whom he thought might in time become very rich, that they should consider giving some of their wealth to medical and kindred causes in which he was interested.

When Osler came to Oxford he was able to persuade some of his rich North American friends to give generously to the University, the Medical School, and the hospitals. Soon, his gentle persuasive charm proved equally effective in Oxfordshire. John Briscoe, a retired surgeon and a bachelor, used to enjoy attending Osler's rounds and would be told of the great need that the Infirmary had for a new and better out-patient department. On his death it was found that he had left to the Infirmary his whole fortune, nearly £70,000, the largest single benefaction the Infirmary has ever received, while the Oxford branch of the British Red Cross, under Osler's encouragement, found that they had a considerable balance and so could purchase for £15,000 the 130-acre Headington Manor estate, on which the new John Radcliffe Hospital now stands.

In 1917 William Morris was not a wealthy man, but the name W.R. Morris appears amongst the subscribers responding to an appeal made by Sir William Osler for a 'curative workshop', which would enable the Oxford Military Orthopaedic Centre to be established.

It was at that same 1957 jubilee dinner that Nuffield, after speaking of Osler, continued, 'Thereafter I started with orthopaedics and moved to various sections of medicine which were Cinderellas. It has given me the greatest pleasure to do what I have been able to do.'

Before the First World War, orthopaedic surgery was not recognized as a speciality in Great Britain, although a Liverpool surgeon, Mr Robert Jones,

Sir William Osler.
[Courtesy of The Wellcome Institute Library, London]

now regarded as the father of British Orthopaedics, was active in this field. The slaughter of the First World War resulted in thousands of soldiers limbless and maimed. Sir Robert Jones persuaded the War Office, with difficulty, that there should be specialized hospitals where these injured soldiers could be properly treated, and that these should be linked with rehabilitation centres, which in those days were called curative workshops.

At that time Oxford was a city of wounded soldiers. The main military hospital was in the University Examination Schools, but soldiers were accommodated in some of the colleges and the Cowley Road Hospital, while at Headington there was the little Wingfield Convalescent Home, which had quite large grounds. One of the medical officers stationed in Oxford was Capt. G.R. Girdlestone, who had been in general practice in Oswestry, where there was one of the first open-air hospitals for children suffering from bone tuberculosis. Robert Jones used to advise on the care of these children, and he had stimulated Dr Girdlestone's interest in orthopaedics, this new branch of surgery. Accordingly, Robert Jones felt that Oxford would be a good place for an orthopaedic centre, but the War Office had insisted that the curative workshop attached to the centre must be financed by the Red Cross and private funds. So Osler was approached to ask if he could organize an appeal for funds for the curative workshop.

Delighted at the idea, Osler organized an impressive meeting in the Oxford Union, at which he gave a moving address 'The Problems of the Crippled and Maimed'. In no time there was enough money for the curative workshop which, with the Oxford Orthopaedic Centre, was established in the grounds of the little Wingfield Convalescent Home, with Capt. Girdlestone in charge. It soon became the 200-bed Wingfield Orthopaedic Hospital.

It is not known whether Morris attended the meeting or just read the full account in the *Oxford Times*, nor what other charitable gifts he made in the next 5 or 6 years, which were critical in his industrial development. It is certain that already his interest in relieving suffering was well advanced. His was not the slightly austere scientific outlook of the Rockefellers. His was the compassionate view of wishing to help and relieve the sick; first individuals, then groups, the workmen in his factories, the blind, the crippled; then a desire to see that there were better hospital facilities for his executive colleagues with the development of private blocks; then improvements in medical education, hospitals, and the health services as a whole. finally the broader concept of a Foundation to facilitate research and education in the whole field of the health sciences.

In his later years Lord Nuffield would say that he had always wanted to be a surgeon but the finances had been lacking. There is no mention of this in his early days. It seems more likely that it was a Walter Mitty fantasy, just as when visiting an Atlantic liner's engine room, he would say that he had always wanted to be a ship's engineer, something he would also tell Mr Jeater, the chief engineer at the Radcliffe Infirmary, a great character, formerly a merchant navy engineer.

However, it is certain that Nuffield had a real interest and quite considerable knowledge of medical subjects, though it must be confessed that some of his theories as to the nature of disease were a little unusual. Next to talking about engineering, medicine was his favourite topic. He greatly enjoyed the company of doctors, young and old, and would not only discuss the nature of his own complaints but of others that he knew. If he thought that one of his workmen was looking a bit out of sorts, he would call him into his office, discuss his symptoms and perhaps examine a specimen of urine, for he had the apparatus at hand.

Arthur Sanctuary, the former administrator of the Radcliffe Infirmary, recalled an occasion when one of Nuffield's relatives was in the hospital. One day Nuffield came into the administrator's office and said he would like to discuss his relative's illness with the physician in charge. Sanctuary quickly summoned the house physician and the registrar, but unhappily the consultant was out of Oxford. So Sanctuary, who had a superb ability for handling any situation with equanimity, rang up the Department of Anaesthestics and asked Professor Sir Robert Macintosh, who was a great friend of Nuffield's, if he could come to the ward to support the junior medical staff. The meeting took place by the patient's bed and as Sanctuary remarked, 'Nuffield stood at the end of the bed holding the patient's notes and gave a clear precise account of the nature of his relative's illness, treatment, and prognosis', and in Sanctuary's view it was done as well as if Nuffield had been the consultant himself. Whether the consultation influenced the outcome of the patient's illness is not recorded.

Lord Nuffield had a medical library of over a hundred volumes. Apart from Osler's works, they were almost all published after 1930 but, in addition to presentation copies, they covered a broad range of works on general medicine and surgery, with a scattering of books on general science and the history of medicine. It is an interesting collection and deserves a more detailed study. But the book that he regarded as the most important and helpful to him was Osler's textbook and he maintained that it was never any use consulting a doctor unless Osler's textbook was clearly at hand in his consulting room.

William Morris's first official link with medicine occurred in 1924 when he was elected a Vice-President of Oxford's Radcliffe Infirmary. It was to prove an epoch-making event both for the medical school and hospitals of Oxford and would lead to very significant changes in the whole medical world.

The immediate reason for Morris's election to the Radcliffe Infirmary was that in the previous year a group of Oxford businessmen had organized the Oxford Motor Ballot, to raise money for the Radcliffe Infirmary and the Oxford Eye Hospital. The tickets cost half a crown; the principal prizes were four Morris motor cars and two motor-bicycles presented by William Morris and there were a number of subsidiary prizes. It had the support of the Earl of Jersey, Lord Valentia, and the Lord Mayor of Oxford. Yielding £9,000, it extinguished the Radcliffe Infirmary's overdraft. The treasurer and the governors of the Infirmary, recognizing that they had in their midst a determined businessman with vision, sympathy, and generosity, felt it was very necessary to have his advice and interest, and they certainly needed it.

The Infirmary site on the Woodstock Road was hopelessly overcrowded and quite inadequate for the increasing hospital needs, while the Radcliffe trustees, who owned the Observatory and all the ground around it, had refused to allot any of it to the Infirmary. The Infirmary had the Headington Manor Estate and they had recently received a further 50 acres in Cowley village for a convalescent home. It was the intention that a tuberculosis sanatorium should be established on the Headington site, but no agreement could be obtained from the Ministry or the local authorities. The Infirmary needed a maternity home and had obtained temporary accommodation in a former University hall of residence in Museum Road; it also required more accommodation for nurses on the Radcliffe site, though it had used some of the Manor House estate for a preliminary training school. But the next new years were to see some remarkable changes.

Lord Valentia, who had been President of the Infirmary since 1916, died early in 1927 and on 15 June of that year Mr W.R. Morris, who would soon be Sir William Morris, was elected to succeed him as President. In August 1927, the Governors learnt from the Radcliffe trustees that they were not prepared to entertain any proposals for giving up any of the Observatory land. So it was decided to see whether a plan could be drawn up to give greater accommodation on the Radcliffe site, and this was attempted.

The Infirmary's treasurer, the Revd Cronshaw, who had by his enthusiasm and confidence led the Infirmary for so many years, was in poor health and would resign in 1928. He decided to approach the new President, Sir William Morris, to ask if he would provide funds for a new maternity home to be built upon the Radcliffe site, as the lease for the home in Museum Road, which in any case was unsatisfactory, would run out shortly. Sir William Morris received him generously, and gave an assurance that he would meet the whole costs of the new maternity home, estimated at just under £40,000.

Oxford was not the only place to enjoy Morris's generosity during 1927. He had factories in Birmingham and in Coventry. So he gave £25,000 towards the rebuilding of the Birmingham General Hospital and a further £200,000 during the next 10 years. The Coventry and Warwick Hospital received £70,000.

Morris also gave £104,000 to St. Thomas's Hospital but the circumstances surrounding this gift are a little obscure. Sir Farquhar Buzzard, the Regius Professor of Medicine, was on the staff of St Thomas's and so it would be logical that this was the first occasion on which he influenced Morris's philanthropy. But chronology does not favour this idea. The St Thomas's Hospital reports state that the Clerk to the Governors, Mr George Roberts, aroused Morris's interest in the hospital in 1926, when he agreed to give £104,000 over 6½ years. The final installment was paid in 1933, when it was decided to commemorate his generosity by renaming one of the wards 'Nuffield'. It is said that on the occasion that this was suggested to his lordship, the then Clerk to the Governors asked whether Nuffield would not be willing to renew the grant, so as to meet the costs of maintaining the ward. Nuffield was not pleased, saying that nobody had ever asked him to do such a thing. It was Guy's Hospital that would enjoy his generosity in the future. It is generally agreed that it was in the summer of 1933, while walking round Huntercombe golf course, that Nuffield suddenly told Professor T.B. Johnston that he would like to provide a private block at Guy's. Mr Burfoot has provided a delightful account of the happy relationship that the staff of Guy's enjoyed with Lord Nuffield (Chapter 16).

Sir Farquhar Buzzard was appointed Regius Professor in October 1927, and early in 1928 took up residence in Oxford. An able neurologist, he was to prove himself one of the greatest medical statesmen of his time. Later in the year, Mr William Goodenough, Manager of the Oxford branch of Barclays Bank, who had been a member of the Committee of Management at the Infirmary for some time, succeeded the Revd Cronshaw as treasurer. Morris, Goodenough, and Buzzard changed the whole character of medical care and medical education in the British Isles.

The appeal for funds for the rebuilding of the Radcliffe Infirmary was launched in the Town Hall on 4 October 1928. Morris, the President, announced that not only would he provide the cost of the maternity home, about £38,000, but if the public subscribed £80,000 or more, he would add to that a further £40,000. The response was excellent and by the end of 1929 the public appeal had reached £45,000, but by that time the prospect for the future of the Infirmary had completely changed.

Buzzard was a convinced and convincing planner. He was aware that in 1923 Dr Abraham Flexner, a representative on the Rockefeller Foundation, was discussing with the then Regius Professor, Sir Archibald Garrard, the provision of a £75,000 grant to build and equip a Department of Biochemistry in Oxford. He suggested that, with the pre-eminent pre-clinical departments, Oxford would be an ideal place to establish an institute of clinical research.

Three years later, representatives of the Rockefeller Foundation came to England, anxious to provide money for such an institute and that it should be in Oxford, but they were unable to get any response from the University, so the scheme was abandoned.

Buzzard was determined that this should not happen again and he saw Morris as a potential benefactor. The Regius had received 'signals' from the Radcliffe trustees indicating that their absolute refusal to consider release of any of the Observatory grounds had softened, and so in June 1929 a letter was addressed to the trustees under the signatures of Morris, Buzzard, and Goodenough, in which they explained that because of the previous information from the trustees the Infirmary had prepared a plan of rebuilding and an appeal had been launched, but owing to the limited space available it was not a satisfactory scheme. They then went on to say that an even more important reason was that there was a possibility of extending the activities of the University's medical school by establishing a postgraduate school of medical research, which should be in association with the Infirmary and could well be centred on the Observatory buildings.

Five months later, in November 1929, it was announced that following negotiations with the Radcliffe trustees, they had agreed to sell the whole of the observatory site, and that Sir William Morris had undertaken to purchase it for £100,000. The site was to be divided between the Radcliffe Infirmary and the Medical School of the University of Oxford. The Trust Deed setting out the details of Sir William's gift showed on the plan a division between the hospital portion and the school portion of the Observatory grounds and Sir William had added to the Trust Deed a requirement that the Observer's House should be known as Osler House. He had not forgotten his friendship and valuable medical and other advice which he had received from the former Regius Professor.

Sir William Morris's purchase of the Radcliffe Observatory and its grounds would completely change the face of Oxford medicine. As the astronomers were still in the building the development of the projected University research institute had to be delayed. But there was no delay over the expansion of the Radcliffe Infirmary on to the former observatory grounds, and the plans were redrawn. The new maternity home of 42 beds, was completed in 1931 and opened on 22 October by the Duchess of York, now Queen Elizabeth the Queen Mother.

Twenty-five years later in 1956, Professor Moir, the Nuffield Professor of Obstetrics organized a ceremony at which Lord Nuffield was present, when the mother of the first baby born in the home unveiled a plaque recording that in the 25 years 18,500 mothers had been delivered, 11,000 nurses had been trained as midwifes, and 500 medical students had had their instruction in midwifery.

In May 1934 the new wards and departments of the Radcliffe Infirmary, built on the old Observatory site were completed. The development had cost £108,000, of which £71,000 was provided by the public, so it was not possible to take advantage of Morris's offer of a £40,000 'cap', and the £37,000 had to be found by selling securities and part of the Manor House estate.

Nuffield's affection for, and generosity to, the Radcliffe Infirmary continued unabated until his death some 30 years later. But it was not the only Oxford hospital to enjoy this.

The Wingfield Orthopaedic Hospital at Headington launched a building appeal in 1929, as the hospital largely consisted of wooden huts built during the First World War, which were rapidly disintegrating. The story goes that William Morris, bicycling home from his factory, stopped at Mr Girdlestone's house and gave him a cheque for £1,000 towards the rebuilding. But the donor was, in fact, Sir William Morris OBE, President of the Radcliffe Infirmary, owner of all the ordinary shares of Morris Motors Limited, value at over £2 million pounds, who had already given nearly half a million pounds for various medical charities. It is certain that Nuffield and Girdlestone became firm friends, for, though there were many differences in character and outlook, they shared a common determination to achieve. Professor Duthie gives an account of what Nuffield achieved for the orthopaedic centre that bears his name (Chapter 19).

But, with any project in which Nuffield was deeply interested, he was not satisfied merely to find money for buildings and equipment, but believed that it was just as important to have scholarships for training and, where necessary, assistance for the patients. He provided orthopaedic scholarships, funds for developing orthopaedic services in the British Empire, and over a quarter of a million pounds for the Nuffield Fund for Cripples.

During the 1930s Lord Nuffield made grants to many medical projects which he found of interest and felt deserved support, but mention should be made of an episode that appeared to be an example of Morris's impulsive generosity but, in reality, was the outcome of a serious decision. The centenary of the founding of the British Medical Association in the city of Worcester was in 1932, and to commemorate the event the Prince of Wales came to the city to open an extension of the Worcester Infirmary. Amongst the honoured guests was Sir William Morris, on whom the Freedom of the City had just been conferred as he had been born there. The extension included an orthopaedic department, which was later named the Nuffield Orthopaedic Department. In the course of his speech the Prince mentioned the serious deficit in the Infirmary's finances and, when he concluded, Morris, with whom the Prince had often played golf at Huntercombe, whispered something to the royal visitor, who immediately announced that Sir William Morris had promised a gift of £26,000 to the Infirmary, which naturally was received with loud applause. After this royal visit, King George V approved the styling of the hospital as the Worcester Royal Infirmary. Several grants provided during this period were to relieve the handicapped and those with other orthopaedic problems.

In 1916 the Tuberculosis Officer for Cambridgeshire, Dr (later Sir) Pendred Varrier-Jones, felt that once tuberculous disease was arrested, further treatment was morally, spiritually, and probably physically harmful, and he believed that an 'opportunity to work' was an essential part of rehabilitation. In 1918 he was able to acquire the Papworth Estate and establish industries there so that patients could live with their families in houses in the village, relieved of financial and social stresses.

In September 1935 Lord Nuffield was approached by the Chairman of the Papworth Trust, explaining that they were hoping to raise £100,000 for various needs in the village and would his Lordship make a contribution? Two days later Lord Nuffield replied, saying that he was very sympathetic to the project but he found that often when a large donation was given, those who might have made smaller contributions felt they were relieved of the necessity. So he offered to give £25,000 once £75,000 had been raised.

Two years later, when there was a festival dinner for the Papworth Centre, Lord Nuffield acted as honorary treasurer and undertook that if the dinner raised £15,000 or more he would give double the amount raised for the charity. Just a fortnight after the Papworth festival dinner, Lord Nuffield was approached by the Chairman of the Enham Village Centre, which already had close links with that of Papworth. The Enham Village Centre had been established in 1917 to provide rehabilitation and sheltered workshops for crippled ex-servicemen, to meet their needs to earn a livelihood after their treatment at an orthopaedic centre and curative workshop, such as that in Oxford. This centre had been the Enham estate in Hampshire, which formerly belonged to the Erale family, and the charity, like Papworth, needed financial support and was seeking to collect £25,000. Lord Nuffield agreed to give £10,000 when £15,000 had been subscribed.

During the Second World War, after the victory of El Alamein, £250,000 was given to the Village Centre as a thanksgiving gift, and the village is now known as Enham–Alamein. Following the successful drug treatment of tuberculosis, so that this disease is no longer the scurge that it was, these two Village Centres, Papworth and Enham–Alamein, continued to provide sheltered and satisfactory occupations for the disabled and their families.

During 1937 Mr Girdlestone told Nuffield of the excellent orthopaedic work being carried out at Exeter by a colleague of his, Mr Norman Capener, and the need for improvement in the hospital, and that as it was a rural area funds were not too easy to acquire. Nuffield wrote to Capener asking for details of their needs and plans for the future, and when these were received he immediately sent a cheque for £15,000, saying that he would give a further £10,000 if £5,000 could be subscribed within 6 weeks by Devonians. This challenge was more than met within the prescribed time and the Princess Elizabeth Hospital had its very necessary extensions completed by 1940.

During the 1930s Lord Nuffield continued to make moderate-sized grants to many medical projects which he found of interest and believed deserved support. It is interesting to note that, time and again, a project that Sir Farquhar Buzzard had been interested in was one that Lord Nuffield supported financially. For example, Buzzard, with his belief in 'positive' health, was greatly interested in the Peckham Pioneer Health Centre, which was established in 1926 by Drs Williamson and Pearse, studying and caring for the well-being of families rather than individuals. Lord Nuffield gave two grants totalling £25,000 and, when the centre was revived after the war, offered a £5,000 challenge if other subscribers gave the same amount. This was achieved but the centre did not survive after 1950.

Sir Farquhar Buzzard was naturally interested in the National Hospital for Nervous Diseases, where he had been a member of the staff. In 1937 the hospital wished to develop their research and surgical facilities. Lord Nuffield contributed £24,000 and a similar sum was provided by the Rockefeller Foundation. Also in 1937, Lord Nuffield contributed £50,000 to the building fund of the Great Ormond Street Hospital for Sick Children, which resulted in the completion of the Southwood Block, which was opened by King George VI and Queen Elizabeth in 1937.

However, it was Nuffield's friendship with Sir Beachcroft Towse that aroused his interest in the needs of the blind, resulting in his great contributions to the 'talking books'. During the South African War Towse, in an engagement for which he was awarded the Victoria Cross, suffered the loss of his sight, and for the rest of his life, some 50 years, he devoted the vigour of his mind and body to the welfare of the blind. Although many books had been printed in Braille, the elderly blind and partially sighted found it difficult to learn, and without a friendly reader the whole world of books and letters was beyond their ken.

In the 1920s there were certain experiments to try to produce some talking machines but these were unsatisfactory and the gramophone-record companies were not interested in producing records running more slowly which could play for a longer time. Accordingly, the Royal National Institute for the Blind and St Dunstan's set up a research committee under the chairmanship of Sir Ian Fraser MP. They devised a record running at about a third of the normal 78 rpm, which seemed to be promising. It was at this stage that Lord Nuffield gave a grant of £6,000 p.a. for 6½ years; this, with other money made it possible to proceed with the experiments and develop the 'talking book service' which was introduced in 1935.

There was close cooperation with the American Blind Association. During the war years the Institute suffered great hardships, with the destruction of their studio by bombings and the lack of gramophone needles, which were made good by the American Association. However, the talking book equipment was costly and difficult to transport; after the war a special cassette and reproducer were designed and, because of Lord Nuffield's gifts, in 1954 it became known as 'The Nuffield Talking Book Library'.

In 1961 Nuffield made a further gift to the Nuffield Foundation, the

Viscount Nuffield Auxilliary Fund, of which one of its main purposes was 'to be the relief of the blind in particular by maintaining and expanding the Nuffield Talking Book Library for the Blind'. This made possible the conversion of the libraries both of St Dunstan's and the Institute from records to tapes, with great advantages from many points of view. While in 1967 a completely new lightweight 'talking book' was introduced which is a great advance on anything available elsewhere in the world.

It was logical after mentioning briefly Morris' renewed interest in orthopaedics, to continue to discuss the various projects outside Oxford, which Nuffield supported at this time. But inevitably this disturbed the strick chronology so now it necessary to return to the Radcliffe Observatory and its grounds.

By 1934 the main Radcliffe Infirmary buildings had been completed, but the Observatory was not to be vacated until 1935. In 1933 the Regius met a committee concerned with the use of the Observatory and put forward his views for making this an institute of clinical research with an adjacent ward. But this was not supported and so it was decided that the institute should be devoted to experimental physiological and pharmacological research.

The first Director of the Institute, Professor J.A. Gunn, had been brought from Edinburgh by Sir William Osler in 1912, to establish a department of experimental pharmacology in Oxford. Not only did Professor Gunn create such a department of outstanding merit, but each of his sucessors in the Chair have advanced the subject further, so that now it is one of the foremost in the world.

In his later years Professor Gunn was well known for his masterly editing of the *British Pharmacopoeia*, which was Lord Nuffield's favorite bedside reading, as he found it was the most effective soporific for his particular type of insomnia. The assistant director, Dr K.J. Franklin was a distinguished physiologist and medical historian. While the third member of the original team, Dr A.E. Barclay was an experimental radiologist with a special interest in studying the gastro-intestinal tract with the aid of barium meals, which particulary interested Nuffield. Barclay was the first to demonstrate a duodenal ulcer by this technique and perfected X-ray cinematography, something which fascinated Lord Nuffield who provided additional funds for the necessary equipment, and visited the institute to see 'moving pictures' of swallowing and digestion. Barclay's technique was also used for studying the changes in the cardio-vascular system before and after birth, which opened the way to the institute's well known work on physiology of the new born. With Professor Daniel and others. Dr Barclay developed a technique of micro-radiography which enabled the study of vascular shunts in the kidney and other organs, which was of considerable importance in understanding conditions associated with this phenomenon. The institute has also been investigating specialised aspects of experimental pharmacology.

When Professor Gunn retired from the Directorship, Osler House became the social and administrative centre of the new Oxford Clinical School, and the grounds of the Observatory provided delightful relaxation. The Nuffield Institute has also moved up to the John Radcliffe and now, under the inspiration and direction of Professor Sir David Weatherall, is incorporated into the remarkable Biomolecular Institute.

The University allotted the Radcliffe Observatory and its grounds to the new Green College and, whether from ignorance of the terms of the Morris Trust or sheer perversity, the designation, 'Osler House' has been abandoned.

Although Buzzard was delighted with the achievements of the Nuffield Institute, he still hankered after that postgraduate medical school to which he had referred in the letter that he, Nuffield, and Goodenough had written to the Radcliffe trustees in 1929. So naturally he was heartened when he received a memorandum 'on the desirability of establishing a complete school of clinical medicine in Oxford' from Mr Hugh Cairns, a surgeon at the London Hospital, formerly an Australian Rhodes Scholar who never took an Oxford degree, but did get his Blue for rowing and married the daughter of the Master of his College, Balliol (Buzzard got a Blue for soccer but only got a fourth class in the Honours School).

A graduate of Adelaide University, Cairns, after his military service, returned in 1917 to take his MB BS degree, but he continued as a Captain in the Australian Medical Corps until the end of the war, when he took up his Rhodes Scholarship and entered Balliol College.

His activities in Oxford were social and sporting rather than academic, then he went to the London Hospital, holding house appointments, gaining his FRCS in 1921, and became a member of the surgical unit under Sir Henry Soutar. Cairns had been up at Oxford when Sir William Osler died; Harvey Cushing's *Life of Osler* appeared in April 1925, Cairns read it, and was fascinated not only by the biography but by the biographer. He made up his mind that he must work with Cushing and take up neurosurgery.

Cushing was in Edinburgh giving the Cameron Lecture in October 1925 when Cairns was able to meet him and was told that if he could get a scholarship, Cushing would be pleased to have Cairns work with him in Boston. Cairns was elected to a Rockefeller Travelling Scholarship and arrived in America in September 1926 to spend a year as Cushing's Junior Resident. Later he admitted that Gallipoli and the Battle of Marne were nothing compared to the physical stress of a year as Cushing's neurological resident.

But Cushing was impressed with Cairns' potentialities and recommended to Sir Walter Fletcher, the Secretary of the MRC, that Cairns should be given support. With the aid of a grant from the Rockefeller Foundation, Cairns set up a unit in the London Hospital, but it was far from satisfactory and he felt that the only way forward would be to have some sort of an institute similar to Cushing's in Boston, and he felt that Oxford might well be the place to establish it. Whether he had heard from his father-in-law about the abortive attempts that Flexner made to set up a unit in Oxford in the twenties is uncertain. But after writing a report, which was published by the Medical Research Council in 1929, of his experiences in Cushing's unit, and taking the advice of several people, instead of thinking of a neurosurgical unit alone, he broadened his ideas, suggesting an undergraduate school of about thirty carefully selected students and postgraduates who might spend 5 or 6 years in training and research.

As Cairns felt that Oxford would be the ideal situation for such a school, he submitted his scheme to Sir Farquhar Buzzard, but where the money was to come from to establish it he had no idea.

Buzzard received Cairns' proposals sympathetically. In December 1935 the Oxford Medical Graduates Club held their winter dinner at which Buzzard arranged that Cairns should meet Sir Douglas Veale, the Registrar of the University, a former distinguished Civil Servant. He was a master of academic politics. Indeed, it was often said that there were usually 'Veales within Veales'. In March 1936 Cairns submitted a more detailed (39-page) memorandum to Buzzard, and copies were circulated to certain people, one of whom was Mr Girdlestone. It was probable that if Nuffield did not actually receive a copy, there were informal discussions about it. Certainly, Nuffield had received a copy before the beginning of the British Medical Association meeting at Oxford in July. The Vice-Chancellor gave a reception in the Ashmolean Museum on Friday 17 July at which Mrs A.L. Smith, the widow of the later master of Balliol and Cairns' mother-in-law, introduced Cairns to Nuffield who invited him to come out to Huntercombe on the following Sunday.

It was a small meeting and Girdlestone was also present. While Cairns was describing his ideas Nuffield suddenly interrupted him and said, 'You're an Australian, you say ee-ther not aye-ther.' Cairns had an almost boyish charm when things were going well but when he thought he was not getting his way he would sit tight and put on his 'tiger grin' thinking out how he could achieve his object. On this occasion there was no need for such strategy, for on the following day Buzzard learnt from Nuffield that he was prepared to give a million pounds towards the scheme. So on Tuesday 21 July, when Buzzard delivered his Presidential Address, 'And the Future', in which, after discussing what was to be the source of the Nuffield Provincial Hospital Trust, he then went on to talk about a postgraduate medical school in Oxford as an 'ambitious dream', he was well aware that Nuffield was going to turn the dream into reality.

Three days later Nuffield again saw Cairns and told him that he himself would provide all the money that would be required for the scheme. Naturally, there followed discussions, often acrimonious, between the Vice-Chancellor, the Registrar, Buzzard, Nuffield, and his advisors. As the proposals were not entirely acceptable either to the University or to the Radcliffe Infirmary staff, Nuffield had to provide 'sweeteners' for both parties.

But there was disagreement on two matters of principal, which threatened to upset the whole scheme. When Morris purchased the Radcliffe Observatory and its grounds for the benefit of the University and the Radcliffe Infirmary, he arranged that it should be administered by the William Morris Trustees and he wished a Board of Trustees, independent of the University Chest, its financial department, to administer the monies of this proposed postgraduate medical scheme. Meanwhile the Nuffield Committee would be responsible for policy. This committee would report direct to the General Board, so that neither the Board of the Faculty of Medicine or the Honorary staff of the Radcliffe Infirmary had any official intimation of what the Nuffield Committee was doing, and the Minutes were marked confidential.

It is true that in Oxford confidential information is usually interpreted as something which should only be revealed to a single person at a time. Nevertheless seeming secrecy of this committee aroused suspicions both in the museum department and the Radcliffe Infirmary as to what the Nuffield Professors were up to. This mutual distrust was not overcome until much later when the Nuffield Committee became the Clinical Sub Committee of the Medicine Board and offical reports as to its decisions were transmitted to the Radcliffe Infirmary Medical Staff Council. But the idea of the independence of the Board of Trustees of the Nuffield Scheme was only accepted grudgingly.

It had been agreed that Nuffield's proposed gift for the postgraduate medical school would be published in a letter written on his 59th birthday, October 10th 1936, addressed to the Vice-Chancellor, setting out a broad outline of the scheme, including establishment in the University of Oxford of three new profesorial chairs of clinical medicine, surgery, obstetrics and gynaecology. A draft prepared by Sir Douglas Veale and Mr Hobbs, Lord Nuffield's private secretary, was submitted to Nuffield early in August. When it was returned it contained in Sir Douglas Veale's words, 'a bomb shell'. Nuffield had added a fourth professorial chair, that of anaesthestics and specified that the first holder, if he were willing, should be Dr R.R. Macintosh.

As was usual, Nuffield had good personal reasons for his charitable acts and the inclusion of a school of anaesthesia in this proposed postgraduate medical scheme was no exception. For until recently his experiences of anaesthesia had been to say the least of them, unpleasant. He recalled nightmares of suffocation, following the pressure of the mask during nitrous oxide anaesthesia for dental extraction and following open ether anaesthesia for appendisectomy, he suffered so much coughing and vomiting that the wound broke down and had to be resutured. Indeed Morris had convinced himself that he was very difficult to anaesthetise.

Then in the thirties he was having a minor operation in London and the anaesthestist was Dr R.R. Macintosh, a member of a very popular and successful group of West End anaesthestists known to their colleagues as the 'Mayfair Gas Fight and Choke Company'. Naturally 'Mac' used as the induction agent evipan (this was pre-pentothal days) – 'a prick in the arm and then you go to sleep'. When Nuffield woke up sometime later, he looked at his watch and asked why the operation had been postponed!

Naturally, Nuffield talked about this scheme of Buzzard's for a postgraduate medical school at Oxford and suggested to Macintosh that he should have the Chair of Anaesthesia and train anaesthetists to be as good as he was, and also to develop research into advances in the subject. Macintosh was far from certain whether he wanted to change his lifestyle or that he would be very good as a professor, but when the appointment was actually made and he resigned from his Mayfair associates he made a proviso that if he found the Oxford post unsatisfactory within a year he could come back to Mayfair.

The reaction to Nuffield's 'bombshell' in the Clarendon Buildings, the

University of Oxford's administrative offices, was amazement, coupled to some extent with annoyance. It was absurd to suggest that anaesthetics, a technical subject, could be of academic status or have a professor, and anyway who was this Scottish anaesthetist friend of Nuffield's? (Robert Macintosh was, in fact, a New Zealander.)

Cairns, who thought that he had convinced Nuffield of the excellence of his scheme, was annoyed; first that a layman had suggested some modification of his scheme and, secondly, that this might mean that instead of having more than a third of Nuffield's 'Golden cake', as he had planned, surgery might have less than a quarter.

But on further consideration, Cairns thought that he might adapt Nuffield's proposals to his advantage. It would be useful to have a School of Anaesthesia in Oxford, because neurosurgery needed prolonged anaesthesia and expert anaesthetists; although he was going to bring his own anaesthetist, Dr Olive Jones, with him, it might well be an advantage to have some development in that field. Furthermore, he might be able to persuade Nuffield to put some more money on the table.

Veale was somewhat perplexed and naturally endeavoured to achieve a compromise. 'Would it not be enough to have a Reader in Anaesthetics or, if there was to be a professor, perhaps he could have a lower salary, only £1,500 against £2,000, to indicate the difference in his status.' But this 'vealing' and 'dealing' had no effect on Lord Nuffield. Either he had a Chair of Anaesthesia, with, if he wished it, Macintosh as the first holder, or he would withdraw his support from the whole scheme.

Buzzard, who had worked with Nuffield as President of the Radcliffe Infirmary for about 9 years, understood him very much better than Cairns or Veale. He knew well that when Nuffield had made up his mind he stuck to it, and that an academic approach to a technical subject, such as engineering, was mutually advantageous and, anyway, was not surgery just as technical a subject as anaesthesia? So he supported Nuffield's decision to add a Chair of Anaesthesia in the new postgraduate medical school, but explained to Nuffield that although it was perfectly possible for the University to confer a personal title of professor to a member of the University, when one was establishing a chair of a particular subject, it was necessary to have a board of electors to determine who should hold the chair. If Dr MacIntosh was as good an anaesthetist as he understood, there was no reason why he would not be appointed to the chair, just as it was extremely unlikely that Cairns would not be appointed to the Chair of Surgery.

Accordingly, Nuffield who trusted the Regius more than he did the University, accepted these assurances and so, on Nuffield's fifty-ninth birthday, 10 October 1936, the public announcement of his gift to the University of £1¼ million to establish this postgraduate medical school, was made.

Two months later, on 12 December 1936 proceedings were to take place approving the decree accepting Lord Nuffield's gifts of £1¼ million and the Chancellor, Lord Halifax, was in the chair. All went smoothly until the Chancellor received a note from Lord Nuffield and announced that Lord Nuffield had asked permission to speak and, contrary to custom, he had granted the request. Only Masters of Art of the University were allowed to make comments at these proceedings and at that time Lord Nuffield had only the honorary degree of DCL, though later on he was created an MA and so became 'one of us'. Lord Nuffield, who had been sitting inconspicuously, stood up and, speaking quietly, explained that he had realized that the gift he had proposed would not be sufficient for what he had in mind and, accordingly, he intended to increase the gift to £2 million, this created scenes of quite unacademic enthusiasm.

The Regius Professor was determined that there should be no delay in getting the Nuffield scheme going. Cairns was elected Professor of Surgery on 27 January 1937 and 5 days later it was announced that the first Professor of Anaesthesia in Great Britain was to be Dr R. Macintosh. In May, Professor Moir was appointed to the Chair of Obstetrics and Gynaecology.

William B. Castle was invited to be the first holder of the Nuffield Chair of Clinical Medicine, but, knowing that he was about to be elected Professor of Medicine at Harvard, he preferred to remain in Boston. Then, much to Sir Farquhar Buzzard's disappointment, Professor Isidore Snapper could not leave his position at the Wilhelmina Hospital in Amsterdam, for, like Buzzard, he had been an enthusiastic player of soccer and, whenever he could, would spend his Sundays refereeing matches. Finally, in November 1936, Professor Leslie Witts accepted the Chair of Clinical Medicine.

The chapters by the present Nuffield professors illustrate the development of the scheme to the present day. It might be interesting to include a comment I made 20 years ago on the occasion of the bicentenary of the founding of the Radcliffe Infirmary.

It has already been suggested that had there been no Nuffield benefaction, Sir Hugh Cairns would have had his neurosurgical teaching

Tea in the grounds of St Hugh's College War Hospital, 1945 (L. to R.): J.R.P. O'Brien, Lecturer in Clinical Biochemistry; unidentified RAF doctor; Robert Macintosh (wearing Air Vice-Marshal's uniform); Lord Nuffield; Mrs Macintosh; Mrs O'Brien.
[Courtesy of Oxfordshire County Libraries]

and research unit somewhere, and it is probably equally true that if Professors Moir, Seddon, and Witts had not been elected to their Nuffield chairs they would have achieved as much, or a little more or a little less, in the fields of research and postgraduate education as they did at Oxford, for they had that gift and would be impelled to us it to the best of their abilities. But the situation with the other two chairs, of Anaesthesia and Plastic Surgery, is very different, not only because Lord Nuffield determined, in the face of academic disapproval, who should be the first holders of these chairs, but also because he had the ability, both in the world of business and in his philanthropic enterprises, to choose the right men to carry out his intentions. Professors Macintosh and Kilner, when appointed to their chairs, were recognized masters of their specialty, in both cases a practical skill in the treatment of the sick, but with no academic tradition, no close links with the biological or physical sciences; neither of them had been trained as teachers or investigators, nor had they carried out any original research. Yet these two men, given the opportunities of a university environment, in a few years transformed their specialties. This was not merely a question of status, dressing-up a practical skill in academic trappings, but they were able to show that with the right attitude and facilities, notable advances and real contributions to knowledge could be achieved. In both cases a dual approach was adopted – education and development of the practical skill by testing out new techniques, and fundamental research. The first approach is inherent in the evolution of a specialty, but there was the opportunity to gather young men and women around the professor to learn from him and one another, so that a progressive and stimulating atmosphere was created, and it was easy to go to the science departments and seek their views and advice as problems arose. In the sphere of fundamental research, Macintosh had the insight to select a physicist as his first assistant, who approached the problems of anaesthesia from a completely different angle, and this resulted in significant advances in the design of anaesthetic equipment and the uses of anaesthetic gases. In plastic surgery less was achieved directly in the field of fundamental research, not from a lack of desire to encourage this field, but because the physical conditions for plastic surgery were even more meagre, if that were possible, than those for anaesthesia; yet Professor Kilner identified the growing point and gave support and encouragement to Peter Medawar and his research team at a time when it was needed, although Medawar's interest in immunology had already been stimulated by his collaboration with Professor Seddon on nerve repair.

In the development of any of Nuffield's major schemes, and the postgraduate scheme was no exception, it would soon become apparent that there were additional needs, and Nuffield was always happy to provide funds for such necessities. He provided scholarships for postgraduates coming from abroad, scholarships for Oxford medical students, additional buildings, etc. All continue to be invaluable to the present day. Nor had Nuffield forgotten to help smaller charities in which he felt a particular interest. For instance, at this time he made a grant of £10,000 to the elderly nurses' national home in Bournemouth and Lady Nuffield established the Elizabeth Nuffield Home for Nurses in Oxford.

By now the magnitude of his munificence was such that he realized that he could no longer make personal decisions on which charities to support, and so with the establishment of the Nuffield Provincial Hospitals Trust in 1939, the Nuffield Foundation in 1943, both of which are described in this book, he recognized that he must delegate this to trustees, although he continued to keep a close interest in their decisions, and still had funds available for particular charities in which he was interested.

In 1942 the Royal College of Surgeons had presented Lord Nuffield, in recognition of his vast gifts to medicine, with their most prestigious award, the Honorary Medal, for which he was only the nineteenth recipient since its inception 140 years ago. In 1948 he was elected an Honorary Fellow of the College in recognition of his support of the College's endeavours in postgraduate education. He had provided funds to convert two houses adjacent to the College as a temporary residential college, designated Nuffield College of Surgical Sciences, which was formally opened in his presence in 1957.

Nuffield had already been elected an Honorary Fellow of the Faculty of Anaesthetists of the College of Surgeons in 1953 in recognition of his support for that Faculty.

Mention has already been made of Lord Nuffield's concern for the blind and his great support for the development of talking books. Later, through the Foundation, there was support given for deaf, dumb, and blind children in St. Dunstan's, Barnado's, and other homes. But Nuffield was also interested in the treatment of eye diseases.

In 1941, with a grant of £25,000, he established the Nuffield Fund for research in ophthamology and, on his seventy-eighth birthday, 10 October 1955, gave £14,000 to provide extensions for the Oxford Eye Hospital. Surprisingly, out of this gift arose a piece of Nuffield 'folklore' and, like all legends, it has its basis of truth.

In *The Times* 'diary' for 19 November 1970, it was stated 'Oxford's Radcliffe Infirmary would probably have been a million pounds the richer if only it had been prepared to change its name.' The diarist had come across a book of essays entitled *Oxford Medicine* (1970), one of which, 'Lord Nuffield and the Radcliffe Infirmary', written by the editor of the *Oxford Medical School Gazette*, stated, 'It was proposed and negotiations reached an advanced stage that the hospital should be renamed the Radcliffe–Nuffield Infirmary . . . Although no precise figure seems to have been mentioned, it was understood that so favourable would his lordship be impressed by this recognition that he would regard the Infirmary as his residual legatee . . .' In the end of the Board of Governors of the United Oxford Hospitals voted against the proposal. In Lord Nuffield's next charitable enterprise, the Nuffield Foundation he invested eleven million pounds.

A week later *The Times* published a letter from a distinguished Oxford historian, and former head of a college, who had been chairman of the Board of Governors from 1950 until 1958. It is a long and involved letter and difficult to comprehend, except that the events took place in 1955, whereas the Nuffield Foundation had been established 12 years' previously. Nuffield had never been informed officially of any project to add his name to that of the Infirmary, but he had been shown some plans, and consequent on this had given £15,000 out of his own pocket.

The records in the minutes are as follows: on 20 October 1955 it was reported that Lord Nuffield had made a gift of £15,600 towards the costs of extensions to the Eye Hospital. The question was raised as to whether some general recognition of Lord Nuffield's generosity to the Infirmary might not be made. When this minute was reviewed at the next meeting on the 16 November, it was agreed that the matter should be referred to the Chairman's Sub-Committee.

At this committee meeting on 15 December the idea put forward that the hospital might be renamed the Radcliffe Infirmary and Nuffield Medical Centre was referred back to the committee from which the suggestion had arisen. This committee received the observations from the Chairman's Sub-committee on 18 January and it was suggested as there were plans to make a new entrance in Walton Street and a quadrangle between it and the Nuffield Department of Medicine building, either the entrance gate or the quadrangle could well be designated the Nuffield Medical Centre. However, it was decided that the matter should be referred to the architects for advice. There is no further mention of the matter in any of the minutes.

It should be appreciated that at this time the Chairman and the members of the Board of Governors, were in the state which, in the First World War was known as 'shell shock' and more recently, as 'post-traumatic neurosis'. They had suffered a severe shock and were unwilling to take any positive action or any decision. This had arisen because it had been indicated by two of the major committees of the board, that there was a lack of confidence in a senior member of the hospital staff and that the appointment should be terminated. The Ministry of Health had been informed of the situation and had approved the Board's proposed action. However the officer did not accede to the Board's directive and demanded a Court of Enquiry. The Ministry of Health then advised the Board that they should withdraw their resolution, which they did; although six members of the Board resigned, amongst them two heads of colleges, two senior professors, and one of the senior physicians. But it was felt by many that the whole Board should have resigned in protest. The senior officer continued in his post until retirement 11 years later.

It was just 3 months after the six had resigned that the information about Lord Nuffield's gift and the suggestion of special recognition occurred. In fact there had been a Morris ward since 1932. There were two Nuffield wards, a Nuffield Maternity Home, and the Nuffield departments of the four Nuffield professors working in the Radcliffe.

The suggestion that Nuffield's name might be associated with a new entrance or a new quadrangle was illusory, as they never materialized. There had been a proposal that there should be a main thoroughfare from the Woodstock Road out to Walton Street, and there was an archway over a road between the Nuffield Department of Medicine and the Gibson Laboratories, but the Walton Street gates and the quadrangle never materialized, and at the moment a rather untidy car park occupies the site.

Consulting the member of the Board who had suggested that Nuffield's name might be associated with these unbuilt structures and other members of the Board at that time, revealed no memory of the event whatsoever. It is unlikely that Lord Nuffield was ever aware that the matter had arisen, and it is merely recorded here because of its appearance in the 'Thunderer'.

It is true that as early as 1950 it had been proposed that the Wingfield Morris Hospital should become the Nuffield Orthopaedic Centre, but the title was not in full use until 1955.

On the eve of his eightieth birthday Nuffield spoke to his old friend, Ralph Brain, the chief reporter of the *Oxford Times*: 'What I have been able to do for medicine and teaching in all walks of life has given me more satisfaction than anything else. I have never allowed anyone to persuade me what I should give money for. I have always decided for myself. In many cases from personal experience of the need.' Meetings took place in his Cowley office which he still went to regularly, and he displayed to Brain the glass case containing the medals he had won as a racing cyclist and also the enormous bicycle, the 27" frame, and 28" wheels, which he had made for the Revd Francis Pilcher, the Rector of St. Clements Church.

Three weeks later he attended the jubilee dinner of the Royal Society of Medicine, mentioned earlier, at which he spoke of the influence Sir William Osler had both on his health and his interest in medicine. But after Lady Nuffield's death in 1959, and with increasing ill-health, he became lonely and withdrawn. The little workshop that he had at Nuffield Place allowed him to repair this and that from time to time, and reminded him of the occasion early in the First World War when there was a sharp frost and he was summoned to 13, Norham Gardens, as Sir William Osler's chauffeur had forgotten to drain the radiator and there was a crack in the cylinder head. Osler had promised to visit some seriously ill soldiers in a country hospital about 30 miles away the following morning. Morris said he thought he could mend the crack in time and this he succeeding in doing. He worked late into the night, drilling holes, on each side of the crack – there were no electric drills in those days. He put screws into the holes in such a way that the heads of the screws overlapped the crack and effectively closed it. So it was that Osler was able to keep his consultation and advise on the treatment of the soldiers.

Lord Nuffield died on 22 August 1963 and, after cremation in Oxford, his ashes were interred in the shadow of the little Norman church, the Holy Trinity, Nuffield, which had enjoyed his generosities since 1931.

Nuffield had said that he would like to die leaving no estate, and his will, a simple one, he had signed on 24 April 1963 with a codicil in July. Nuffield left £3,000,264 2s gross. The duty paid was £2,424,364 4s. There were bequests of £10,000 each to Worcester and Pembroke Colleges and to relatives, business colleagues, and former servants. But the residual legatee, Nuffield College, received Nuffield Place and the whole of his money and the income derived from it (about £500,000). As the Warden of Nuffield College said, 'The business of early years had sometime ago disappeared and it shows that the College which Lord Nuffield founded stood outstanding in his last thoughts.'

The will was simple because in his lifetime Lord Nuffield had made financial provision for his relatives, his friends, and his staff, and had given some £30 million away to charity. His prime interest being to relieve suffering, help the crippled and the blind, ensure that those who devoted themselves in this field should enjoy continuing education and frequent 'brain dusting', an attitude of mind that he had learnt from Sir William Osler. He told his trustees to peer into the crystal ball and seek out and support projects and improve the quality of life, perhaps by means as yet unthought of.

The London memorial service was held at St Paul's Cathedral on 10 October 1963 and it would not be inappropriate to apply to Lord Nuffield the epitaph that Christopher Wren composed for his father: '*Si momentum requiris, circumspice*'.

Chapter 16

Lord Nuffield and Guy's Hospital

A.H. Burfoot

The golf course at Huntercombe provided the setting that led to Sir William Morris's appointment as a governor of Guy's Hospital in January 1934. Later in 1935, as Lord Nuffield, he became Treasurer, and in 1944, as Viscount Nuffield, he succeeded Viscount Goschen as President. At Huntercombe a group of Guy's doctors, among them John Josias Conybeare, Herbert Eason, George Doherty, and T.B. Johnston, relaxed at weekends and were inevitably attracted to Morris, whose interest in medical science had already led to a gift of £104,000 to St. Thomas's Hospital.

Conybeare's name is for ever linked with *Conybeare's Textbook of Medicine*. Eason, an ophthalmic surgeon, was Superintendent of Guy's and subsequently became Vice-Chancellor of the University of London. Doherty, a noted rugger player and GU surgeon, was later also to serve as Superintendent, while TBJ, as he was always known, an anatomist, became Dean of the Medical School, and later he, too, was to serve as Superintendent. Their youthful enthusiasm and love of, as well as concern for, Guy's infected Morris, already disillusioned with St. Thomas's following receipt of a printed reminder that he had not paid his annual subscription.

It was inevitable that Morris became privy to the financial problems with which Guy's was beset in the 1930s. Thomas Guy, a governor of St Thomas's Hospital, had, in the early years of the eighteenth century, wished to fund a ward at St Thomas's for those 'incapable of relief by Physick or Surgery'. St Thomas's had turned down his offer and so he decided to build his own hospital 'for incurables'. Guy, like Nuffield, was a man of immense wealth and foresight, a shrewd entrepreneur who made his money in printing Bibles and grammars, and invested it to good effect in South-Sea Stock; he was also a man of great compassion, whether it was in relieving prisoners in the Borough Prison of their debts or debating with a St Thomas's physician, Dr Mead, the need for lunatics to be cared for in his new hospital. His plans for this were completed in 1721 but he died before the building was finished 4 years later. The balance of his fortune, after paying for the hospital and meeting innumerable small bequests, became the endowment that was to maintain Guy's for more than a century and a half.

It was not until the latter half of the nineteenth century that the cost of running a large teaching hospital outstripped the rents from the land that Guy had instructed his executors to buy from the balance of his fortune. By the time Sir William Morris began to examine the financial plight of the hospital 'founded at the sole costs and charges of Thomas Guy Esquire', wards were closed, a debt of £165,000 existed, and Guy's own building had reached the end of its useful life in housing operating theatres and surgical beds.

Lord Nuffield's first major gift was to provide a building for paying patients, which in turn would encourage the medical staff to carry out their private work at Guy's and be at Guy's for more of their working time. Before the National Health Service, a consultant gave his services, apart from a token honorarium, to the hospital, and his income was derived solely from private fees.

Nuffield House was completed in 1935 at a cost of £75,000. Within the entrance to the building hung a portrait of Lord Nuffield by Beatrice Nermberg. She described him as 'shy, rigid, and self-conscious' while sitting, and it was some time before she broke through his reserve and he finally said that he like talking to 'down-to-earth people like you.'

When, in 1935, Lord Nuffield became Treasurer he rarely missed a monthly meeting of the Court of Committees, and became increasingly involved in the business of the hospital. An appeal for £500,000 was launched with the object of rebuilding Thomas Guy's original building, discharging the hospital's massive debt, and meeting other pressing needs. In the hospital's archives is a film in which he pleads eloquently for public support.

The growing shadow of war hung heavily over the appeal and it failed to reach its target. But in 1938 the Treasurer gave further support by purchasing land off Borough High Street. An anonymous donor provided funds for the subsequent building of a clinic for psychiatric patients on part of the site, echoing once more the intentions of Guy himself.

While the Second World War was still in progress, Lord Nuffield's optimism and influence were evident in the setting up of a Post-War

Planning Committee to determine the shape and content of a new building to house Guy's when the war was over. Lord Nuffield had already financed the erection of a new nurses' home, which was completed in 1940. When, in 1944, he became President of the Corporation his thoughts were concentrated upon turning the plans that had been formulated into reality, and these led on to his major gift to Guy's. Before the war he had made a massive contribution to the country's Distressed Areas Fund. In the changed circumstances of war this money was not used and he arranged for the gift to be transferred to the King Edward's Hospital Fund for London, with the proviso that £250,000 was passed straight away to Guy's to form the solid base of the rebuilding fund.

An interesting insight into Lord Nuffield's character followed the Governors' publication of *A History of Guy's to 1948*, written by Hector Cameron, a former Dean of the Medical School. A beautifully tooled leather-bound copy was sent to the President and, a day or so later, the office telephonist told me that Lord Nuffield was on the line. I expected some words of congratulation upon the book, which indeed there were, but followed by the comment 'I found no mention of the gift of a quarter of a million pounds which I made to the hospital.' Indeed there was not, because the clerk who entered the gift in the hospital's accounts had regarded it as coming from the King Edward's Hospital Fund for London, and the author had not been aware of the background. Great as the number of Lord Nuffield's benefactions had been over the years he had not forgotten the way he had helped Guy's and the enormous significance of this gift to the hospital. Needless to say my apologies were profuse. He returned the book at my request, the page with the omission was removed by the printers, a new one was bound listing this final major benefaction, and the book was sent back to Lord Nuffield. Unfortunately it was not practicable to do this for all the copies already printed and distributed, and it was too late for an erratum slip. Significantly enough, the *British Medical Journal* on 31 August 1963, in detailing Lord Nuffield's benefactions to medical charities, also missed this gift to Guy's.

In 1948 the National Health Service was introduced. The old Corporation of Guy's was dissolved and a new Board of Governors set up. Lord Nuffield continued as President and was honoured in the summer of 1949 by the erection of his statue in the west quadrangle of Thomas Guy's hospital. Maurice Lambert had been commissioned by the Court of Governors as far back as 1944, and the statue was to be similar in size and material to that of the founder by Peter Scheemakers, which stands in the

The unveiling ceremony of Lord Nuffield's statue in Guy's Hospital.
[Nuffield Place collection]

Lord Nuffield in the company of HM the Queen Mother.
[Courtesy of Oxfordshire County Libraries]

front quadrangle. The statue was unveiled by Lord Nuffield himself during a garden party in the hospital grounds, when the wards and other departments were open for inspection. The proceedings were started by a grand procession led by the head porter carrying the hospital mace, followed by the Chairman Lord Cunliffe, Lord Nuffield, governors and academics, doctors, and nurses, many in brilliant academic dress. The simple inscription read 'Viscount Nuffield – President, Benefactor and Friend of Guy's Hospital'. It was equally appropriate that in November 1957 Lord Nuffield should lay the foundation stone of New Guy's House, the first stage of rebuilding the hospital to which his major benefaction had contributed. Also in the hospital's archives is a tape-recording of the ceremony, which was attended by the Minister of Health, and subsequently a silver statuette of Thomas Guy, a miniature of the Scheemaker's statue, was presented to Lord Nuffield by Sir John Conybeare, one of the doctors who had first interested him in Guy's more than 20 years before.

Finally, in 1961 Lord Nuffield attended the opening of New Guy's House by the Queen, and joined her for tea after the ceremony. I was at that time clerk to the governors and he arrived early in my office to be briefed on the proceedings, accompanied by his secretary, Mr Kingerlee. His grey hair was resplendent in a blue rinse and his faith in the medical profession appeared by that time to have been somewhat diminished – he relied on more homely remedies, demanding a dose of bicarbonate from the bottle which Mr Kingerlee bore with him before he sat down to talk. This was a happy occasion with the Queen attending as Patron of Guy's, and Lord Nuffield with her as Honorary President. There was an amusing incident at tea when the architect of the new building, Mr Alexander Gray, presented a silver cigarette box to Lord Nuffield. Unfortunately a mistake had been made in engraving Lord Nuffield's title on the box, and instead of crediting him with an Honorary FRCS he had been made an Honorary FRICS. The embarrassed architect, after he had made the formal presentation, quietly asked His lordship if he might kindly have the box back, explaining the reason and his wish to correct the mistake. 'Certainly not', said Lord Nuffield, 'I always wanted to be a Fellow of the Institute of Chartered Surveyors and now I am!'

In retrospect, an assessment of the enormous impact of Lord Nuffield on the affairs of Guy's Hospital has two major facets. First, his personal contribution as a born entrepreneur and shrewd businessman. He came when Guy's fortunes were in many respects at a low ebb – debt and poor management were facts. He spearheaded the search for new funds and helped to bring a new sense of purpose to the organization and practical reality in its management, with the appointment of my predecessor, Mr Bertie Lees Read, as clerk to the governors. Secondly, the huge benefactions which he directed towards vital areas of the hospital. He met, within the hospital grounds, the needs of the honorary medical staff for the most up-to-date facilities for treating their paying patients upon whom they depended for a livelihood. This, in turn, enabled them to give more of their time to patients in wards and departments. He provided more than 100 additional single rooms for the accommodation of nursing staff on the site, making it no longer necessary to house nurses in what rooms could be hired in various parts of London. Finally, he made the initial major contribution towards the complete rebuilding of the clinical facilities of the hospital, so essential if the treatment of patients and clinical research were to be carried out in suitable accommodation.

Guy's was the first London undergraduate teaching hospital after the Second World War to commence rebuilding and so to provide modern facilities for its patients. It came into the National Health Service well organized and directed, leading the way over succeeding years both in its medical achievement, research, and management. With Lord Brock, it pioneered new techniques in heart surgery. Psychiatric patients were for the first time, cared for within a major undergraduate teaching hospital. Other outstanding advances in medicine and surgery followed and its organization became a model that bears some relationship to present-day plans for self-governing hospitals. Guy's has for ever benefited from the unique personal and financial contributions of its former 'President, Benefactor and Friend' – Lord Nuffield.

Chapter 17

The Nuffield Department of Clinical Medicine

Sir David Weatherall

In 1966 Leslie Witts, the first Nuffield Professor of Clinical Medicine, reflecting on his years in Oxford, wrote: 'It is difficult for newcomers to realize how great is the change that has come over the Oxford medical scene in the last 30 years. When I was appointed in 1937, doctors in Reading or Northampton would no more have thought of sending a patient to the Radcliffe Infirmary for advice and treatment than of sending him to the moon. Between the wars Oxford citizens had managed to build themselves the largest theatre in the country and at least two lavish cinemas but medical facilities were inadequate. Today Oxford is a great medical centre to which patients are sent from all parts of the world. This change is largely due to the Nuffield Benefaction.' The complete story of how the establishment of the Oxford Clinical School brought about this remarkable transformation in such a short time is for a historian of the future to tell. But when it is told, there is little doubt that much of it will revolve round the activities of the founder departments.

The Nuffield Department of Clinical Medicine (better known as the 'NDM') is the largest of the five clinical departments which were established as the result of Lord Nuffield's far-sighted gift to Oxford University in 1936. The department is now 56 years old. In this short essay I shall outline the way that it has developed and a few of its achievements, touching along the way on some of those who made them possible.

Before describing the NDM, it may be helpful for non-medical readers to understand what an academic clinical department does; even those in government who are responsible for funding our universities and National Health Service (NHS) seem to have only the flimsiest idea of what goes on in these places! In Great Britain such departments are usually quite small. Traditionally they are headed by a professor and have a handful of permanent senior clinical staff who, although employed by the university, also have honorary contracts within the NHS. Thus they form a relatively small part of the total staff of teaching hospitals, most of whom are consultants or junior hospital doctors employed directly by the NHS. Academic clinical departments, which form the direct link between university and NHS, have three main responsibilities. First, they must play their full role in looking after patients in exactly the same way as the other staff in the hospital. In this context they should set standards of clinical care and develop new specialities for the hospital. Secondly, they are responsible for organizing undergraduate and postgraduate teaching; although much of this is done by the NHS staff it is the responsibility of the academic departments to ensure that standards are maintained and that there is a uniformity of purpose in teaching, both for medical students and for the many young doctors who come to the hospital for training. Finally, they are expected to carry out a programme of medical research. Thus, although numerically small, they play a central role in the life of a teaching hospital.

THE EARLY YEARS

The NDM was founded in November 1937 following the appointment of Leslie Witts as the first Nuffield Professor of Clinical Medicine. Witts, a native of Warrington, had read modern languages at Manchester University before the First World War but, as the result of his service experiences, re-entered Manchester to study medicine and graduate in 1923. After a particularly brilliant early career he was appointed Professor of Medicine and Head of the Department of Medicine at St Bartholomew's Hospital, London in 1935. It was from there that he moved to Oxford late in 1937.

Witts came to Oxford fully expecting to establish a postgraduate research department, as originally conceived by Lord Nuffield, but his plans for building the wards and laboratories necessary to develop a unit of this kind were interrupted by the outbreak of war in 1939 when it became necessary to make some rapid *ad hoc* arrangements for accepting medical students from London and elsewhere. To deal with this unexpected problem an undergraduate clinical school had to be improvised in Somerville College. Because many of the clinical teachers had joined the forces, some eminent physicians were recruited from retirement to lend a hand with teaching. This was not without its problems. For example, Sir Arthur Hurst took a weekly round on cases which had to be carefully selected so that they did not required the use of a stethoscope for diagnosis; Sir Arthur was extremely deaf. Even though the first priority was to attempt to organize some kind of teaching for students, a few research projects were started during the war period. The medical students participated as (presumably) willing guinea-pigs in this work. For example, some of them went for several weeks to a TNT factory so that a team headed by Dr Alice Stewart could study the effects of the chemicals involved on their blood and body chemistry. Others took the antimalarial drug mepacrine so that its side-effects could be analysed. And because of concern about hepatitis in the forces, the NDM, in collaboration with Dr Fred MacCullum, became one of the principal centres involved in the study of the mode of transmission and long-term follow-up of cases. During the war the facilities of the department were extremely limited: a ward of 21 beds, two tiny laboratories, and a desk in the corridor where all the blood analyses were done. The research assistants shared a room in a hut.

Despite these difficulties, the NDM was already developing a reputation for clinical training and research, and after the war many young doctors who had been in the forces returned to the department. In addition, there was a steady flow of British Council and Rhodes Scholars from abroad who wished to work with Witts. All this caused considerable congestion, which was relieved to some extent when the Americans, who had occupied the Churchill Hospital during the war, left. Twenty-four beds were made available for longer-stay patients. It was here that the first important clinical research in the NDM was carried out during the post-war period, in particular the study of bone disease and the pioneering work which was later to make the department famous for its management of inflammatory disease of the intestine. The NDM also started to study the important anaemias due to deficiencies of iron and vitamin B^{12}. Gradually the research activities of the department became focused on the blood and intestine.

After the war it became clear that Oxford would have to maintain and develop its undergraduate clinical school. Hence the Nuffield Departments had to take on the responsibility for organizing medical-student teaching programmes as well as postgraduate work. By the mid-1950s the stage was set for expansion and the development of a modern department of medicine. Witts, who had been constantly battling for better facilities, finally achieved his goal in 1958.

1958–1965

In 1958 a new department was built to house the NDM in the Radcliffe Infirmary. Two purpose-built wards were constructed on top of the old Private Block, which in turn was converted into offices. The house officers' rooms, which were originally part of this building, were converted into laboratories, and a seminar room and further laboratories were built to provide more space for research. The temporary wards and laboratories at the Churchill Hospital were vacated and the entire department was now housed in excellent accommodation in the Radcliffe Infirmary. Its wards were named after two of Oxford's great physician-scientists, Thomas Willis and Richard Lower. The latter was particularly appropriate for a department with an interest in blood diseases; Lower gave the first blood transfusion in this country, and the second ever, in 1667. Before an admiring audience at the Royal Society, and uninhibited by the attentions of a modern-day ethics committee, he injected a small quantity of sheep's blood into a clergyman who was said to be suffering from a brain that was 'a little too warm'. Remarkably, the patient survived.

In these new surroundings the NDM flourished. Witts had three main aims. First he wished to build a top class department in the physical sense. Second, and probably based on his knowledge of Johns Hopkins Hospital in the USA, he wanted to develop an integrated division of medicine including semi-autonomous departments such as dermatology, paediatrics, neurology, general practice, and so on. He realised that these would be ultimately separate departments, but that through his sphere of influence as Professor of Medicine he might be able to create an environment in which there could be mutual stimulation. Ultimately, a wide variety of patients was attracted for a flourishing undergraduate teaching programme and for the type of clinical research which characterized the department during the Witts' period.

During his 27 years as the first Nuffield Professor of Medicine Witts saw the development of a large and active department of medicine that, because of its excellence and of the quality of people that it trained, had an enormous influence on medicine in Oxford, the United Kingdom, and abroad. The NDM was well and truly established.

1965–74

The appointment of the second Nuffield Professor of Clinical Medicine, Paul Beeson, was largely the work of Sir George Pickering, the Regius Professor of

Medicine in Oxford who did so much to develop the Oxford Clinical School. At the time he came to Oxford Beeson had just completed his thirteenth year as Chairman of the Department of Internal Medicine at Yale. He was recognized as one of the most successful departmental chairmen in the USA, and had trained many residents who had gone on to achieve distinction in academic medicine. But, like Sir William Osler before him, he had become rather disillusioned with the enormous administrative load in running a very large American department and was not spending as much time as he would have wished with patients or medical students. Thus, although he only had about 10 years to retirement, he decided to make the break with the United States and was appointed to the Nuffield Chair in 1965.

Beeson decided to maintain the general pattern of departmental activities that had been established in Witts' time. Being an excellent physician he had no difficulty in maintaining the clinical standards of the NDM and of expanding its sphere of influence among the clinicians within and outside Oxford. His main research interests were in immunology and metabolic disease. On arrival in Oxford he recruited some excellent clinical research fellows in these subjects, both from the United Kingdom and abroad.

The 9 years during which Beeson was Nuffield Professor of Clinical Medicine saw a continuation and expansion of the department which had been so ably established by Witts. Beeson was a superb and highly respected clinician who was able to draw together the Oxford physicians into a more unified team of the type to which he had been accustomed in the United States, and to have a major influence on the development of the Clinical School. Although he was not able to make many senior appointments during his time, he attracted a continual stream of talented young research workers who were able to provide the department with an international reputation in two new areas, metabolic medicine and infectious disease. In incorporating the group of Hans Krebs, a Nobel Prize winner and the most distinguished name in biochemistry of his generation, he was able to sow the seed for the development of the strong basic science presence which was to be so critical for the further development of the department.

Towards the end of the Beeson's period in Oxford plans were well advanced for a new teaching hospital in Headington, the John Radcliffe Hospital. In typically generous fashion, Beeson retired one year earlier than he needed so that his successor could be involved in planning the transition from the Radcliffe Infirmary to the John Radcliffe Hospital, a move that included the construction of a new NDM on the Headington site as part of the John Radcliffe Hospital development.

1974–89

The way in which I followed Paul Beeson as the third Nuffield Professor of Clinical Medicine reflected a degree of eccentricity which could only be achieved by Oxford University. I was a Liverpool graduate, had only been to Oxford on a day trip with my parents, and knew nothing whatever about the University. I had spent a considerable part of my postgraduate training at Johns Hopkins Hospital in Baltimore, came back to Liverpool in 1965, and built up a Haematology Department within the Department of Medicine. In the spring of 1973 a member of the NDM came up to Liverpool to give a lunchtime seminar, and as he was leaving, mentioned that some of his colleagues in Oxford were interested in the possibility of my putting my name forward for the Nuffield Professorship. I thanked him, made a mental note to double his honorarium, and told him that I wasn't interested in moving from Liverpool. However, a few days later I was invited to dine with some of the Electors to the Chair. After a particularly dyspeptic evening spent playing academic cat-and-mouse I visited Sir Richard Doll, the Regius Professor, and several other electors, and was encouraged to post a copy of my curriculum vitae to Oxford.

I heard nothing more from Oxford for several weeks and had almost forgotten the episode when I received a phone call from the University Offices saying that I had been elected to the Nuffield Chair that morning; could I tell them whether I would accept it – there was no hurry but they would like an answer by the following day. After an all-night sitting with my wife and a long talk with my close friend and research colleague John Clegg I rang up Oxford and said that I would come provided they could meet certain requirements, in particular that it would be possible to move some of my research group with me. This appeared to present no difficulties and so I agreed to come.

These quaintly informal arrangements were made well over a year before Paul Beeson was due to retire. However, by the spring of 1974 I thought it about time to resign my appointment in Liverpool but realized that I had heard nothing formally from Oxford except for the original phone call. Thinking that I might sound a bit foolish if I rang Oxford University to see whether my appointment was real or imagined I delegated the task to my secretary. She rang up the University Offices and asked whether I had actually been appointed to the Nuffield Professorship, because I had heard nothing more from them. There was a long pause interspersed with much muttering and shuffling of papers and then a rather irate voice came on the phone and said 'It was announced in *The Times* wasn't it, what more does he want?' So it was that one morning in September 1974, with no contract and much trepidation, I made my way up the long corridor at the Radcliffe Infirmary. About half way along I was stopped by an extremely agitated old gentleman. 'You must be Weatherall; my name is Krebs and I examined you in biochemistry in Liverpool in 1954.' 'Yes', I replied, 'I remember it well' (which I did). 'Your predecessor gave me space in the Nuffield Department when I retired from the Chair in Biochemistry; I hope that you are not going to take back any of it.' 'Of course not' I replied, and bolted for the safety of my new office. Life in Oxford had begun.

To carry out good basic research in a clinical setting a very professional laboratory is required, together with continuity of technological expertise. The only way to achieve this is to create a mixture of clinical and non-clinical scientists. This raises all sorts of problems, not in the least the difficulty of finding suitable career posts for non-clinical scientists in a clinical setting. I was fortunate to be able to transfer my Medical Research Council programme grant from Liverpool and thus it was possible to bring my friend and long-term collaborator John Clegg with me, the man who has been the key figure in developing laboratory science in the NDM over the past 15 years. Later we were joined by John Old, a molecular biologist, and Bill Wood, one of our old PhD students, both from Liverpool. In 1979 the Medical Research Council recognized the work of these people by setting up the MRC Molecular Haematology Unit in the NDM, thus giving us long-term support for its basic science activities, particularly in the field of the inherited anaemias. This led to the recruitment of a number of outstanding young research workers, including Douglas Higgs who has remained with the Unit. Over the past 10 years work by the Unit has unravelled the molecular basis for many of the inherited anaemias that affect millions of children throughout the world, and shown how these conditions can be avoided by prenatal diagnosis.

The latter half of the 1970s saw increasing problems for both the clinical services in Oxford and for the Clinical School. In the early 1970s a decision had been made to increase the number of clinical students to 100 and it soon became apparent that there were insufficient beds for acute patients, who were needed for the teaching of this number of students. The pressure on the acute services was increasing year by year, many of the old hutted wards in the Radcliffe Infirmary were falling apart, and the morale of the clinical staff was declining. All this reflected the total inadequacy of the Radcliffe Infirmary for its new role as an internationally famous teaching and research centre. Perhaps this is not suprising when it was remembered that the hospital originally started out as a small building to serve the needs of Oxford. It was never designed for the clinical school as envisaged by Lord Nuffield, let alone the great international centre which it had undoubtedly become. It seemed essential, therefore, to move to the new facilities in Headington as soon as possible.

The move to the new John Radcliffe Hospital site in Headington was not without its problems, however. The District Health Authority were extremely short of money and there were several months of heated debate as to whether the new hospital should he opened. I chaired a committee called the Central Oxford Hospitals Working Party, which attempted to rationalize the move and, in the end, we developed a plan which enabled the new hospital to open. The NDM moved to the Headington site in June 1979.

At the John Radcliffe Hospital site the NDM had larger laboratory facilities. The MRC Unit was expanded and Kay Davies joined the department from St. Mary's Hospital Medical School, bringing with her a very talented group of young people working on the molecular biology of muscular dystrophy. Work on inherited diseases expanded rapidly. The DHSS asked the department to take on the National Haemoglobin Reference Laboratory and, over the next few years, it developed a programme for the prenatal diagnosis of the inherited anaemias for the whole of the UK, a service run by John Old. In collaboration with Professor Peter Morris of the Nuffield Department of Surgery, an immunology research laboratory was set up, initially for Ian MacLennan. However, he was offered the prestigious Chair of Immunology in Birmingham before he could move into his new quarters, but we were fortunate enough to be able to attract Andrew McMichael to Oxford from the USA. He became an MRC Research Professor and rapidly built up an outstanding team of immunologists which now includes Alain Townsend and John Bell. These young men are making major advances in our understanding of how the cells of the immune system work, in the inheritance of diabetes and arthritis, and in the way in which viruses cause chronic disease.

One of the major roles of a department of medicine is to develop new specialities and research activities which are lacking in a particular teaching centre. We decided that we should expand the department's activities in infectious disease and, in particular, attempt to develop tropical medicine research in Oxford. In 1979 David Warrell (later to become Professor of Tropical Medicine in the NDM), Peter Williams, Director of the Wellcome

Trust, and I travelled to Thailand to complete negotiations to set up a tropical medicine unit jointly between the NDM, the Wellcome Trust, and the Tropical Medicine Faculty of Mahidol University. David Warrell went out to Bangkok to run this unit and was joined by several young men from Oxford, including Nick White and Rodney Phillips. Over the next few years, together with their Thai collaborators, they built up an international reputation for clinical research in the tropics, particularly in the fields of malaria, rabies, and snake bite. In the past few years a second NDM Wellcome Tropical Unit has been set up in Kalifi, Kenya to study the cause of death in childhood malaria, and another group is working in Nairobi on the interaction between AIDS and tropical diseases. As part of this programme the NDM was fortunate enough to recruit Chris Newbold on the government's 'new blood' lectureship scheme and he had been able to build up a very strong basic science team for malaria research to back up the field programmes in Thailand and Africa.

Other developments in the NDM in the 1980s reflected changing needs in clinical practice. The problems of the aging population loomed increasingly large and were becoming responsible for many of the difficulties being encountered by the NHS. For this reason it seemed important to try to create an academic sub-department of geriatric medicine. With the help of the Regional Health Authority it was possible to establish a Chair of Geriatric Medicine and to entice John Grimley Evans from Newcastle to be its first holder. He has built up an excellent team with a major interest in the community care of the elderly. Another neglected area in academic medicine is terminal care, and with the generous help of the Macmillan Trust, we were able to appoint Robert Twycross to the Macmillan Readership in Terminal Care within the NDM.

Over the years after the move to the John Radcliffe Hospital the NDM continued to play a full role in the general acute medical work and specialized medical services for Oxford. It was reponsible for providing specialist care in a number of areas, including blood diseases and marrow transplantation (the latter being developed by Christopher Bunch), high blood pressure, infectious disease, and diabetes.

The teaching programme for undergraduates and postgraduates also evolved after the move to the new hospital. The NDM was responsible for organizing undergraduate teaching in medicine and for assessing the progress of the students thoughtout their course. It was also involved in running many of the postgraduate teaching programmes. One of its major undertakings in postgraduate education has been the *Oxford Textbook of*

Medicine. This enterprise followed an approach by Oxford University Press who asked the department to edit a completely new textbook of medicine to take the place of the rather aged British postgraduate textbook which the Press had published previously. John Ledingham, David Warrell, and I undertook the edit this book which, in fact, turned out to be an enormous task. However, we gradually amassed a team of authors and the first edition appeared in 1983 to embarrassingly good reviews. The second edition had to be started almost immediately and this two-volume work, which included over 400 authors from 20 different countries, saw the light of day in 1987, with an equally good press; work is already starting on the third edition!

Clearly, the NDM was very active in the early 1970s and 1980s and had expanded enormously. Unfortunately, at the same time, government cuts of university support hit Oxford. The department lost several key posts and there was a gradual decline in its annual support from the University. Because the smaller clinical departments were even worse off, and following the cuts were in a negative financial balance, the NDM had to donate some of its running costs to bail them out. Thus, this period of expansion occurred in the face of a decline in the funding of the department by the University. In fact it now depends heavily on outside support and it would not have been possible to achieve any of these developments without generous help from the Medical Research Council, Wellcome Trust, the major cancer charities, Rockefeller Foundation, National Institutes of Health, and many other bodies. The annual income from outside research grants broke the £1 million barrier in 1979, and in 1987 rose above £2 million, thus promoting the NDM to the rank of one of the 'big spenders' in the University science departments.

Fund raising and handling these large grants greatly increased the load on the NDM's administration. The fact that it was possible at all was entirely due to the superb management of Gerry Warner and the loyalty and extreme hard work of its underpaid secretarial staff, notably Janet Watt, Liz Rose, Jeanne Packer, Linda Roberts, Lyn Davis, Eunice Berry, and Judy Last.

THE FUTURE: THE INSTITUTE OF MOLECULAR MEDICINE

The period of rapid expansion of the Oxford Clinical School had been exciting, but if the School was to survive and continue to flourish it could not stand still. And if the NDM and other academic clinical departments were to remain internationally competitive, there had to be some serious

The Nuffield Department of Clinical Medicine in the Radcliffe Infirmary, 1957.

The Institute of Molecular Medicine at the John Radcliffe Hospital. The building was completed in 1989 and opened by HRH The Princess Royal on 17 July that year.

rethinking about how their research was organized. One of the great potential strengths of the Oxford Clinical School was the application of the new tools of cell and molecular biology to clinical practice. It had already led the way in this field and has the added advantage of having first-class basic science departments in the University with which to interact.

In order to rationalize the development of molecular medicine, the NDM took the lead in setting up the Institute of Molecular Medicine (IMM) on the John Radcliffe Hospital site. In 1984, at the time of the retirement of Professor Geoffrey Dawes, the University decided that it could no longer support the Nuffield Institute of Medical Research. This Institute was first housed in the Observatory building which was bought for the university by Lord Nuffield in 1930; later it was rehoused at the John Radcliffe Hospital site and became a famous fetal physiology research department. We therefore approached the Medical Research Council with the idea that the Institute might be refurbished, and that a completely new wing could be added to it. This would provide a building in which the new techniques of molecular biology would be applied to medical problems. The Council liked the idea but could not afford it at the time. It was decided, therefore, to try to develop a partnership programme between the Council and various charitable organizations.

The capital development for this building, approximately £7.2 million, was raised by generous support from the Medical Research Council, the Wolfson Foundation, the E.P. Abraham Research Fund, and the Imperial Cancer Research Fund. By the middle of 1989 a very elegant building was finished, consisting of a refurbished Nuffield Institute for Medical Research joined to a completely new, three-storey research block. The IMM has been developed on a 'research hotel' concept. Several different groups from the Clinical School will move their laboratory activities into the Institute. Each will maintain a close link with their parent clinical department and will apply similar techniques of cell and molecular biology to medical research. It is hoped that the Institute will create an environment in which both clinical and non-clinical scientists can work together using the same kind of technology to study a wide variety of different problems of clinical importance. As well as providing a very good environment for basic science as applied to medicine, it is hoped that this development will continue to attract top-calibre non-clinical scientists into medical research. Because of the major role of the NDM in initiating and developing the IMM, workers from the department will play a major part in its research activities. The MRC Molecular Haematology Unit will be rehoused in the Institute and will expand its studies of the inherited anaemias and how they can best be prevented and treated. Dr Kay Davies' team will also move into the new building and continue their work on inherited muscle diseases and mental retardation. Andrew McMichael's group will work on the basic mechanisms of the body's immune system and study common diseases, including diabetes and rheumatoid arthritis, that are thought to result from abnormaltities of these mechanisms. A group headed by Chris Newbold will study the molecular aspects of malarial infection and provide a laboratory base for the field units of the NDM which are studying this disease in Thailand and East Africa. Other groups based on different clinical departments that will form the founding staff of the Institute include Professor Newsom-Davis's team from the Department of Clinical Neurology, which studies muscle disease; Dr Colin Jones' group, which is interested in the chemistry of early development; Dr Brian Sykes' group, which studies inherited abnormalities of the skeleton; and a large Imperial Cancer Research Fund Unit, which will include the newly appointed Professor of Clinical Oncology, Adrian Harris, and Dr Christopher Higgins.

These new developments mean that the NDM is now a large and broadly based department. It will continue to carry out its major clinical and teaching activities at the John Radcliffe Hospital, and house its research facilities at the Radcliffe Infirmary, the John Radcliffe Hospital, and in the IMM. As it moves into the next decade the department will span work ranging from epidemiology and the care of the elderly, through a variety of aspects of clinical research at the bedside, to the study of disease at the molecular and cellular level. This is all compatible with the hopes of Witts when he first set up the department in 1937. He envisaged that it should gradually take on the broad-based role of large academic departments like those in the best American centres. Within the constraints of the British system this is what it has done and, hopefully, will continue to do in the future.

WHAT HAS BEEN ACHIEVED?

It is likely that Lord Nuffield would be satisfied with the results of his generosity to Oxford University in 1936. If he were able to visit the NDM in 1994 he would see a large department with a very good track record of producing young people for every branch of medical practice; in the past few years a former member of the department has been appointed to the first Chair of Haematology in Scotland, and others have taken; prestigious consultant physician posts in major London and provincial teaching hospitals. He might also be interested to hear of the appointment of an ex-NDM member as the only doctor on the new management committee set up by government to run the NHS. He would note that, in 1988, the NDM admitted 2,272 patients to its forty beds, over 30 per cent of the total workload of the hospital. He would compare this with the 1,100 patients admitted to its forty-eight beds in 1964, and start to understand some of the problems of the NHS. But he would find a very lively clinical school with an outstanding intake of new undergraduates selected from among the cream of the Cambridge and Oxford pre-clinical schools. And he would be shown many thousands of scientific papers and books published by members of the department over the past 50 years.

Undoubtedly Lord Nuffield would ask what all this activity amounts to in terms of medical progress. A great deal of medical research consists of adding small pieces of knowledge to the enormously expanding base of information that underlies the medical sciences. But, just occasionally, a single piece of work, or a body of work carried out over a few years, makes a major contribution that genuinely advances clinical practice or clarifies a previously obscure area of human pathology. In this context Lord Nuffield could be proud of some of the achievements of the department: the development of rational forms of treatment for certain forms of anaemia and inflammatory disease of the bowel; the use of molecular biology to elucidate the cause of some of the common, inherited anaemias of childhood that affect many millions of children throughout the world, and the application of this work to the prenatal detection of these diseases; the development of more rational approaches to treating the serious complications of diabetes; the discovery of the location of the gene for cystic disease of the kidney, the disorder that affects 15 per cent of the patients who have to survive on kidney machines in the UK; the development of better ways of treating cerebral malaria and the other complications of malaria, which are now used throughout the world; the organization of clinical trials, in collaboration with the Department of Cardiology, that have changed the management of serious heart disease; the clarification of the genetic basis of common diseases such as diabetes, allergy, and rheumatoid arthritis; and fundamental discoveries about how the cells of the immune system work, and so on.

Lord Nuffield might also be impressed with the enormous amount of money that is raised each year to support research in the NDM. But he might be less happy about the declining support for the department from the University following government cuts, and the gradual erosion of its staff which has resulted. And he might wonder how the department will maintain clinical standards now that it has fewer beds and over twice the number of patients to look after. With his businessman's eye he might look at the Oxford Clinical School and decide that it was living dangerously because of the decreasing base of university support on which to raise the large amount of money required to pursue modern research, and hence to remain internationally competitive. He might even decide that what the School needs is a new benefactor to put it on a healthy financial footing as it moves into the next century. But he could certainly take justifiable pride in the results of his far-sighted generosity in 1936.

ACKNOWLEDGEMENTS

In writing this short account I was helped enormously by some notes that were prepared for the fiftieth anniversary of the NDM by Sheila Callender and Paul Beeson. Strictly speaking, they should have been co-authors of this chapter, although their modesty would have made it difficult for me to put their contributions to the department in true perspective. I was also helped by a number of essays prepared by Leslie Witts after his retirement and which were published in the *Oxford Medical School Gazette*. But any factual inaccuracies must be ascribed to the present author.

Chapter 18

The Nuffield Department of Surgery

Peter J. Morris

When the Nuffield Department of Surgery was founded in 1937, Hugh Cairns, an Australian, became the first Nuffield Professor of Surgery. Cairns was born in 1896 in South Australia in a small country village called Riverton and was educated at the new Adelaide High School, from which he won a scholarship to the University of Adelaide Medical School. He served in the First World War in the Dardanelles as a medical orderly in the middle of his medical course, but was repatriated because of illness, to Adelaide where he completed his medical studies. He then returned to France as a captain in the RAMC. During his final year as a student he had won a Rhodes Scholarship, and as soon as the war was over, in 1919, he came to Oxford as a Rhodes Scholar and became a student at Balliol.

After the war the social life in Oxford must have been a culture shock for Cairns, but he survived it and, indeed, married the daughter of the Master of Balliol. Following a brief period at the Radcliffe Infirmary, he went to the London Hospital to train as a general surgeon, but with the ambition to become a brain surgeon at a time when there was nobody specializing in this area in England. However, in 1926 he was awarded a Rockefeller Travelling Fellowship to train with Harvey Cushing in Boston. Cushing was the world's most eminent neurosurgeon and was Chief of Surgery at the Peter Bent Brigham Hospital in Boston. Cairns returned to London as a consultant surgeon at the London Hospital, and established a neurosurgical unit at the hospital, the first in England. He restricted his own practice to neurosurgery both at the London and in private, at a time when any surgery within the skull was performed by general surgeons who had no special training in this increasingly important and relatively unknown area of surgery.

In 1935 and 1936 Cairns had written to Sir Farquhar Buzzard, the Regius

Professor of Medicine at Oxford, suggesting that Oxford was the ideal site for an outstanding postgraduate medical school. Indeed, his second letter, written early in 1936 as he was making a return trip to Boston to examine certain aspects of Cushing's work on brain tumours which he had reviewed during his first stay, was a long document entitled 'Second Memorandum from Mr Cairns to the Regius Professor of Medicine on the desirability of establishing a complete school of clinical medicine at Oxford' which Buzzard passed on to Lord Nuffield around the time of the BMA meeting in Oxford in July of 1936. As a result, Cairns was asked to meet with Nuffield and several long discussions took place which played a significant part in influencing Nuffield to create the benefaction to the University, resulting in the establishment of the Nuffield Chairs of Surgery, Anaesthesia, Obstetrics and Gynaecology, Clinical Medicine, and, a little later, Orthopaedics.

Although the medical school at Oxford dates back for many hundreds of years, it is fair to say that the modern medical school, as we know it, arose as a result of Nuffield's benefaction, for really before this the Oxford clinical school was little more than a country district hospital associated with a major university, despite the distinction bestowed on it by Osler, at the beginning of the century.

The main thrust of the Nuffield Department of Surgery under Cairns, after he took up his appointment in 1937, was in neurosurgery, although he did appoint general surgical senior lecturers to ensure that there was a general surgical element to the department's activities, for he never fogot his responsibility for the teaching of undergraduates. Indeed he was very keen for the school to become a major undergraduate medical school, which had not really been Nuffield's intention.

Under Cairns the department flourished and eventually became a mecca for neurosurgeons from all over the world. Many notable contributions were made by Cairns and his department, primarily in the treatment of head injuries. During the Second World War he became responsible for the organization and provision of neurosurgical care, both at home and in the field, for the British Army. He established a magnificent Military Hospital for Head Injuries at St Hugh's College, where he gathered the cream of neurologists and neurosurgeons in the UK. He was responsible for designing mobile operating theatres, which could move around a field of combat and which became widely used throughout the Western Front. He was also alarmed by the high rate of head injuries and deaths resulting from motorcycle injuries, particularly amongst army couriers, and as a

Sir Hugh Cairns, c. 1945, in Army uniform.
[Courtesy of the Wellcome Institute Library, London]

result designed a crash helmet which all motorcycle couriers in the army had to wear. Following the war he continued his work with head injuries and also developed a major interest in the diagnosis and treatment of abscesses and tuberculosis of the brain, both being common and usually lethal conditions in those days.

His name had reached the public eye to some extent early on in his career, for while an assistant surgeon at the London he was called in to see T.E. Lawrence (Lawrence of Arabia) following the motorcycle injury in 1935 which lead to his death. Lawrence was a legend in his own time and no doubt this favourable publicity for Cairns helped to establish his reputation as a leading neurosurgeon before he came to Oxford. Another well-guarded secret at the time was that early on in the war Unity Mitford, a devotee and allegedly a girlfriend of Hitler, was flown into Oxford from Munich to be cared for by Cairns with a bullet in her head following an attempted suicide.

Although Cairns made many contributions to neurosurgery, probably the most notable of which was his approach to head injuries, his most significant contribution to surgery was the establishment in England of neurosurgery as a specialist discipline requiring specialist skills and training. As a result, the unit in Oxford became a centre for training for neurosurgeons, not only in England but from all over the Commonwealth. He was ably assisted in this respect by Joe Pennybacker who evidently was a superb technical neurosurgeon and who had come from the London Hospital to Oxford with Cairns in 1937 and stayed. There was a time when a whole generation of neurosurgeons, particularly in the Commonwealth, had been trained in Oxford, and this particularly applied to neurosurgery in Australia and New Zealand.

In 1952 the Cairns era ended prematurely when he died quite quickly at the age of 56 following diagnosis of an abdominal lymphoma. Phillip Allison was then appointed as his successor and took up his appointment in 1954. Allison was a surgeon in Leeds who at that time was considered by many to be the top surgeon in the United Kingdom. He had made an international name for himself for his work on surgery of the oesophagus and thorax. When he came to Oxford he found conditions not to his satisfaction and while two wards and operating rooms were being built at the Radcliffe Infirmary, he went away for 2 years to work both in Cambridge and at the Johns Hopkins Hospital in the USA. This long absence following his appointment did not endear him to his clinical colleagues and the rift that arose as a result tended to become wider with time. Despite the frustrations of his early years as Nuffield Professor of Surgery he did establish cardiothoracic surgery in Oxford, and indeed the first use in England of the Gibbon heart-lung machine, which allowed open-heart surgery, was pioneered in Oxford by the Nuffield Department of Surgery.

One of the young men Allison brought with him from Leeds as First Assistant, Alf Gunning, who was both a qualified dentist as well as a surgeon, made many seminal contributions to surgery. For example, Gunning, with Allison, designed the heart valve homograft, the first of which was implanted in an emergency in London by Donald Ross. He then went on to develop a pig xenograft valve for the heart, and the first valves prepared in Oxford were implanted by French surgeons. With Pickering (the Regius Professor) he also described the embolic nature of amaurosis fugax, a temporary loss of vision in the eye due to the passage of thrombi from either the heart or an atheromatous lesion at the origin of the internal carotid artery. The interest in the carotid artery within the NDS continues to this day. He also described, with Pickering, the embolic nature of Raynaud's phenomenon in patients with aneurysms of the subclavian artery in the neck. This was a spastic condition of the blood vessels of the hand which could arise occasionally from the passage of emboli from the more proximal aneurysm. He carried out quite extensive studies on experimental lung transplantation in the dog, long before most people were considering this as even a remote clinical possibility. Peripheral vascular surgery started in the NDS, and the first abdominal aortic aneurysms were operated on by Gunning in the late 1950s and early 1960s. The NDS also made major contributions to surgery in the haemophiliac. Allison, who was due to retire in 1974, died unexpectedly early in that year following an operation for bowel obstruction.

In the tradition of appointing Nuffield Professors who would open up new areas in medicine, the author (Peter J. Morris), another Australian who was Reader in Surgery at the University of Melbourne, was appointed to the Nuffield Chair of Surgery in 1973 and took up his appointment towards the end of the 1974. The author's own specialist interest were in transplantation, both at a clinical and research level. A renal transplant unit was established in Oxford together with a major research programme in tranplantation biology. This programme, too, has made many major contributions to the field and its international reputation draws people for training in research and transplantation from all over the world.

Another major interest of the Nuffield Department of Surgery, apart from its general surgical commitment, is in arterial surgery, in which it provides a regional service as well as being involved in an active programme of research in various aspects of arterial disease, especially aneurysmal disease of arteries and carotid artery surgery.

The Nuffield Department of Surgery has maintained its reputation as one of the leading departments of surgery in the UK, with an outstanding international reputation. The original department, which commenced at the Radcliffe Infirmary and was based there until 1979 when the new John Radcliffe Hospital opened, now has its major clinical and research base at the new hospital on the sixth floor. The transplant unit is situated at the Churchill Hospital and towards the end of 1990 a new Oxford Transplant Centre with its own purpose-built laboratories for applied research in this field opened, also at the Churchill Hospital. It would seem highly unlikely that a university department of surgery of the stature and reputation of the NDS would ever have developed in Oxford without the benefaction provided by Lord Nuffield in 1936.

Chapter 19

Lord Nuffield's benefaction to orthopaedics

R.B. Duthie

Orthopaedics in Oxford began in 1870 as a humble and Christian convalescent home in Headington, based upon an Appeal by the Revd J. Rigard of Magdalen College. Miss Wingfield gave the freehold of the land, with money to endow it. The Wingfield Convalescent Home was opened on Whit Monday, 1871 and continued its vital, albeit not glamorous, role in convalescing patients discharged from the Radcliffe Infirmary, 'cured' but yet unfit to return to active life and labour.

Soon after the start of the First World War a sectional military hospital of 20 beds was opened and in 1915 an anonymous gift provided a new wing. Gathorne Robert Girdlestone was posted to the Third Southern General Hospital as Captain in the RAMC. He was dynamically in charge, with strong support and inspiration from Miss Feilden, the matron. In 1919 GRG and Miss Feilden continued the running of the now civilian hospital, which had been handed over to the Ministry of Pensions, for the care not only of wounded soldiers but also of crippled children. It soon was approved by the Ministry of Health and Board of Education as a Hospital School for recovery of children suffering from tuberculosis, deformities and paralysis.

In 1922 G.R. Girdlestone had given a lecture on 'The care and cure of crippled children', stating that hospitals are best placed 'near a university town where there is a good general hospital. The staff cooperate, teamwork is developed in staff and students, and a spirit of total care is created.' This led to the charity foundation called the Wingfield Orthopaedic Hospital.

Expansion in all directions took place. The hospital still used the old wooden army huts, but in 1931 a splendid gift from Sir William Morris allowed the Wingfield Morris Hospital to be rebuilt.

On 30 June 1933 HRH, the Prince of Wales opened the new hospital and described it as 'the latest; a most up to date hospital for this important work in Great Britain. Orthopaedics is one of the most promising departments of surgery'.

The friendship between Sir William Morris and GRG flourished steadily. It was said that the benefaction from Lord Nuffield of £2 million, establishing chairs for a postgraduate medical school, originated from meetings between Hugh Cairns, surgeon; Sir Robert Macintosh, anaesthetist; G.R. Girdlestone, orthopaedic surgeon; and Sir Farquhar Buzzard, Regius Professor of Medicine – the leader/negotiator. Girdlestone and Macintosh were personal friends of Lord Nuffield.

Initially G.R. Girdlestone was satisfied with the support for the Wingfield Morris Hospital, but when he saw the growth and development of the other Nuffield Departments, he returned to his benefactor with the chair of orthopaedic surgery in mind. There is a note from Mr Hobbs (Lord Nuffield's secretary), 'Lord Nuffield had talked to Goodenough about it and that it was perfectly plain to him [Nuffield] that he wished provision to be made for this. Mr. Hobbs said that the matter could now be regarded as settled.' Following that, a decree was passed by Congregation, 4 May 1937, stating that G.R. Girdlestone, BM, MA (New College), be constituted Nuffield Professor of Orthopaedic Surgery, holding the office as Clinical Director at the Wingfield Morris Hospital, but with the provisions: (a) he should receive no enrolments as Professor, (b) he should not be debarred from engaging in private practice; and (c) he should retain the title Professor until 31 July following his sixty-fifth birthday, or until such a date he should cease to be Clinical Director of the Wingfield Morris Orthopaedic Hospital.

The Lord Nuffield Scholarships in Orthopaedic Surgery and After-Care for nurses was set up with a special donation of £22,500. Lord Nuffield established a Fracture Clinic with a gift of £10,000 in the Albert Dock Hospital, London and a gift of £25,000 was given to the Princess Elizabeth Orthopaedic Hospital, Exeter.

In 1938 there was an extensive infantile paralysis epidemic throughout the world. A trial of convalescent serum had been administered in the pre-paralytic state to prevent paralysis, but without success. One whole ward in the Wingfield had been taken over for the care of paralysed patients and, adjacent to this, the first warm-water bath was built for remedial swimming for victims of the disease. Lord Nuffield saw the destruction and disablement associated with poliomyelitis, and built, in his Oxford factory, Bath respirators or 'iron lungs', which were delivered to hospitals in Great Britain and throughout the Empire with a benefaction of £62,620.

This interest in world orthopaedics was continued by his supporting and donations of £500,000 to orthopaedics in Britain, Australia, New Zealand, and in South Africa. Indeed, GRG had gone out to South Africa to establish a similar scheme of orthopaedic organization to that found in Oxford.

As the Second World War loomed, GRG began to negotiate a change in the Nuffield Professorship from a non-stipendiary into a salaried position. To facilitate this he offered his resignation. Numerous discussions, memoranda and papers were exchanged and, on 13 March 1938 G.R. Girdlestone met with Dr Lindsay, Vice-Chancellor of Oxford University, in Balliol and explained that money necessary for a chair had been set aside for this purpose. GRG then wrote a memorandum to Lord Nuffield on 2 May 1939, pointing out that the title should be that of the Lord Nuffield Chair in Orthopaedic Surgery, to bring it in line with the Lord Nuffield Scholarship in Orthopaedic Surgery. After much discussion, counselling, and heart searching, Professor Girldestone withdrew his letter of resignation on 31 March.

A letter addressed to the Chairman of the Nuffield Committee for the Advancement of Medicine, dated 31 March 1939, stated 'the results of a meeting of the Regius Professor of Medicine, Professors Cairns, Florey and Gunn with Mr. Harry Platt, acting as an outside advisor and myself [GRG].' They discussed a full-time professorship with a salary of £2,500, and this was accepted. £11,000 was set aside for the chair, for the provision of a new building to include X-ray and photographic departments, and for the appointment of the first research fellow. Lord Nuffield continued to give his strong support to GRG and added to the development of the Wingfield Morris Orthopaedic Hospital. On 28 October 1938 he personally opened the new Nuffield block and gave £31,381 for additional nurses' quarters and new beds on site.

Girdlestone resigned his professorship again but maintained a powerful influence in running the Wingfield Morris Orthopaedic Hospital, writing, 'I am not, of course, resigning my position as Honorary Surgeon to the hospital, which I hope to retain for many years. It is a great relief to feel that I will have time to work at a reasonable rate and to keep in closer personal contact with my patients, both in the ordinary and private wards of the hospital. It was given to a few to see their dreams come true and then to have the happiness of handing over the reins of leadership, with perfect satisfaction to my successor, Professor Seddon, so admirably fitted for the task.'

The war years were bleak. Professor Seddon took over on 14 January

1939, established an academic orthopaedic unit, unique in the country, and research was begun.

In the early 1940s Professor Florey in the Dunn School of Pathology had developed penicillin from a cheese mould. For a therapeutic trial he placed small quantities of this most vital substance at the disposal of Professor Seddon in the Wingfield Morris Orthopaedic Hospital. In January 1944, a 10-year-old boy with osteomyelitis of the femur was treated, the drug being given by a duodenal tube, placed into the stomach. Sadly, it was not effective because it became inert. However, the next patient, who had an infection following a bone operation, received the dissolved, deep-orange-coloured powder by an intravenous route. Within 36 hours the total supply of penicillin had been used up; the patient's temperature had returned to normal and the wound had healed. This unprecedented miraculous result was recorded by the house surgeon at that time, Dr R. Lourie, who described how the bed pans containing the urine specimens of these patients were transported by Professor Seddon himself in his Austin car down the Headington Hill, so that the penicillin could be recycled in the laboratories of Professor Florey in South Parks Road. This led on to an official trial of penicillin as a therapeutic agent.

Another important field of research was the development of an X-ray apparatus for cine-radiographic recording of movements in normal joints. This was conducted by the Nuffield Institute for Research, in collaboration with Dr Barclay.

Following visits of Professor Seddon to Malta, to consult on a very severe epidemic of poliomyelitis, Lord Nuffield gave further funding to bring surgeons, who were in the poliomyelitis field, from other countries to train in Oxford.

Through Lord Nuffield's endowment establishing a nursing school within the Wingfield Morris Hospital, orthopaedic nursing was accepted as a specialty within nursing.

The war ended and the surgeons J. Scott, R.G. Taylor, and Edgar Somerville returned to the Wingfield Morris Hospital. The arrival of John Mullins, a young ex-officer, was of great significant for the hospital. He took over as secretary at the Wingfield Morris Orthopaedic Hospital and held this post for the next 30 years. Another important appointment was John Thomson as the treasurer of the Wingfield Morris Hospital, on the retirement of his father. Sir John Thomson (a personal friend of Lord Nuffield) held this post for over 30 years.

In the post-war period, before the introduction of the National Health

Service, strains and stresses began to appear in the working relationships of the professor and his colleagues, particularly in the allocation of beds. Unfortunately this led to certain demands by Professor Seddon, which his colleagues refused to meet (although the University strongly supported Professor Seddon's position). He resigned to take up an appointment as Director of Clinical Services at the Royal National Hospital. Once again, because of interpersonal relationships, the chair was being used as a bargaining point.

Following the resignation of Professor Seddon, there was a vacuum, and Emeritus Professor Girdlestone, who was still a senior surgeon of the hospital, was heavily involved in discussions (letters flying backwards and forwards to the University and, indeed, to Lord Nuffield). One of these letters was a passionate appeal by GRG, that the chair must continue, saying: '. . . there is no argument for deferment of an appointment.' GRG was still very active with his ideas and ambitions for the Wingfield Hospital.

Finally, however, a public advertisement for candidates went forward and in 1949 a University Electoral Body elected Dr J. Trueta as the Nuffield Professor of Orthopaedic Surgery. Shortly before this, at the beginning of the National Health Service on 5 July 1949, the 'Red House', which had been owned by Girdlestone, was bought from him by Lord Nuffield, and then handed back to the managment committee of the Wingfield Morris Orthopaedic Hospital. This was to become a centre to provide housing for clinical staff and postgraduates from abroad; it also had teaching facilities and research rooms. The Wingfield Morris Orthopaedic Hospital became part of the Regional Hospital Board structure and organization, still maintaining a separate and autonomous position as a teaching hospital but being regionally based. In November 1949 Professor Trueta, Professor Girldestone, and Mr John Thomson went to see Lord Nuffield about improving the department, with a request for £250,000. Lord Nuffield immediately gave them £50,000 and the rest of the money came from the University and the University Grants Committee. Within a year GRG was dead and Lord Nuffield gave a further donation of £10,000 to the Wingfield Morris Orthopaedic Trust Fund for the purpose of establishing a scholarship to commemorate his old friend.

One year later, because of the generous support and benefaction from Lord Nuffield over all these years, the Wingfield Morris Hospital was renamed the Nuffield Orthopaedic Centre. This name having been suggested by GRG before he died.

The work expanded particularly in research methods, the treatment of congenital deformities and of bone infections by penicillin. Because of the increasing numbers of scholars, particularly from abroad, there was not enough space. At the beginning of 1955 Lord Nuffield was again approached for further donation of about £200,000 to expand the building. Lord Nuffield agreed to this and in his letter to his legal advisors he stated 'I shall be quite happy as long as the Trustees decide the donations already mentioned in my deed make clear my wish to create and perpetuate an orthopaedic training centre under the guidance of the Nuffield Professor of Orthopaedic Surgery and the University of Oxford.' From this money a three-storey building was completed to house the University Department for Orthopaedic Surgery, with laboratories, a new NHS out-patient department, an X-ray department, and a lecture hall. The Oxford Regional Hospital Board gave £90,000 to furnish the new building, and to cover and maintain expenses, and £30,000 for new X-ray apparatus and a Department of Radiology.

On 27 October 1958 her Majesty Queen Elizabeth the Queen Mother honoured the hospital in the names of Lord Nuffield and Professor Girdlestone when she opened the new academic block. She said, 'successful treatment depends so much on the opportunities for research and it must be of equal importance that these two activities should be carried out in the same place at the same time by the same doctors. From this centre, will come a great enrichment of our knowledge of prevention and treatment of all those crippling diseases which affect both the young and old. What you do will affect the scholars who will come to you from all parts of the world. Researchers will return to their own countries and thousands of people all over the world will reap the benefit of your work.' Lord Nuffield, representatives of town and gown, and over 700 guests attended this magnificent occasion.

Through the Nuffield benefaction, the Nuffield Chair and all research activities and teaching were strongly supported and extended. In 1962 the Vice-Chancellor of the University of Khartoum visited Oxford with a view to setting up a professional relationship to train orthopaedic surgeons from the Sudan.

In the following year Lord Nuffield died, and thus ended the era of his personal support for the professors and staff of the Nuffield Orthopaedic Centre. It is interesting to note the comments of Professor L.G. Witts, the first Nuffield Professor of Clinical Medicine, writing in the *Oxford Medical School Gazette*, Trinity Term, 1966. In considering his 27 years of being a first incumbent of a Nuffield Chair, he wrote on 'the great value of the Nuffield benefaction funds to education and scientific medicine': 'A post-graduate centre had been formed for postgraduate teaching and research for the established hospitals of Oxford. Indeed,' he declared, 'this is what Lord Nuffield favoured and had given his monies for, although Professor Hugh Cairns with his American experience and training wanted to develop a University Hospital along American lines with a limited entry of students. The decree accepting the Nuffield benefaction has meant different things to different people, most of whom were not trained in subtleties of the law.' Professor Witts had hoped to see the completion of the buildings and staffing of the Nuffield Departments before undertaking the teaching of undergraduates, but Professor Hugh Cairns was not so easily persuaded and it was said he would not be happy until he had broken a bottle of champagne over the head of the first undergraduate clinical student. The Second World War solved this particular dilemma as undergraduates were transferred from the teaching hospitals in London to work in Oxford, where there have been undergraduates ever since. Lord Nuffield always thought he was doing enough for any government by paying his taxes. He believed in using his donations for postgraduate education and that the government should pay for undergraduate schooling. He lost interest in Oxford medicine when the clinical school for undergraduates was continued after the war but, because of his friendship with Professor Girdlestone, he continued to support orthopaedics, unlike other Nuffield Departments, and this in time produced conflicts. Professor Witts emphasized that Lord Nuffield had been disappointed over the foundation of the new Nuffield College which he also had endowed, instead of becoming a postgraduate science/engineering college it had been altered to accept undergraduates for history and social science subjects.

In 1964, committees were set up to consider the impending vacancies of the four Nuffield Professors.

Professor Loewi from the Presbyterian Hospital, New York, as external advisor, said there was a real future need and necessity for the continuation of the Orthopaedic Chair, because of the modern epidemic of trauma. It was noted by the University Committee that the Professor of Orthopaedic Surgery was housed under the auspices of the Regional Hospital Board in the Nuffield Orthopaedic Centre and new premises had specifically been provided for him by the benefaction of Lord Nuffield. The report mentioned that the Nuffield Professor of Othopaedic Surgery should have adequate facilities in the Accident Service in the Radliffe Infirmary or wherever that function might be situated in the United Oxford Hospitals.

On the retirement of Professor Joseph Trueta, Professor Robert Duthie returned from the University of Rochester Medical Center, Rochester, New York, to take up the chair on 17 March 1966, with a Professorial Fellowship in Worcester College which had always held the chair. In the past 20 years there has been a marked expansion, both in the number of undergraduates and postgraduates being taught, and of the extended research programmes in the Nuffield Orthopaedic Centre and in the Nuffield Department of Orthopaedic Surgery.

Between 1966 and 1968 under the Regius Professor, Sir George Pickering, the Nuffield Benefaction for the Advancement of Medicine Fund was incorporated into the University Chest in order to stabilize and expand the Clinical Faculty of Medicine. The Nuffield Committee for Advancement of Medicine was disbanded. The Nuffield Benefaction began to provide additional finances for the extension of the new clinical school, which was enlarged to accommodate 100 undergraduates, necessitating new clinical departments.

Professor Sir Humphrey Waldock was asked to give his opinion of the terms of the trust deeds and to comment upon financial needs of the new Medical Faculty. His opinion was that such needs should be met from the benefaction, and for widening the scope of the Medical School, with the provision of special facilities for such a school and for those who work in the field of research, including postgraduate students undergoing instruction in modern methods of investigation. This was the end of all the work, negotiations, and donations handsomely given by Lord Nuffield and built upon by the founding five Nuffield Professors.

In the following years in the Nuffield Orthopaedic Centre new fields of practice and research have been opened in rheumatology, in bone metabolism, and in the development of artificial limbs; all with various external fundings.

Biochemistry laboratories and staff have been added, and the MRC Bone Research Unit has been transferred from the Churchill Hospital and rebuilt within the grounds of the Nuffield Orthopaedic Centre, to provide a stronger clinical link for the fundamental work, under the new Director, Dr Maureen Owen.

Research workers have come from all over the world to participate in this unique setting. In 1974 with the reorganization of the National Health Service Act, the Nuffield Orthopaedic Centre management committee was disbanded, with administration being allocated to the new Area Health Authority. The NHS budgetary support decreased in spite of increasing demands from ever-increasing numbers of patients, particularly those with degenerative diseases.

The Board of Governors at the Radcliffe Infirmary also became part of an Area Health Authority. Funding from elsewhere has had to be achieved to maintain progress and to contribute to the many few fields in the musculoskeletal system.

The new Accident Department in the John Radcliffe Hospital was successfully re-organized, so that junior house staff trained in rotation with the NOC.

In 1977 both Professor J. Trueta and Professor Herbert Seddon died. These two great men, through personal friendship, had the direct support of Lord Nuffield, and through this achieved many great things.

The Nuffield Orthopaedic Centre, and the Nuffield Department have changed over the past 20 years. Significant research has been carried out requiring the use of specialized techniques in bioengineering, biochemistry, tissue culture, isotope bone metabolism, ultrastructural and electron microscopy and, more recently, in MR spectroscopy. This has necessitated the formation of teams with scientists to provide a broad base for young clinicians to make a contribution to fundamental knowledge of the musculo-skeletal system. The Nuffield Department and its professor have made a direct and significant contribution in developing sixteen chairs of orthopaedic surgery, (eight professors having received all or part of their training in Oxford). In 1966 when Professor Duthie returned from the United States there were only six. The generosity of Lord Nuffield from the beginning and the drive and inspiration of Gathorne Robert Girdlestone established the Nuffield Chair for Orthopaedic Surgery, and with it the modern Nuffield Orthopaedic Centre. Obviously the beginning was rough, untidy, full of strife and personality clashes, but it has been a remarkable achievement to build and develop an orthopaedic teaching hospital with all its allied specialists in rheumatology, bone metabolism, rehabilitation, orthopaedic engineering, and orthopaedic workshops.

The requirements of any academic department have been made more complex by the demands placed upon it by the National Health Service. The responsibility of maintaining and developing high standards of clinical practice often appeared to have been compromised by the stringencies of the NHS.

The goals and achievements of the past 50 years, the discoveries, the alleviation of human suffering, the training of young undergraduates and specialists, and the participation in research by postgraduates from all over the world has surely justified Lord Nuffield's belief in orthopaedics and the NOC.

It has been calculated that from 1930 to 1958, Lord Nuffield's benefactions to orthopaedics in Oxford and elsewhere in the world amounted to £1,128,000 (Table 19.1). Over 317 postgraduate fellows from over 20 countries have worked in the NOC and the Nuffield Department of Orthopaedic Surgery and have returned to their own countries to provide leadership and a great service, 40 becoming professors.

All in the Nuffield Orthopaedic Centre have striven to uphold the philosophy of a great and generous man, who, by his legacy has helped so many of us to achieve so much.

Table 19.1   Lord Nuffield's benefactions to orthopaedics in Oxford and elsewhere*

		£
1930	Sir William Morris, Bt, for the Building Fund	1,000
1930–39	Rebuilding the NOC (Wingfield Morris Orthopaedic Hospital 1931-55, NOC 1955 to date)	117,381
1935–37	Nuffield Fund for Cripples	275,000
1935–45	Nuffield Fund for Orthopaedic Services in Australia, New Zealand, and the Union of South Africa.	321,500
1936	St Thomas's, Albert Dock Hospital, Fracture Clinic	10,000
	The Lord Nuffield Scholarships in Orthopaedic Surgery and After-Care, NOC	22,500
1937	Princess Elizabeth Orthopaedic Hospital, Exeter	25,000
1938–44	Bath respirators, 'iron lungs', given to hospitals in Great Britain and the Empire	62,620
1944–45	NOC extensions to buildings	10,000
1949	NOC Trust	50,000
1951	Girdlestone Memorial Scholarship in Orthopaedic Surgery	10,000
1956	NOC Trust, Collateral to the 1949 Trust	200,000
1958	Nuffield Committee out of Lord Nuffield's Building Fund for the Research Building	31,000

* From Andrews and Brunner. This table contains one correction and one addition. The amount given towards rebuilding the hospital has been increased to tally with

the total sum donated for this purpose. The addition is a further benefaction made in 1956 a year after the biography was published (1955).

FURTHER READING

R.B. Duthie and J. Mullins, *Fifty years of the Nuffield Professorship of Orthopaedic Surgery in the University of Oxford* (Oxford, 1987).

R.B. Duthie, *Orthopaedic services in Oxford and the Region: the past 100 years* (1988), pp. 98–117.

In a County Hospital 1920–88, C. Miles (ed.). A collection of Essays about the history, changes and development of the hospital in Oxford.

Chapter 20

Lord Nuffield and anaesthesia

Keith Sykes

In the foreword to the fiftieth anniversary volume, *A history of the Nuffield Department of Anaesthetics, Oxford 1937–1987*, Sir Robert Macintosh, the first Professor, wrote: 'Lord Nuffield always showed great independence of thought, on no occasion more so than when he founded the first fully endowed Chair of Anaesthetics in the World. As far as I know, not a single person saw any merit in the idea. He realized it would take some years to raise the existing standard to bring it to the level of other university departments but, as he said, "If I do not found a Chair now, who will do it in the future?"'

This was the situation that existed in Oxford when Lord Nuffield announced his gift of £2 million to the University to create the first four Nuffield chairs. Chairs in Medicine, Surgery, Obstetrics and Gynaecology created no comment, for these were core subjects of the medical curriculum. However, the proposal to create a Chair of Anaesthetics met with strong opposition from within the University. Attempts were made to downgrade the chair to a readership and, initially, it was proposed that the Professor of Anaesthetics should receive a lower salary than that paid to the holders of the other three chairs. The reason for the opposition was that anaesthesia had not really developed as a speciality. Although there were some specialist anaesthetists, the majority of anaesthetics were given by junior house staff or by general practitioners who undertook anaesthetic sessions in local hospitals. There were no academic departments in England or the rest of Europe, and in the United States, where academic anaesthesia was somewhat more advanced, there were some academic departments but there was no independent chair. It was, therefore, remarkable that Nuffield not only succeeded in persuading the university to create a Chair of Anaesthetics but also that he managed to secure the appointment of Macintosh to the post.

Macintosh was a New Zealander who had joined the British Forces during the First World War and had been shot down over Germany, where he subsequently spent a period as a prisoner of war. He qualified in medicine at Guy's Hospital and began giving anaesthetics while training to be a surgeon. He rapidly became a very skilled anaesthetist and soon established a large practice in Harley Street. However, he had received no formal academic training and, when he moved to Oxford, he enlisted the help of scientists from other disciplines to initiate research in the department.

Shortly after his appointment, Macintosh received an invitation to anaesthetize for an American plastic surgeon, Eastman Sheehan, who was treating victims from the Spanish Civil War. This experience convinced Macintosh that there was a need for simple vaporizers which would produce known concentrations of ether and, on his return to Oxford, he invoked the assistance of physicists from the Clarendon Laboratory to design such a device. The result was the Oxford Vaporizer No. 1. The problem with previous vaporizers was that the liquid ether cooled as it vaporized. The cooling reduced the concentration of ether vapour above the liquid so that the concentration received by the patient was very variable. The Oxford vaporizer overcame this problem by utilizing a chemical thermostat which kept the ether at a known and constant temperature. Since the concentration of ether vapour at this temperature was known, it was possible to construct a device which mixed ether vapour and air in known proportions so that the final concentration could be varied by the anaesthetist. The vaporizer was described in the *Lancet* in 1941 and within a year, over 1000 of these vaporizers had been produced in the Morris Motor Factory at Cowley and distributed to the services, after stringent testing in the Nuffield Department. By the end of the war some 2,700 Oxford Vaporizers had been produced at Cowley at a total cost of £46,600. The majority of these were used in the armed forces but a number were also distributed to mission hospitals, production ceasing finally in 1947.

The use of these vaporizers greatly increased the safety of anaesthesia, for the anaesthetist knew for the first time what concentration of ether was being given, and, in addition, the vaporizer was fitted with a bellows which enabled the anaesthetist to supply artificial ventilation if the patient's breathing was inadequate. In later years, a number of other vaporizers were developed in the department. There was, for example, the ESO vaporizer, which was designed to be carried by paratroopers, chloroform being chosen as the anaesthetic because it was non-explosive. After the war, a more refined ether vaporizer, the EMO, was developed. this utilized a car radiator thermostat to alter the proportions of air and ether vapour in the gas mixture in order to compensate for the changes in temperature of the ether. The department also produced the EMOTRIL vaporizer, which enabled patients to self-administer low concentrations of trichloroethylene to achieve pain relief without loss of consciousness when in labour. The vaporizer was designed to be used by midwives when a doctor was not present and represented a significant advance in obstetric pain relief. Still later, the Oxford Miniature Vaporizer was designed for use with the newer non-explosive agents such as halothane, and it was a development of this vaporizer which was used with great success in the emergency operating theatres in the Falklands War. Although modern apparatus uses much more sophisticated technology, there is still a place for this type of simple vaporizer for, in many Third World countries, oxygen and anaesthetic gases are unobtainable or the sources unreliable, and anaesthetics may still be given by nurses or relatively untrained assistants. Such personnel can be trained to use these relatively simple vaporizers in a safe manner, and the cost of the apparatus and anaesthetic agent is within the reach of most mission hospitals.

Since there is still a great need for training in the use of this type of equipment, the department has continued to play a major part in the teaching of anaesthetists who are prepared to spend periods in Third World countries or in disaster situations. We, therefore, continue to run special courses in this field and one of the consultants, Dr M.E. Dobson, has set up an organization which keeps a register of anaesthetists prepared to undertake this type of work and which provides help and guidance for both the anaesthetist and host department. The Nuffield Department thus continues to maintain and develop the enormous network of international connections which has characterized the department since its inception.

Another result of Lord Nuffield's benefaction was the provision of 'iron lung' ventilators for the treatment of paralytic poliomyelitis. The 'iron lung' consisted of a large metal cylinder which surrounded the trunk and limbs of the patient with an air-tight seal at the neck. The interior of the chamber was connected to a large bellows which intermittently lowered the pressure inside the chamber and so caused the air to flow in and out of the lungs. Lord Nuffield's interest in this device was stimulated by a film made in the department which reviewed all the known methods of providing respiratory assistance to the paralysed patient. It was apparent that the iron lung was the best machine available at that time, but the original design was complicated and expensive. The department identified a much simpler design in plywood by an Australian engineer called Both, and Nuffield immediately seized on this design and started to manufacture it at Cowley. In 1938, one week after Lord Nuffield had decided to build 5,000 iron lungs, costing £98 each, he was pictured in the local newspaper with Professor Macintosh lifting a volunteer (the Chief Technician, Mr Richard Salt) into one of the Both machines. Subsequently, every hospital in the Commonwealth was offered one of these devices and members of the department spent a greal deal of time teaching other doctors how to use them.

The onset of the Second World War had an enormous impact on the department, for it was necessary to train a large number of anaesthetists quickly. The department therefore organized a number of courses which were run throughout the war. Other members left to join the Forces, and Macintosh became an Air Commodore in the Royal Air Force with responsibility for anaesthesia. Those who were left behind became drawn into physiological research relevant to the war effort. The submarine *Thetis* sank in Liverpool Harbour in 1939 and this stimulated a great interest in submarine escape apparatus. Three members of the department, C.F.G. Pratt, S.F. Suffolk, and S.L. Cowan, worked on improvements to air purification systems in submarines and devised an instrument which indicated the level of carbon dioxide in the atmosphere. Later, they evolved new submarine escape apparatus utilizing principles previously developed for some of the breathing circuits used during anaesthesia. Another important project was the determination of the maximum height at which a pilot could safely bail out of an aircraft without oxygen. This involved breathing very low concentrations of oxygen in order to reduce the oxygen pressure in the lungs to that existing at an altitude of 40,000 feet. In other experiments volunteers were suspended from scaffolding to study the effects of the pressure exerted by a parachute harness on respiration.

Another remarkable series of experiments was concerned with the design of life-jackets. At that time there were no suitable models of human bodies which could be used to test how these devices performed, so E.A. Pask, who later became Professor at Newcastle, had himself deeply anaesthetized with ether and then thrown into a swimming pool to see how the standard life-jackets turned the subject so that the face was submerged. This showed that an unconscious airman would have drowned. As a result the life-jacket design was extensively modified and re-tested on the unconscious Pask, not only in the local swimming pools but also in the pool studio at Ealing film studios where there was a wave-making machine. The department still has a film record of these remarkable experiments which resulted in Pask being awarded an OBE in the Honours List in January 1944. Another member of the Department, Dr C.F.G. Pratt, was also awarded the OBE for an act of bravery not connected with his research.

It will be apparent from this brief description of some of the research projects undertaken by the department that it has had an enormous impact on the development of anaesthetic apparatus and on the teaching of simple methods of anaesthesia. Macintosh was also a great proponent of safety in anaesthesia and travelled the world teaching simple, safe methods which were applicable even in quite primitive surroundings. He produced a number of books on anaesthesia and, in the immediate post-war period, members of the department did much to promote the use of regional anaesthesia as an alternative to general anaesthesia. These books were superbly illustrated and have remained classics. The presence of a physicist, H.G. Epstein, greatly influenced the teaching and research in the department and resulted in another classic volume, *Physics for the Anaesthetist.* This book firmly established physics as a core subject in the anaesthetic curriculum. The subsequent application of the physical principles so clearly outlined in this book not only resulted in the development of new apparatus for the administration of anaesthetics but also led to the development of new methods of measuring the patient's condition during anaesthesia and surgery.

Since the war there have been a number of developments in the activities of anaesthetists outside the operating theatre. The first of these was the anaesthetist's involvement in long-term respiratory support. Prior to 1952, patients with poliomyelitis or other paralytic diseases were treated with 'iron lungs'. During 1952 there was a large epidemic of poliomyelitis in Copehagen with a particularLy severe form of the disease which could not be treated successfully with 'iron lungs'. It was the Danish anaesthetist, Dr B. Ibsen, who suggested that patients could be kept alive by squeezing air into their lungs from a bag, rather than by enclosing them in an iron lung. In the initial epidemic, relays of medical students were used to provide this form of respiratory support, but within a year mechanical ventilators had been designed to take over this task, and special respiration units were developed to treat this kind of patient. One of the first of these was at the Churchill Hospital in Oxford where Drs Ritchie Russell, J.M.K. Spalding, and Professor Crampton Smith (the second Nuffield Professor of Anaesthetics) treated patients with the new kind of therapy. Within a few years, patients who had sustained severe chest injuries and patients who had undergone severe thoracic surgery were also being treated with mechanical ventilators. Later, with the advent of open-heart surgery, intensive care units were formed. In this country, over 80 per cent of such units are now directed by anaesthetists.

Another field where anaesthetists have played a major role is in the development of centres for the treatment of chronic pain. Dr John Lloyd was one of the first anaesthetists to enter this field and he set up the Oxford Regional Pain Relief Unit in Abingdon Hospital in 1977. He and his colleagues have pioneered many new forms of treatment for both cancer and non-cancer pain and the unit now has an international reputation, not only for the care of patients but also for research into pain-relieving drugs and other types of treatment.

Finally, one must consider the role of the Nuffield Department in the development of anaesthesia worldwide. When the Nuffield Chair was founded in 1937 there were no other chairs of anaesthesia in the world. Although the Harvard Chair had been funded in 1924, and H.K. Beecher had been appointed to the headship of the department in 1936, it was not until 1941 that he became Henry Isaah Door Professor. The second chair in this country was created at Cardiff in 1953 and was occupied by W.W. Mushin, who had been Macintosh's first assistant at Oxford. A.E. Pask was the next to be appointed to a chair, at Newcastle, and other chairs, both in this country and abroad, rapidly followed. The first chair in Europe was founded at Innsbruck, Austria in 1959 and was a direct result of a speech made by Macintosh when he visited the city. In subsequent years there was a rapid proliferation of chairs, both in this country and overseas, and academic departments are now found in the majority of developed countries. A large number of holders of these chair obtained some training in Oxford, and at the recent fiftieth anniversary celebrations of the Nuffield Department of Anaesthetics there was a remarkable gathering of anaesthetists from all over the world.

The national and international reputation of the Nuffield Department continues to grow. The department currently consists of some fifty clinical anaesthetists, and approximately thirty academic anaesthetists, scientists, secretaries, and technicians. The scientists include physicists, electrochemists, electronic and mechanical engineers, a mathematician, a physiologist, and pharmacologists. Research programmes are concerned with the effects of anaesthesia on the heart and the lungs, methods of providing articifial support for patients with acute lung disease, and the pharmacology of anaesthetic and analgesic drugs. There is a major interest in new methods of post-operative pain relief and their effects on post-operative complications and outcome from surgery. There is, in addition, a continued programme of apparatus development. The department has recently completed clinical trials of the new sophisticated microprocessor-controlled anaesthetic machine which is being developed in association with local industry. The department continues to play a major role in undergraduate and postgraduate teaching and runs a number of residential and other courses. Its members are active in national and international organizations and receive many invitations to speak at overseas meetings.

Lord Nuffield displayed great courage when he insisted on the creation of a Chair in Anaesthetics at Oxford. However, it is doubtful if even he could have recognized what a major impact this chair would hae on the development of anaesthesia worldwide. Thanks to his vision, the United Kingdom now has enough highly trained anaesthetists, not only to provide high-quality anaesthetic care in even the smallest hospital, but also to look after patients in intensive care units, in pain clinics, in hospices, and in accident and emergency departments. Anaesthetists are active in the organization of advanced life-support programmes and many anaesthetists have used their skills in mass disasters or in the transport and resuscitation of the seriously ill. Anaesthetists now play a major role in hospital and university administration and anaesthesia is now the largest single speciality in the National Health Service. Seldom can such a single idea have had such a great impact on society.

Chapter 21

Plastic surgery's first professor

T.J.S. Patterson and A.H.T. Robb-Smith

During the Battle of Britain, pilots would fly their crippled planes to Cowley and wait for them to be repaired while sleeping exhausted in accommodation that Nuffield provided for them; but as soon as their planes were ready they would fly back to battle. Nuffield was well aware of the terrible facial injuries that the pilots often suffered and wanted to do something more than his revival of the RAF Benevolent Fund. He knew that Sir Archibald McIndoe was doing magnificent work in plastic surgery at the East Grinstead Hospital and, with his 'guinea-pigs', was restoring the confidence of these disfigured young men, while Sir Harold Gillies, the doyen of British plastic surgeons, was fully occupied with the Army and Navy.

In the early years of the war Lady Nuffield, who was far from strong, was in America and a close friend Professor Robert Macintosh, the Oxford Nuffield Professor of Anaesthetics, arranged that an American plastic surgeon, Mr Eastman Sheehan, should keep an eye on her, and he was most kind and assiduous in this matter. Indeed, when Lady Nuffield was returning to England he came with her on the ship and arrived in London in 1942. Lord Nuffield sent him a letter expressing his gratitude for the care and help he had given to Lady Nuffield, and that he would be happy to arrange for Sheehan to be given a chair of plastic surgery in Great Britain. In those days almost all the English plastic surgeons were extreme individualists with something of the prima donna complex and Sir Harold Gillies was no exception. Gillies disapproved of Sheehan as an American 'beauty surgeon' who had served in the Spanish Civil War on the wrong side, and he made it very clear to Sir Winston Churchill that any appointment of Sheehan to a British post would be most undesirable. Nuffield learnt of these observations and, to say the least of it, was displeased. On the other hand Sheehan, who had a highly successful cosmetic surgical practice in New York, had no intention of remaining in England and it is probable that he spoke about Nuffield's offer to tease his English colleagues. However, he suggested to Nuffield that Mr Pomfret Kilner might well be suitable for such a post.

Kilner, a dapper and, in his younger days, very peppery Manchunian, had done much work with Gillies. Gillies, while serving as a major, had persuaded the authorities during the First World War that a separate surgical speciality was needed to treat the large number of maxillo-facial injuries resulting from Trench warfare. Towards the end of the war, Gillies had been joined by Kilner, and the two of them continued to practice the speciality after the war, applying the lessons learned to the casualties, deformities, and diseases of peacetime. Kilner had made important contributions to the repair of fractures jaws by bone-grafting, and, during the 1930s, he established the principles of the management of hare lip and cleft palate deformities. Eventually, they parted in a flaming row and Kilner became consulting plastic surgeon to St Thomas's and in charge of the plastic surgery unit at the Ministry of Pensions Roehampton Hospital. Nuffield immediately took to Kilner and felt that the University of Oxford would be proud to have an experienced plastic surgeon of such eminence as the first professor of that subject. The Nuffield Provincial Trust agreed to provide funds to cover the expenses of a department for some 10 years. Sir Farquhar Buzzard warned that it might not be so easy to persuade the University to carry out his lordship's wishes, but Sir Arthur Ellis, the Regius Professor, who never understood Oxford University politics, was delighted with the idea.

However, Hebdomadal Council questioned whether the money was sufficient for establishing a chair and whether plastic surgery warranted a chair. Would it not be better just to have a unit in the department of surgery directed by a reader?

Naturally this was not to Lord Nuffield's liking and, in the end, it was agreed that there should be an academic unit of plastic surgery with Kilner in charge with the personal title of Professor but no established chair. Thus, in 1944 Thomas Pomfret Kilner was appointed Professor of Plastic Surgery in Oxford – the first professor of plastic surgery in this country. The unit was set up with a grant of £56,000 from Lord Nuffield, which was designed to cover the period of 13 years before Kilner would be due to retire.

Some concern was felt amongst the Radcliffe staff when it was learnt that Pomfret Kilner was to direct the new plastic surgery unit. For he had gained the reputation of being difficult and that even the most stalwart

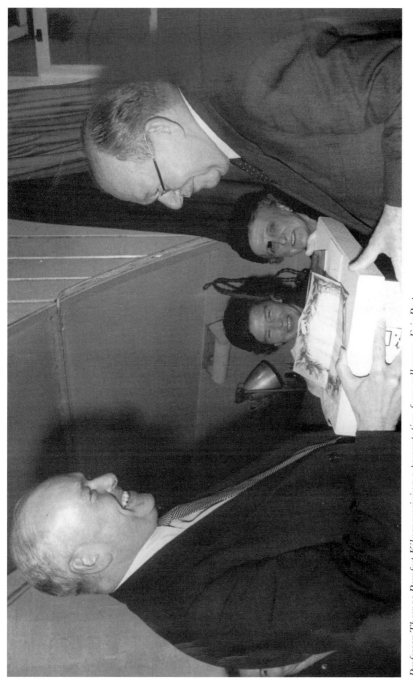

Professor Thomas Pomfret Kilner receiving a presentation from colleague, Eric Peet. [Courtesy of the Kilner Library, Radcliffe Infirmary, Oxford. Previously published in the British Journal of Plastic Surgery]

theatre sisters could dissolve in tears when Kilner was on form. But these were folk tales of a brash young surgeon of the 1920s, very different from the wit, charm, and ability of the little puckish Lancastrian who delighted not only the medical staff but also the Senior Common Room of St John's College to which he had been elected. Of course, he had no beds and no department. There was only a miniscule room in one of the derelict telescope towers of the old Radcliffe Observatory and a fortnightly out-patient clinic in the Ear, Nose, and Throat Department; all his patients had to be admitted to his beds at the Ministry of Pensions section of Stoke Mandeville Hospital at Aylesbury. But he was not impatient, for he knew that several of the original Nuffield Professors had still inadequate accommodation and he could but hope that things would improve, and they did. St John's College provided him with more spacious office accommodation and he had with him his secretary, who had looked after his needs for many years; with efficiency and charm, she was able to produce the various pieces of office and photographic equipment that he required. For Kilner was meticulous in his clinical notes and insisted on having photographs of the injuries of his patients and the progress of their repair.

It was at this time that Peter Medawar, a Fellow of St John's College, was working with little support on his epoch-making studies on the immunobiology of homografts. Kilner at once recognized the importance of this work and gave Medawar financial support at this critical period in his scientific achievements.

Late in 1945 the Radcliffe Infirmary took over the responsibility for the Churchill Hospital, which had been occupied by American Army medical staff for some time. Soon Kilner had twelve beds in the hospital and a Nissen hut which was converted into departmental offices, a library, a photographic department, and a number of study rooms for visiting workers. In February 1946 Kilner was joined by Mr Eric Peet as assistant director of the unit on the latter's return from war service in India where he had been in command of a maxillo-facial unit. J.S. Calnan was appointed first assistant to the professor; after Kilner's retirement he went to Hammersmith Hospital as Professor of Plastic Surgery – the second such post in this country. The staff of the department was increased to include a senior registrar, a senior house officer, and a research assistant. Steadily, the fame of the unit as a training centre spread all over the world.

Two wards were made over to the department – an adult ward, and a childrens' ward. The adult ward was unusual at that time in that it housed both male and female patients. The ward was divided into four-bedded cubicles, each cubicle being allotted either to men or to women; but all cubicles opened on to a common corridor, and the recreation and eating and bathing areas were shared by all patients. This was a particular policy of Kilner's – many of the patients were visibly disfigured or deformed, and their re-integration into the community was an important part of their treatment. As soon as they were fit enough after their operation, they were encouraged to get dressed in their ordinary clothes, and to mix freely with patients in other cubicles. This was the first step in giving them the confidence to return to a more normal life.

The childrens' ward contained a number of individual cubicles for nursing very small babies, and close cooperation was developed with the Paediatric and Anaesthetic Departments to deal with the problems that they posed. Here, among the many other injuries and deformities of childhood requiring plastic surgery, Kilner's absorbing interest in cleft lip and palate was continued and developed, and, in cooperation with the X-ray and speech-therapy departments, valuable research was carried out in the evaluation and treatment of patients with speech defects.

Joint clinics were set up with the dental department at the Churchill Hospital for the management of maxillo-facial injuries and deformities, and members of the department were always 'on call' for the Accident Service at the Radcliffe Infirmary, to help in the management of patients with multiple injuries and burns. There were always a number of patients under treatment by the plastic surgeons in beds in other wards in the United Oxford Hospitals, such as the Cowley Road Hospital and the Nuffield Orthopaedic Centre.

Joint clinics were also set up with the Radiotherapy Department and with the dermatologists for the management of malignant disease, particularly of the head and neck and of the skin. There was close liaison with the ENT department at the Radcliffe Infirmary, and important advances were made in the treatment of deaf children with deformities of the ears.

Teaching was an important part of the plastic surgeons' function, not only of medical students and nurses, but of postgraduates and relatively experienced surgeons from all over the world, and Oxford became well known for the part that it played in the training of plastic surgeons.

Thus there was developed a central plastic surgery unit at the Churchill Hospital with approximately forty beds – an unusually large complement for this speciality in a teaching hospital at this time. In addition, patients were being treated in most of the other Oxford hospitals, and the out-patients drawn from the whole of the Oxford region. Links were established with many of the other medical and surgical departments, so that common problems could be discussed, and the benefits of early plastic surgical treatment applied. This expertise was passed on in multiple teaching sessions.

When Professor Sir Hugh Cairns died in July 1952 it was natural that Kilner should become acting head of the Department of Surgery and he was able to weld those individualists into a more harmonious group than had ever occurred before. Five years later Kilner retired from the directorship and handed over to Eric Peet. By now he had a medical staff of seven, the majority of whom were supported by outside grants as the unit had become a mecca for the training of plastic surgeons and these trainees would go out to the corners of the Earth.

When Kilner reached retirement age, in 1957, the chair was not renewed by the University, and the department came wholly under the National Health Service. Under Kilner's careful management some funds still remained, and these were used for a time to continue the research activities of the department, until these could be taken up by the University. The department is now based at the Radcliffe Infirmary, and continues to maintain the fine traditions established in those early days.

It was unfortunate that Kilner had been so occupied in teaching and practising his speciality that he never had time to write on the art and science of plastic surgery, and after his retirement ill-health dogged him until his death in 1964.

However, Mr Peet, before his untimely death, had provided some accounts of the Kilner technique. Kilner himself, in the last report of the academic unit, wrote 'it was a venture without doubt that had served a very useful purpose and is worthy of repeating at some future date when financial restrictions on progress are less frustrating. It would be no exaggeration to say that of the various Nuffield Professorial Units established in Oxford, that of anaesthestics had the greatest influence on the practice of its speciality, but the plastic surgery unit though in existence for such a short time was a worthy companion in influencing the art of that branch of surgery.

Plastic surgery had been developed in the First World War as a result of the demands of mass casualties; after the war, its potential for treating civilians was not fully appreciated. But after the Second World War it was realized that the principles of repair and reconstruction that had been worked out in wartime should not be allowed to disappear. Lord Nuffield's benefaction enabled a relatively large department to be developed in Oxford, which played a leading part in the application of wartime skills to civilian patients.

Chapter 22

The Nuffield Provincial Hospitals Trust

A.H.T. Robb-Smith

The Nuffield Provincial Hospitals Trust was created in December 1939 by an endowment from Lord Nuffield of one million share units in Morris Motors Limited (£1,200,000). The object of the Trust being 'the co-ordination on a regional basis of hospital and ancilliary medical services, throughout the Provinces and the making of financial provision for the creation, carrying on, or extension of such hospitals and ancillary medical services as in the opinion of the governing trustees are necessary for such co-ordination.'

Up to this time virtually all of Lord Nuffield's benefactions, to medicine had been for specific purposes, often with trustees to ensure that the donor's intentions were properly carried out. But in this Trust and the Nuffield Foundation created 4 years later, the function of the charity is expressed in very broad terms and it was left to the governing trustees, advised by their Medical Advisory Council and other advisory bodies, to determine in what fields the funds of the Trust should be directed.

ROOTS

In order to comprehend the circumstances that led Lord Nuffield to establish this Trust it is necessary to return to the period shortly after the First World War.

Many of the voluntary hospitals found themselves in grave financial difficulties and the Radcliffe Infirmary at Oxford was no exception. Up to this time the income of a voluntary hospital had largely been derived from bequests and the annual subscriptions of the governors, which gave them the privilege of providing 'turns', enabling a deserving patient to be admitted to the hospital. It was a tradition amongst the county families to support their hospital in this way, which also ensured that their sick and needy would be cared for. But now that so many of their sons had been killed in Flanders there were few left to maintain this charitable endeavour.

In 1920 Dr Collier, one of the senior physicians at the Radcliffe Infirmary, suggested that they might follow the example of the associations which were fairly common in the Midlands and initiate a contributory scheme of two pence a week which would render the contributor eligible for admission to the Infirmary. The idea was welcomed by the treasurer, the Revd Cronshaw, and soon there were collecting committees in every village and also in the Cowley factories. So that by 1923 60 per cent of the Infirmary's income was derived from the contributory scheme. It was natural that this self-help attitude was welcomed by William Morris and, in 1924, as a result of the Oxford Motor Ballot, he presented the Infirmary with £9,000 which extinguished their overdraft, and, in recognition of his generous interest, he was elected a Vice-President of the Infirmary. On the death of Lord Valentia, in 1927, Morris succeeded him as President, an office which he held for 21 years, until the 15 September 1948 when Lord Nuffield took the Chair at the final Court of Governors of the Radcliffe Infirmary, as the Corporation had ceased to exist on the 4 July when the Board of Governors of the United Oxford Hospitals, appointed by the Ministry of Health, took over responsibility for the hospitals in the city.

Throughout the 1920s the weekly contributory scheme continued to relieve to a large extent the financial problems of the Radcliffe Infirmary, while the subscribers knew that if they or their family required to be admitted to hospital there would be a bed for them. But a group of Oxford businessmen, led by William Goodenough and Alderman Hyde, were concerned about the financial stresses sometimes faced by professional middle-class families when they suffered serious illness, and believed that a provident scheme might circumvent some of these difficulties. Goodenough, director of Oxford's 'Old Bank' (absorbed by Barclay & Co. in 1900) who had recently been elected Treasurer of the Radcliffe Infirmary, approached his president for financial support for the project; Morris immediately responded by providing £1,000, as an initial reserve fund, thus enabling the Oxford and District Provident Association to be set up in 1927. As this gave financial security to the subscribers, Morris recognized that it was equally important to ensure that the hospitals should not only be able to provide the necessary medical skill but also the accommodation that would provide the comfort and facilities that these patients would expect. So it was that from 1934 with the founding of Nuffield House at Guy's, Nuffield began to provide private accommodation in hospitals and enlargement of nursing homes.

Not that he neglected the insurance aspect of the Provident Schemes. In 1941 he created the Provident Guarantee Fund, and 6 years later The British United Provident Association (BUPA) was established. It is probable, as Mr Webb suggests, that the hundreds of thousands of BUPA subscribers form the largest group enjoying a benefit from Nuffield's generosity. On the other hand, there is a little doubt that the meeting that Morris had with William Goodenough and Alderman Hyde in 1927 had a greater impact than anything else on the character of Lord Nuffield's philanthropic achievements.

Goodenough came from a banking family with strong charitable interests. For his father had been the architect, and later the Chairman, of Barclays Bank, with a great interest in helping and encouraging young people. William Goodenough had served with the Guards at the latter part of the First World War and after reading history at Christ Church, took charge of the Oxford branch of the family's banking interests. Then, as Treasurer of the Radcliffe Infirmary, he came into contact with the new president, and Morris quickly appreciated not only his financial ability but also his quality of outward looking and enthusiasm for compassionate activities. Goodenough became Chairman of all Lord Nuffield's major trusts, both those concerned with medicine end education, and others such as the Nuffield Fund for the Forces of the Crown. The association of Nuffield and Goodenough reached its ultimate achievement in the formation of the Nuffield Foundation in 1943.

THE PHILOSOPHY OF REGIONALISATION & BUZZARD'S HEALTH CENTRES

Though very different in character William Hyde, like Nuffield, was of humble origin, and had made his way upwards in the world of insurance. A traditional Liberal, Hyde took an active interest in a wide range of local affairs, but like Nuffield he had deep emotional concern for the care of the sick. He was convinced that one of the most effective methods of achieving this was to co-ordinate the activities of hospitals and ancillary services in circumscribed areas of the country. It was not difficult to convince Morris of the rightness of this view, for in his motor industry it had been the integration of various aspects of engineering and manufacture which had rendered the Nuffield Organisation so successful.

There had been several Governmental atttempts to achieve some degree of co-ordination all of which had come to nothing. The Dawson report of 1919 advocated the amalgamation of voluntary and municipal authorities in the field of health care and a section of the 1929 Local Government Act had also attempted to implement these ideas.

However Sir William Morris learnt from his friend Mr Girdlestone, the Oxford orthopaedic surgeon, that at the Wingfield Orthopaedic Hospital there had been a co-ordinator of hospital services of a rather specialised kind for some fifteen years. At the end of the First World War the Military Oxford Orthopaedic Centre, and curative workshops, to which in 1917 W.R. Morris had made a contribution, had been transferred to the Ministry of Pensions which had arranged that the Radcliffe Infirmary should administer the hospital on their behalf. However, the Wingfield Committee insisted that 22 beds should be reserved for crippled children, and the first group arrived on 20 November 1919. At the present day, orthopaedics is thought of as dealing mainly with injuries, and arthritis of the hip and knee. Whereas in the twenties apart from war-ravaged cripples, othopaedics did in fact mean the straightening of children, for apart from remedying club foot or hunchback, it was mostly the treatment of tuberculosis of the spine and hip requiring children had to remain in hospital for months, sometimes even years.

Early in October 1919, shortly before the crippled children arrived at Headington, a paper entitled 'A Proposed National Scheme for the care of Crippled Children' appeared, written by Sir Robert Jones, the creator of the speciality of orthopaedics in the British Isles and G.R. Girdlestone, his pupil, who was to become one of the leaders of British orthopaedics. The scheme proposed that the British Isles should be divided into a number of orthopaedic districts centred on an orthopaedic hospital, linked with general hospitals in which there were orthopaedic departments and also linked with local orthopaedic clinics in smaller towns and villages. The Oxford District, later called a region, embraced the three counties of Oxfordshire, Berkshire, and Buckinghamshire, and, by 1930, when Sir William Morris called on Mr Girdlestone at his home in Headington with a cheque for a £1,000 to asssist the hospital's rebuilding, the scheme was fully operational, with peripheral clinics and orthopaedic departments in the general hospitals, all linked with the Wingfield Hospital. This was associated with the educational authorities and also with the workshops special transport.

Rapid progress was being made in a more general form arising out of the Radcliffe Infirmary Contributory Scheme. In 1935, the cottage hospitals joined, forming the Radcliffe and Associated Hospitals Contributory Scheme. It was from Mr Arthur Sanctuary, the Radcliffe Infirmary's administrator, that Nuffield gained a balanced insight into the potentialities of hospital coordination and he could not have been enlightened by a better informant.

Arthur Sanctuary felt that it was his privilege, using charm, firmness, and tact to blend together the able but often individualistic staff of doctors, nurses, and ancilliary workers, backed by work staff who felt themselves to be part of this devoted family, so ensuring that the function of the hospital was to relieve the sick in the best possible manner.

During his 30 years as administrator Arthur Sanctuary was involved in the most remarkable and headlong hospital development ever known. On his appointment in 1921 he was in charge of 214 beds and an annual expenditure of £35,000. On his retirement in 1951 he was responsible for 1,260 beds with an annual budget of just over £1 million. It was on this occasion that Nuffield wrote to Sanctuary 'my own association with the Infirmary has been one of the pleasantest in my life and your invaluable help and advice went very far in assisting the success of my endeavours'.

But it was in 1936, when the British Medical Association held their annual meeting in Oxford with the Regius Professor, Sir Farquhar Buzzard, as President, that a more definite scheme for integrating general hospitals and general practitioners was outlined and even more exciting proposals were touched on.

Buzzard called his address 'And the Future'. He started by pointing out that the war against disease had been conducted in a wasteful and unorganized system. There should be integration of preventative and curative services on a regional basis, coordinated by a Board on which there would be representatives of both the voluntary and the local authority hospitals and also the medical school. Coordination would reach from the general practitioners, whom he called 'the fingers of the profession, its most sensitive parts, trained in the ability to detect disease in its early stages', through to the hospitals and then to the research centres where fundamental work on the cause of disease would be carried out. Buzzard called this coordinated scheme a health centre and, as is so often the way, the phrase has changed its meaning.

Naturally he felt that it was desirable that there should be private practice alongside a state service and he wished to see that general practitioners were responsible for both preventative and curative medicine. In the latter part of his speech, which he called an 'ambitious dream' he discussed the possibility of the development in Oxford of a postgraduate medical school of a new type. Lord Nuffield, who had recently been made an honorary member of the British Medical Association, was sitting by his side and the first part of Buzzard's speech produced an immediate impact and an even more fundamental reaction to the 'ambitious dream'.

THE OXFORD AND DISTRICT JOINT HOSPITAL BOARD

Lord Nuffield once remarked that all his best decisions had been made very quickly, though he did admit that his subconscious, which he maintained was his best guide, had been considering the matter for a while. So it was not altogether surprising that a little over a month after Buzzard's address, it was announced that Lord Nuffield had established a trust to create the Oxford and District Joint Hospital Board to perform for the Oxford area the functions of Buzzard's 'Health centre' as an experiment in hospital cordination, while it was on his fifty-ninth birthday, 10 October 1936, that Nuffield wrote to the Vice-Chancellor of the University of Oxford, informing him of his wish, with a donation of a little over a million pounds, to establish a postgraduate medical school and so provide something which had been going through his mind for some time and which Buzzard had put into words.

The establishment of the Oxford and District Joint Hospital Board proceeded rapidly, as its framework and was already there. Lord Nuffield became the president, Goodenough the chairman and Alderman Hyde the honorary secretary. A memorandum was drawn up which stated frankly that there was a possibility that in the not too distant future legislation might be introduced to abolish the voluntary hospitals, which would soon be replaced by a system of state-run hospitals. Although the memorandum did not explain why this would be so undesirable, it suggested that if the existing voluntary system was to be maintained, the hospitals must show themselves to be efficient in providing the necessary care to a high standard with the greatest of economy and also to ensure collaboration with the local authorities concerned with the public health. It seemed that the Oxford area was peculiarly suitable for a demonstration of this type. The Board, which was advisory rather than executive, would consist of representatives from the associated hospitals and the medical profession in the area, the local authorities concerned with public health, and the medical school of the University. It was intended to arrange that the locally available accommodation would be used to the maximum advantage, there would be central coordination with regard to specialist services, so as to minimize the risk of wasteful overlapping or duplication, 'only by this means can progress be maintained and each unit be enabled to attain to the full measure of its capacity in fulfilling its duty to the community.'

Oxford was perhaps too good an area for an experiment in hospital regionalization, and the triumvirate often found themselves preaching to the converted. The integration of the smaller and cottage hospitals into the Radcliffe Infirmary Contributory Scheme had created a sense of community amongst the hospitals. Since early in the century the local authorities, in spite of ministerial disapproval, had largely delegated the responsibility for the care of tuberculosis, antenatal, and child health care to the voluntary hospitals and general practitioners. Dr Geoffrey Williams, the Medical Officer of Health of the city, was a coordinator rather than an empire builder. Indeed, he became the first senior medical administrative officer of the Oxford Regional Hospital Board. In the mid-thirties he persuaded the city to make good the relative imperfections in the care of infectious diseases by building a first-class hospital, which he largely designed.

However, the reaction of the Radcliffe Infirmary medical staff to Lord Nuffield's other proposal to create an Oxford postgraduate medical school was anything but favourable. They were far from convinced of their good fortune in having 'their hospital' invaded by high-powered academic professors of the Nuffield postgraduate scheme.

Nuffield as president of the Infirmary was aware of this and Goodenough, as his treasurer, spoke to the staff about their attitude in a very straightforward manner. Soon it became apparent, not only to the Radcliffe but to the smaller hospitals and the county as a whole, of the advantages they were enjoying by the provision of first-class anaesthetic, midwifery, and pathological services available locally from the Nuffield departments.

Nuffield himself added some sweeteners, giving £30,000 for enlargement of the Acland Nursing Home which was immediately adjacent to the Radcliffe Infirmary, and an endowment fund of £300,000 to the Oxford and District Joint Hospital Board for improving the facilities in the associated hospitals. So it was that the philosophy and achievement of the Joint Hospital Board attracted considerable interest, and similar but different schemes were started up in various parts of the country.

Although the Government proposals for some sort of National Health

Service in the 1920s came to nothing, the Hospital Board were quite right in stating that the introduction of a nationalized hospital service was still under discussion.

The Public Health Act of 1936 made it obligatory on local authorities if they were planning hospital development, to consult with the representatives of the voluntary hospitals in the area. But, a year before this Act was passed, the British Hospital Association had established the Sankey Commission, to look into the question of hospital coordination, and recommended that the country should be divided into hospital regions with voluntary community hospitals to correlate hospital needs in the area and a central committee to coordinate this work.

A Provisional Council was appointed to consider how this should be implemented, but it was clear from their recommendations in 1938 that the prospect of anything being achieved was very remote, partly through lack of finance and partly for lack of willingness on the part of the local authorities to collaborate, while there was little enthusiasm on the part of the voluntary hospitals. However, the Commission did point out the successful experiment of the Oxford and District Joint Hospital Board and one or two other local coordination systems.

FROM OXFORD'S HOSPITAL BOARD TO A REGIONAL HOSPITAL TRUST

Lord Nuffield, recognizing the success of the Oxford scheme and the impasse which had arisen as to a national scheme, wrote to the Minister of Health, Walter Elliot: 'it is my hope that a truly national hospital service may be evolved which will embrace all that is best of both public and voluntary effort with the maximum economy to the State and to the private purse'. He then outlined his proposals, which were welcomed both by the Minister and his Chief Medical Officer, Sir Arthur McNalty. Elliot lost his place in the Cabinet when Chamberlain fell in 1940 and McNalty, who had been the architect of the emergency medical service which enabled the voluntary hospitals to survive financially throughout the war years, retired in 1941.

This was the political scene when Nuffield announced the establishment of the Nuffield Provincial Hospitals Trust in December 1939, although the Trust Deed was not completed until 25 June 1940. During the first three months of the Second World War, Germany and Russia had overrun Poland, we had lost two battleships, HMS *Courageous* and HMS *Royal Oak*. German magnetic mines had caused the loss of 60,000 tons of British shipping in a week, the battle of the River Plate had ended in the scuttling of the *Graf Spee*. This was the background against which the Trust started its first six creative years.

It might appear in those early days of the Trust that all that happened was that those who were responsible for the Joint Hospital Board, had left their Oxford office in King Edward Street and moved into the Trust's offices in London's Mecklenburgh Square, but this is far from correct. It is, of course, true that Lord Nuffield, who was President of the Joint Hospital Board, became one of the three ordinary trustees, though it is certain that not only did he take a very close interest in the activities of the Trust, but on occasions made recommendations as to particular grants or matters in which he was interested.

Sir William Goodenough, who had been Chairman of the Hospital Board, was now chairman of the governing trustees. The governing trustees were for the most part men of affairs with philanthropic interests, but there were also two medical men, Sir Farquhar Buzzard and Dr A.Q. Wells, a distinguished Oxford bacteriologist who took a considerable interest in the health matters of the city and county of Oxford.

Alderman William Hyde was the first secretary of the Trust, and brought to it his enthusiasm for hospital cooperation and his knowledge of the problems that had to be overcome. The Trust had appointed as their accountant Miss Livock, who had come to the Radcliffe Infirmary in 1937 when the Nuffield Postgraduate Scheme was about to commence and it was essential to know which part of the hospital expenditure should be allotted to the Nuffield Professors and which to the general hospital funds. Miss Livock was a brilliant mathematician as well as an experienced accountant: but like Dr William Farr, the nineteenth century founder of British Vital Statistics, she could see the laughter and the tears between the lines of figures. She introduced to the Infirmary a system of current costing, so that within a fortnight of the end of a quarter costing sheets would be available to the heads of service departments, giving details of allocated expenditure to the various wards and departments. So the effect of changes would be apparent within 3 months. This type of current costing was very necessary when cooperation and coordination between hospitals was being introduced. It was a matter in which the Trust would take considerable interest and would be able to give advice.

Until she retired from the Trust in 1952 Miss Livock was much concerned in enlightening both hospital administrators and ministerial officials as to the value of standard costing in the control of hospital expenditure. Something which was not adopted initially by the Ministry at the start of the National Health Service. In 1949 the Trust completed a study of standard costing based on the experience in the Radcliffe Infirmary, but also from other hospitals which had adopted it, and this was submitted in November of that year to the Committee of Hospital Administration of the Central Health Services Committee which advised the Minister on problems of the health service.

In May 1950 the Minister invited the Trust and the King Edward's Fund to undertake experiments in hospital costing. The Trust published its own report of an experiment in hospital costing in 1952, which produced convincing evidence that the system proposed by the Trust was not only economically practical but valuable in providing important information for control of hospital expenditure. But it was not until 1955 that the Stationery Office published the findings of the Joint Working Party on hospital costing.

Unhappily there is such a delay in the publication of the Department of Health's annual reports on hospital costing, that although they may be historically interesting, they serve little useful purpose in the control of hospital expenditure.

But to return to the early days, the trustees appointed a number of committees and councils to carry out the Trust's policy, and the most significant was the Medical Advisory Council, gathering under the chairmanship of Sir Farquhar Buzzard some thirty outstanding medical men, representing all branches, selected for their forward-looking attitude to developments in preventative and curative medicine. They met regularly at Oxford in Christ Church, considering both proposals for projects that might be supported by the Trust and their own ideas of the way in which the Trust Funds could best be expended.

HOSPITAL SURVEYS AND CLOUDS FROM WHITEHALL

There were also Regional Advisory Councils for England and Wales, Scotland, and Northern Ireland. It was plain to the Trust that before one could achieve a successful regional coordination of hospitals, both voluntary and local authority, it would be necessary to determine what was the range of hospital care available and what was required. This could only be determined by carrying out surveys by knowledgeable men and women in those areas which were designated as regions. So the Trust started this task and by 1941 had already completed three surveys, while the Medical Advisory Council had published *A National Hospital Service* setting out in broad terms the Trust's regionalization policy. Many of the ideas were incorporated into the Government's National Health Service, though not improved by bureaucratic concepts.

It was in October of that year that it was announced in the House of Commons that the Ministry of Health in connection with its plans for a post-war organization of the Health Service was intending to carry out hospital surveys, starting in London but ultimately throughout the country.

Following Walter Elliot's departure from the Ministry of Health there had been a kaleidoscopic series of ministers, but Sir Arthur McNalty's successor as Chief Medical Officer, Sir Wilson Jameson had, before he joined the Ministry, been quietly preparing his plans for the introduction of a National Health Service. 'Protomedicus Anglorum' as the *Lancet* called him, for by his tact, geniality, and ready helpfulness, he had avoided any fatal split with the medical profession during the negotiations. He had vast experience of medical administration and how to deal sensibly with his medical colleagues. He never hesitated to absorb from others ideas which he felt were useful and would adopt them quietly as his own.

Consequent on Mr Ernest Brown's statement, there were discussions between the officers of the Trust and the Ministry of Health and it was agreed that these surveys should continue, the majority being carried out by the Trust alone. But the same principles applied whether surveyors were appointed by the Ministry or the Trust. Ultimately these surveys were published by the Stationary Office in 1945 and year later the Trust issued *The Hospital Surveys, The Doomsday Book of the Hospital Services.* It was natural that these surveys revealed many centres of excellence but also grave deficiences and provided the future Regional Hospital Boards with invaluable blueprints for action.

THE TRUST'S WITHDRAWAL

In 1942 when the Trust agreed to the Government's request that they should not proceed further with their plans for coordination of hospital services, the Trust had already organized four regional and eleven divisional councils in England and Wales, while in Scotland and Northern Ireland there were either regional councils or advisory councils. The Berks, Bucks and Oxon Regional Council was one of the earliest to be fully organized because the existing Joint Hospital Board had become the Oxfordshire Divisional Council, while all the hospitals had considerable experience of coordination in the orthopaedic services; certainly in Oxfordshire and to some extent in the other divisions there had been for a very long time close coordination between local authority Health Services and the voluntary hospitals. The Council was also fortunate in that they had a powerful and active medical advisory committee under the chairmanship of Professor George Gask, with Dr Williams, the Medical Officer of Health for Oxford City, as vice-chairman.

THE REPORTS OF THE MEDICAL ADVISORY COMMITTEES

Professor Gask, who had recently retired from the surgical Professorial Unit at St Bartholomew's Hospital, had responded to Sir Farquhar Buzzard's appeal for experienced teachers to strengthen the clinical school, established in 1939 at the Radcliffe Infirmary, to meet the needs of Oxford clinical students evacuated from the London teaching hospitals. Gask took a full share in the teaching and clinical work at the Radcliffe Infirmary but it was his catalytic influence on the Regional Medical Advisory Committee that was outstanding. Reports on the regional coordination of cancer treatment, child health and maternity services, ophthamology, orthopaedics, pathology, and psychological medicine were produced, many being outstanding and serving as an inspiration for studies in other areas. They were gathered together and published as a single volume in 1947.

One might take as an example the cancer survey. In November 1944 a widely based conference was held in Oxford to consider the implications of the Cancer Act of 1939. It was agreed to ask the Medical Advisory Committee to carry out a survey and make recommendations how best the care of cancer patients in the region could be achieved. By using clinical, pathological, and mortality data the size of the living cancer population in the area was determined; something which had never before been attempted in Great Britain, although there had been previous studies in the United States. The Oxford figures were comparable. It was also possible to assess the number of patients requiring treatment for different types of cancer, the probable number of beds required, and bed occupancy. This report, like many of the others, proved invaluable when actual planning of services was carried out.

THE ACCIDENT SERVICE

Until 1945 the Trust allotted to each Regional Council administrative costs and also a yearly block grant to allow the development of individual projects. But in 1941 the first grant was made to the Oxford, Bucks, Berks Regional Council to establish an accident service at the Radcliffe Infirmary. This evolved in the following manner.

In 1940 the Radcliffe Infirmary decided, with support from the Medical Research Council, that it would be advantageous both from the point of view of treatment and research if patients suffering from burns, instead of being scattered through the various wards of the Infirmary should be gathered together in a single ward as a burns unit. This proved so successful from every point of view that Professor Seddon, (orthopaedics) Professor Cairns (neurosurgery), and Mr Corry (fractures) agreed that an attempt should be made to draw together accidents, burns, and infected hands into a single accident service. The proposal was submitted to Sir Farquhar Buzzard who found that the Nuffield Provincial Hospitals Trustees were sympathetic to the idea and made a grant of £1,500 to establish the service, which was opened under the direction of Mr J.C. Scott on the 1 July 1941. This was the first comprehensive accident service in a teaching hospital.

There had been accident units in some of the London county council hospitals and the Birmingham Accident Hospital which was opened as an experiment in a redundant hospital on 1 April 1941, but it was not until October of that year when the hospital had received considerable financial support from the Nuffield Provincial Hospitals Trust and Mr Gissane had become Director that the hospital gained fame as did the Radcliffe. Indeed, it used to be said that if you were going to have a serious motor accident it would be as well to have it in the vicinity of Oxford as the prospects of survival would be much greater.

In subsequent years the Trust made studies of these two accident services and their relationship to various types of injury and rehabilitation.

The Trust also gave money to the Radcliffe Infirmary to establish a diabetic clinic which would serve the whole region, and this, under the skilled direction of Dr A.M. Cooke and his successors, has continued to be a valuable part of the regional service.

STUDIES ON NURSING

In 1941 the Trust made its first grant in relation to nursing. This would prove to be one of the more important and long-standing interests, studying enrolment, education, and duties of nurses, with recommendations for improvements, in all these aspects, although it was not able to overcome the defects in the nursing service consequent on the Ministry's adoption of the recommendations of the Salmon report. The starting point in the Trust's nursing interest occurred in 1941 when it provided funds to extend to the provinces the work of the recruitment centre organized by the King Edward's Hospital Fund for London, and to arrange for similar recruitment centres in Scotland and Northern Ireland; incidentally this was the first occasion on which the 20-year-old Nuffield Hospitals Trust collaborated with the long-experienced King Edward's Fund and the association was to continue to the present day.

PENICILLIN AND THE NUFFIELD TRUST

In both Lord Nuffield's biographies there is mention of his interest in the development of penicillin, but the account in the *Nuffield Story* is clearly illusory as the dates are incompatible with facts. However, it is certain that during a critical period in the development of penicillin, the Nuffield Trust played a helpful, supportive role.

Howard Florey first arrived in Oxford from Australia in 1922, a brilliant young Rhodes Scholar aged 24. He returned as Professor of Pathology in 1935, determined to restore the department as part of the centre of excellence, the Oxford School of Experimental Medicine, which Osler had initiated when he brought Dreyer from Copenhagen, Gunn from Edinburgh, and Sherrington from Liverpool. Professor Georges Dreyer, Florey's predecessor in the Oxford chair, was an able experimental pathologist, recognized for the careful planning of his experiments, and had carried out some important work for the Air Force during the First World War and in immunology. He was a Fellow of the Royal Society and member of the Medical Research Council, on whose behalf he established a standards laboratory to ensure the quality and reliability of bacteriological diagnostic agents, something which would nowadays be called quality control.

In recognition of Dreyer's achievements, the Sir William Dunn Trustees offered the university £100,000 to establish a Department of Experimental Pathology, which was accepted in November 1922. Unhappily, unwanted press publicity forced Dreyer into publishing experimental results before they were properly controlled, and they were subsequently unable to be confirmed. Ashamed and humiliated, Dreyer virtually abandoned any further experimental work and devoted himself to the planning and supervision of the new Sir William Dunn School of Pathology, with the same singleness of purpose that he had shown in his experimental work, determined to provide the finest Department of Experimental Pathology in the British Isles. But when it was opened in 1927 Dreyer was an exhausted and ailing man, unable to enjoy the fruits of his labours.

Florey was delighted with his new department, for in addition to excellent laboratories and classrooms, there was a magnificent workshop for making apparatus for experiments and superb accommodation for experimental animals. Very soon the somewhat somnolent atmosphere of the Dunn School completely changed. Florey brought some of his staff from Sheffield, but other able young men and women were soon clamouring to join the department and a completely new pattern of lectures and practical classes was evolved. Though the Dunn School was magnificently designed, the University's financial allocation for its staffing and equipment was quite inadequate and so Florey had to spend much of his time trying to get grants in order that his research programme could proceed.

On 22 November 1935 Florey received a letter suggesting a meeting to discuss the future of medicine in Oxford from Hugh Cairns, a fellow Australian Rhodes Scholar, who had come to Oxford in 1919 and was now a surgeon on the staff of the London Hospital. Early in the summer Cairns had received a favourable response from Sir Farquhar Buzzard, the Regius Professor, to his proposal for a complete clinical school in Oxford, which, of course, was the germinal idea behind the Nuffield Postgraduate Medical Scheme. It is not known whether there was a meeting at this time between Cairns and Florey and what Florey's initial reactions were. But it is virtually certain that Cairns' rather more detailed memorandum, which was circulated informally in the spring of 1936 to members of the Board of Faculty Medicine and hospital consultants and also to Nuffield, had been seen by Florey. For Dr Gardner, Florey's reader in bacteriology, not only saw it but made criticisms of some details within it. The first public indication of what was afoot occurred during the annual meeting of the British Medical Association in Oxford in July 1936, when Buzzard, during his presidential address 'And the Future', after outlining his ideas on the regional coordination of hospital services, out of which the Nuffield Provincial Hospitals Trust arose, then went on to speak of ambitious dreams of a postgraduate medical school in Oxford, though in fact he was well aware by this time, that not only had Cairns met Nuffield but Nuffield had agreed to finance the scheme.

In the course of his address Buzzard remarked that observations were

Howard Florey (centre), with J.F. Falton (L.) and K.D. Keale (R.), (c. 1958).
[Courtesy of The Wellcome Institute Library, London]

being constantly made in the wards which would bear rich fruit if cultivated in a pharmacological, physiological or biochemical laboratory, and that the result of many laboratory experiments would stimulate new branches of enquiry at the bedside, if only the clinician and his scientific colleagues were more closely associated in their daily work and had the time and opportunities to discuss their problems.

Although Buzzard did not mention pathology, there is no doubt that Florey believed that he and his pre-clinical colleagues had been promised a share of the expected Nuffield benefaction to help pay for their own research and to encourage collaboration between the science departments and the new clinical units. He stated this in writing as late as 1952. However, when the university statute dealing with the Nuffield benefaction for the advancement of medicine was published at the end of 1936, it was clear that the income from the Trust funds was to be devoted to the clinical medical school, though funds were to be allotted to the fluid Research Committee to promote research in the whole field of medical science. Small annual research grants were allotted to the preclinical departments to be used at their own discretion.

In addition, there were, at any one time, three dominion demonstrationships which could be held in any of the preclinical departments, but this was not the sort of share of £2 million that Florey had imagined.

Florey had a low opinion of the intellectual ability of clinicians, and was in no doubt that it would be better for medical science if a larger portion of the benefaction had been allotted to the University scientific departments. So it was not altogether surprising that he was extremely annoyed when the Nuffield Committee rejected his application for a grant of £200 a year to facilitate his studies on the functions of the gastrointestinal tract, and he obtained an apology for the committee's actions from Sir Farquhar Buzzard. It so happened that this work led in a somewhat indirect way to the demonstration by Florey and his team that pencillin was indeed a wonder drug, the most powerful antibacterial therapeutic agent known at that time.

For some years Florey and his team had been studying the bacteriocidal activities manifested by certain bacteria and fungi, including *Penicillium*. It was not until 6 September 1939 that Florey, in an application to the Medical Research Council for a grant for Ernst Chain, his biochemist, revealed he intended to investigate the therapeutic activities of penicillin. Florey wrote 'the properties of penicillin hold out promise of its finding a practical application in the treatment of staphylococcal infections . . .

penicillin can easily be prepared in large amounts . . . in our opinion the purification of penicillin can be carried out easily and rapidly . . .'. In his covering letter to Mellanby, Florey observed 'I can get clinical co-operation from Cairns for any products which we produce . . .'. By this time there were excellent relations between the newly established Radcliffe Department of Pathology and Florey's university department; Macfarlane and I were taking part in his lecture courses; and there were free interchanges between the staff of both departments. Furthermore, the first Nuffield Orthopaedic Research Fellow, Dr J.M. Barnes, after 6 months at the Wingfield Hospital, had been working in Florey's department since 1938 learning experimental techniques.

It is remarkable that Dr Barnes, almost by chance, played a part in the early stages of the two major contributions to medical knowledge achieved in Oxford at this time. On 19 March 1940, Chain provided rather more than half (about 50 mg) of the total amount of the most purified preparation of penicillin he had yet made, so that Barnes (as Chain had not a licence for animal experiments) could inject it into two mice to see whether or not it was toxic; the mice were quite unaffected. Chain described it as the most crucial day in the history of penicillin, but Florey was not exactly pleased as it had been agreed that Chain would concern himself solely with the chemical aspects of the investigations and Florey with the biological. So Florey used the remains of Chain's penicillin to inject a mouse intravenously and, again, there was no untoward reaction.

Dr Barnes' second involvement in a major scientific achievement, occurred 18 months later. He had been put in charge of the burns unit at the Radcliffe Infirmary in May 1941 and one of the first patients he had to look after was a young electrician who had suffered severe burns involving nearly two-thirds of his body surface, which in the 1930s would certainly have been fatal. But this patient was surviving, partly because of chemotherapy, controlling sepsis, and transfusions, replacing the fluid lost from the raw skin surfaces. Under ordinary circumstances grafting of skin would have been carried out to assist the healing, but in this case there was so little normal skin available it was a problem. When Barnes was at the School of Pathology there was also a young zoologist, Peter Medawar, who was working on tissue culture. In September 1941 Barnes asked Medawar to see the patient in case he could think of some method of increasing availability of skin for grafting. Medawar was most distressed at the patient's condition and was determined that he should try and ameliorate it. But in spite of all his endeavours it was not possible in this particular case. However, a combination of the patient's confidence in survival and skilled plastic surgery, he left hospital 2 years later and when last heard of, a year or so ago, was in Canada selling kitchen furniture. He was proud that he had been a useful guinea-pig.

Forty years later Sir Peter Medawar FRS, Nobel Laureate for his achievements in immunobiology, recalling this period, said, 'I believe I saw it as my *métier* to find out why it was that it was not possible to graft skin from one human being to another and what could be done about it.' He continued, 'If anybody had then told me that one day in Oxford kidneys would be transplanted from one human being to another, not as a perillous surgical venture but as something more in the common run of things I would have dismissed it as science fiction.' But Sir Peter's progress was not always easy and in 1944 when little interest was taken in his research, as will be mentioned later, it was the financial support of the Trust, inspired by the enthusiasm of Professor Kilner, the Nuffield Professor of Plastic Surgery, that enabled good progress to be made in Medawar's work at this time.

Having considered the influence, indirect though significant, of Lord Nuffield's benefactions of one of Oxford's great contributions to medical science, the possibility of organ transplantation, we must return to the other, the clinical use of antibiotics.

On 25 May 1940, just 10 weeks after Florey and Barnes had carried out the toxicity test, enough purified penicillin was available for the crucial experiment, which neither Fleming nor anyone else had yet performed, to see if penicillin would protect animals against a fatal bacterial infection. Eight mice were each given a carefully calculated lethal dose of staphylococci; four were left as controls, two were given a single dose of penicillin, and two a graduated dose over a period. After 15 hours all the control mice that had received no penicillin had died. Whereas those that had received penicillin appeared perfectly well, though one of them died after 3 days. It is said that Florey described the result as a miracle and that a devout Roman Catholic hearing this some years later said how surprised Florey would have been had it really been one!

The results of these experiments were published in an article in the *Lancet* of 24 August 1940, entitled 'Penicillin as a Chemotherapeutic Agent', which concluded 'the results are clear cut and shows that penicillin is active *in vivo* against at least three of the organisms inhibited *in vitro*'. It was accompanied by a short and cautious editorial and, as Macfarlane remarks, 'indeed it is ironical that for the next two years

Florey was to spend much of his time and energy in trying to persuade people to take notice of what he felt to be the medical discovery of the century.'

Naturally, the next step was to see whether the effect of penicillin in animals would also be true in man. In those days there were no ethical committees or watchdogs, official or unofficial. The medical profession as a whole had a compassionate moral attitude to their patients and their patients trusted them. Of course there were black sheep, but they were seldom to be found in medical teaching schools. Florey turned to Professor L.G. Witts, the Nuffield Professor of Clinical Medicine at the Radcliffe Infirmary for help in the clinical trials, and he was given it in full measure.

Witts decided that Dr Charles Fletcher, a Cambridge medical graduate, who had recently been his house physician and was now a Nuffield Graduate Assistant, should be responsible for selecting the cases and supervising the trial. Dr Fletcher showed great skill in selecting the cases because it was essential, owing to the very limited amount of penicillin that it should be tried on patients with infections so severe that a fatal outcome was almost certain. Indeed, in the first case selected, a man aged 41 with streptococcal and staphylococcal septicaemia, treatment had to be abandoned after 5 days because of lack of further supplies of penicillin, and although there was a definite and transient improvement, he succumbed a month after the start of penicillin therapy. However, the outcome of the remaining five cases was even more miraculous than that of the animal experiments.

The results were published in the *Lancet* in August 1941, but even then there was little appreciation that a new era in medicine was about to begin.

Under wartime conditions the British pharmaceutical firms felt they could not undertake the experimental production of penicillin and so Florey with one of his colleagues, Dr Heatley, went to the United States and, after some difficultly, convinced the Americans of the importance of the work and production on a fairly large scale got under way.

By 1942 the prospects were so good that before long there would be enough penicillin available for more extensive clinical trials, and in March Howard Florey was elected a Fellow of the Royal Society, a fulfilment in his scientific career for he had been accepted by the country's leading scientists as one of themselves.

Professor Alexander Fleming, bacteriologist at St Mary's Hospital, who had discovered penicillin in 1928, visited the Dunn School shortly after publication of the first penicillin paper in 1940, and on 5 August 1942 Fleming rang Florey telling him that he had a friend seriously ill with a severe infection and would it be possible to let him have some penicillin as he believed this was the only hope of his recovery.

Florey took almost all his stock of penicillin up to London and explained to Fleming how it should be used and the results were spectacular, for the patient who had been at death's door recovered completely. The results caused great excitement amongst the medical staff at St Mary's Hospital.

On 30 August a leading article in *The Times* headed 'Penicillium' drew attention to the remarkable new therapeutic substance and, without mentioning names, referred to work in Oxford. The following day a letter appeared from Sir Almroth Wright, the Director of the Bacteriological Research Institute at St Mary's Hospital, in which he explained that Professor Fleming was the original discoverer of penicillin and had suggested its therapeutic possibilities. The press immediately stormed St. Mary's Hospital; there were interviews with Fleming and he was described as 'the man of the week'. Naturally there was no mention of Oxford or Florey.

On 1 September Sir Robert Robinson, the head of the Dyson Perrins Chemical Laboratory at Oxford wrote to *The Times* pointing out that it was Professor Florey and his colleagues in Oxford who had carried out all the preparatory work which turned penicillin into this outstanding therapeutic agent. Florey was both annoyed and alarmed when the reporters rushed down to Oxford. He told his secretary to send them away. So naturally they returned to St Mary's and were regaled with further achievements of Fleming and his hospital.

Florey was alarmed because he recalled that nearly 20 years before, when he was an undergraduate at Magdalen, taking his final examinations in physiology, the lay press was full of reports that the Oxford Professor of Pathology, Georges Dreyer, had discovered a cure for tuberculosis, a diaplyte vaccine. Indeed, Florey had written to his fiancée in Australia 'it holds forth an extraordinary promise of success, though at present owing to its limited trial they are very cautious. If it should be so it is the greatest discovery since Lister'. It transpired that Dreyer had given a lecture at St Mary's and without authority, Sir Almroth Wright had embroidered his lecture to the lay press. Unhappily the clinical trials did not uphold the reports in the lay press and Dreyer was quite unjustifiably blamed. Ashamed, it put an end to his scientific career.

This was the background to Florey's seemingly high-handed treatment of the reporters which certainly did not endear him to the gentlemen of the press.

He had sought, without avail, the help of the Secretary of the Medical Research Council and the President of the Royal Society, and when he proposed writing a correct account of the penicillin story, he was advised that this would be inexpedient. However, in March 1943 the *Lancet* published an article by Howard and Ethel Florey on 187 cases of sepsis successfully treated with penicillin. Without any lefthanded comment it made the situation as to the remarkable effectiveness of penicillin perfectly clear.

It was understandable that the members of Florey's staff were puzzled and somewhat disheartened at his failure to react to the Praed Street publicity and he himself was far from happy about how the affair was being handled. There was another more parochial matter that was worrying him, as the key members of his team, Abraham, Chain, Jennings, Heatley, and Sanders, were not holding university appointments, but were on Medical Research Council grants, which were renewed annually but gave no security of tenure. Sir Farquhar Buzzard was well aware of the unhappiness in the Sir William Dunn School, but he could do nothing in the academic sphere as he had retired from the Regius Chair in April 1942. His successor Sir Arthur Ellis, a delightful Canadian, had been Director of the Medical Professorial Unit in the London Hospital, but he was never able to comprehend the finesse of university politics and was beginning to show signs of what has been called 'the stateman's disease' hardening of the cerebral arteries.

Sir Farquhar Buzzard was a master in the tactical approach to a problem and though he realized that Florey disliked him, personal matters of this sort did not worry him. He was determined that the Oxford Medical School should regain the credit for its considerable achievements and, if possible, to restore the morale in the school of pathology.

First, Buzzard arranged that Lord Nuffield should come to the Dunn School, meet Florey and see what was going on there, which impressed him greatly. Secondly, the Medical Advisory Council of the Nuffield Provincial Hospitals Trust, of which Buzzard was chairman, agreed with the Medical Research Council that the Trust should be responsible for 5 years for the salaries of the five key members of Florey's team, at present being paid by the Medical Research Council, but the Council would continue to be responsible for equipment and other expenses in connection with their work.

In 1947 when the five years were coming to an end, Lord Nuffield himself endowed, at Lincoln College, Oxford, of which Florey was a

Professorial Fellow, three Nuffield Research Fellowships, to be held in the first instance by Abraham, Heatley, and Sanders. Chain and Mrs Jennings had already been appointed to college fellowships. Nuffield had already endowed a research scholarship, which was held between 1942 and 1945 at the School of Pathology by Dr Trevor Williams, who later became a scientific consultant and editor; he wrote the second volume of the Florey biography, very different in character from the first volume, Gwyn Macfarlane's brilliant *The Making of a Great Scientist*.

Sir Farquhar's endeavours to restore to Oxford and Florey the credit for the 'magic drug' were not restricted to creation of academic posts and financial adjustment. In April 1942 at a meeting of the Medical Research Council's War Wounds Committee, Major General Poole, the director of pathology in the War Office, reported that he had received from Florey sufficient penicillin to justify trials of its effectiveness in controlling infection in wounds occurring in the North African campaign. Brigadier Cairns, the Nuffield Professor of Surgery who, in addition to being in charge of the Military Head Injuries Hospital at St Hugh's College, Oxford, was also consulting neurosurgeon to the army, he was already receiving a grant from the Nuffield Trust for a study of the effects of penicillin in meningitis. In the late autumn of 1942, Buzzard, ever the strategist, suggested to Cairns that it might well be useful if Florey could go out to North Africa and see how penicillin was working under field conditions.

In November 1942 Florey was invited to the War Office for a meeting at which Cairns was also present, and it was agreed that a penicillin team consisting of a surgeon, bacteriologist, and technician with an issue of ten million units of penicillin, should go to Algiers, and that Florey and Cairns should go out at a later date to see how the arrangment was progressing. It took some time to arrange the final details, but Florey arrived in Algiers at the beginning of May 1943 and Cairns a little later. They returned to England at the beginning of September and quickly submitted reports both to the Medical Research Council and the War Office. There was no doubt that the visit was a great success, as it had been possible to determine what was the most effective method of using penicillin under active service conditions and the importance of training staff in its use. Florey had made a very favourable impression and it was not surprising that with his personal knowledge and experience in the properties of penicillin and the prestige that his recognized achievement had given him, that it was he who would be turned to for direction and advice in the new field of antibiotic therapy.

Nor is it surprising that when the Russians invited an Anglo-American scientific mission to visit their country at the end of 1943, it was Florey and Sanders who were selected as the British representatives.

Though Nuffield's and Cairns' ready response to Buzzard's suggestions had a notable impact on Florey and his team, the Praed Street ghost continued to irritate them for years.

THE SAD STORY OF THE OXFORD INSTITUTE OF SOCIAL MEDICINE

Sir Farquhar Buzzard resigned from the Regius Professorship in April 1942 and was suceeded by Professor (Sir) Arthur Ellis and it was in the same month that Professor John Ryle was appointed as the Professor of Social Medicine in the University of Oxford, with an institute to carry out his work, the first professorship in the subject in the United Kingdom and funded by a grant of £100,000 from the Nuffield Trust.

It was Sir Arthur McNalty, the former Chief Medical Officer at the Ministry of Health, and a member of the Trust's Medical Advisory Council, who was very anxious that social medicine, which like democracy meant many different things to different people, should gain an air of academic respectability by the establishment of a professorial chair. Sir Farquhar Buzzard was not in sympathy with this as he felt that what was meant by social medicine should not be an isolated discipline, but should be the attitude which doctors recognized as the background to their understanding of their patient's health or ill-health. Buzzard instanced the work of William Pickles in general practice and Professor Spence in child health. But his objections were overruled, though as it proved, in Oxford the appointment was not a success. John Ryle had been a highly successful physician but developed strong socialist views, and, in order to escape from the difficulty of Harley Street consulting practice, accepted the Regius Professorship of Physic of the University of Cambridge, but found he was out of sympathy with Cambridge academic life. So he hoped that the Oxford appointment would give him that intellectual satisfaction which he had lost.

Unfortunately, his institute, a former private college, was some distance from the Radcliffe Infirmary, with which he achieved little contact. Various projects were started in the institute but they came to little and Ryle's health was steadily deteriorating.

Another project supported by the Trust in association with the Institute was the Bureau of Health and Sickness Records. A good but premature idea. The proposal was to create curricula vitae of a whole section of the population by integrating health records (perinatal, child welfare, school medical examinations, etc., and illness records of general practitioners and hospitals), so that one could analyse possible factors determining the ill-health of an individual as well as providing demographic and epidemiological information, and to estimate probable demands on health care of various sorts.

The Trust was interested in the idea of linking records and established two bureaux, one in Oxford the other in Glasgow. It soon became apparent when the Oxford Bureau was started that the quality of hospital records in the area, with the exception of the Radcliffe Infirmary, was quite inadequate for such studies. So attention was turned to the improvement of hospital records, which was most successful and valuable. In Glasgow, individual studies of certain conditions were made but in neither bureau was the background available to achieve what had been propounded. It was some years later that Record Linkage, which was a reintroduction of the bureau idea, was supported by the Nuffield Trust and was facilitated by computer programmes.

On Professor Ryle's death in 1950 the University decided not to continue the chair; the institute was occupied by the Department of Mathematics, and accommodation for the Reader in Social Medicine, Dr Alice Stewart, was found elsewhere. She carried out important work on the radiation risks of exposing a fetus to obsetric radiography, and this led on to investigations about the radiation hazards to the population at large, which she continued after she had resigned her readership, though her work has been more widely appreciated in the United States than in this country.

THE FOUNDATION OF THE BRITISH STUDENTS' HEALTH ASSOCIATION

This gloomy account of the Oxford Institute of Social Medicine can be relieved by a single episode for which the Nuffield Trust was responsible.

In July 1947 a conference was held at the Institute on student health, attended by representatives from universities, colleges, and medical schools throughout the British Isles. This was the first occasion on which there was such a gathering.

In 1944 the Goodenough Committee stated that universities had a responsibility for the health of their students and should provide a properly organized student health service; views endorsed in a memorandum compiled at the Oxford Conference.

It was appropriate that this conference should have taken place in Oxford, for earlier that year the Radcliffe Infirmary had appointed a full-time Medical Officer to look after the health of the nurses, medical students, and other hospital staff, as well as the health of the whole hospital viewed as a living community. This was a novel appointment and Dr Clement Wells was a wise choice. He had served in the First World War for a short time then had been in general practice in Banbury and again became a Medical Officer in the Second World War. As a regimental medical officer and a school medical officer he had a real interest in healthy young people and would be understanding of their ailments, slight or severe. As a member of the Health and Hygiene Committee he could investigate the hygienic conditions of the wards and other hospital departments, bringing a practical view into the sometimes unrealistic recommendations of the bacteriologists. His room soon radiated the comfortable reassurance of general practice with the brass plate on the door, the consulting room with its eighteenth century furniture providing a relaxed atmosphere, while the efficient surgery with a carefully selected sister, who, as she served meals in the nurses' dining room, would notice the girl who looked worried or out of colour, and encourage her to see Dr Wells. From every point of view the appointment was a great success and when Dr Wells retired in 1961 his successor, Dr Juel-Jensen, continued the tradition, but now he was also Medical Officer to the University and developed a wide knowledge of tropical medicine so that undergraduate exploratory groups could be advised as to what the medical risks were and what precautions should be taken.

A consequence of the Trust's sponsorship of this conference was the foundation of the British Students' Health Association, which fulfilled much of what the Goodenough Committee felt was necessary.

THE SUCCESS OF THE BIRMINGHAM CHAIR OF SOCIAL MEDICINE AND THE REVIVAL OF THE OXFORD CHAIR

In 1972 the Trust made a grant of £35,000 over 5 years to re-establish in the University of Oxford a Chair of Social and Community Medicine, which shows every indication of serving a very valuable purpose in the Clinical school.

It was fortunate that the Nuffield Trust endowed their second chair of social medicine in Birmingham before the failure of the Oxford chair became apparent. For the University, in selecting Thomas McKeown for the chair, could hardly have made a better appointment and it would be no exaggeration to say that with this chair the Nuffield Trust established the academic status of community medicine.

McKeown, an Irish Rhodes Scholar from British Columbia, had his laboratory training in physiology and biochemistry, developed an enthusiasm for demography and medical history, and so recognized that the achievements of the Victorian social epidemiologist were thwarted by the uninspired bureaucratic medical officers of health, only interested in sanitation, and the consignment of the chronically sick, the aged, the physically and mentally defective to unsuitable and inadequate institutions. On the portals of their 'homes' were inscribed, for those who could see, the letters of Dante's 'Abandon Hope, all ye who enter here!'

McKeown's philosophy was that medicine should not try to create health but assist us to come safely into the world and comfortably out of it, and during life to protect the well and care for the sick and disabled. He was forthright in his views and did not mince his words, and so was not universally welcomed. But it was difficult to evade the logical clarity of his observations.

In 1976, just before he retired from his Birmingham chair, McKeown was elected to the Rock Carling Fellowship and spoke on 'the role of medicine: dream mirage or nemesis?' It was translated into French, Italian, and German. A man as forward looking and disturbing as Tom McKeown induced a good deal of wishful misunderstanding but received no civil honours. For example, he once wrote 'Our habits begin as pleasures of which we have no need and end as necessities of which we have no pleasure.'

Dr George Knox, his successor in the Birmingham chair, had been guided into community medicine by the humanity and intellectual stimulus of Sir James Spence, who had been his lecturer in paediatrics at Durham.

REACTIONS TO THE GATHERING CLOUDS FROM WHITEHALL

By 1943 the Regional Councils were not only coordinating their functions but beginning to make positive suggestions as to additional needs. For example, in Scotland there was a report on the whole question of staffing, both medical and administrative in the various hospitals. In Manchester the University received assistance in the expansion of their neurology department, and the department of education was supported in some pioneer work aimed at minimizing the isolation problems of the deaf.

The Nuffield Provincial Hospitals Trust had been characterized as provincial, because Nuffield had been convinced that coordination of the various hospital services in a limited area would be both more economical and enhance the quality of medical care provided. In the thirties it was clear that the London teaching hospitals, those indiosyncratic monoliths, would not consider any coordination one with another. Futhermore, there was already in existence the King Edward's Hospital Fund for London.

This charity, apart from its important colleges for training of administrators and senior nurses, had funds at its disposal and the independence to undertake projects for the betterment of hospital services in London, which no government department would dare to consider. Early in 1942 it was apparent that the Ministry of Health intended to create a national health service in the post-war period, and had made it clear that they did not wish the Nuffield Provincial Trust to continue its activities in the coordination of local authority and voluntary hospitals in the provinces, which had been the essence of Lord Nuffield's benefaction and had already proved so successful. Emasculated in this way, the Trust had to look to those endeavours which were aimed at improving medical services for the country as a whole and would not impinge on the Government's plans. On the other hand, Lord Nuffield hoped that the King Edward's Fund, untrammelled by ministerial restrictions, would support some of his medical charitable projects, if they were sympathetic to the ideas, as would prove to be the case at Guy's Hospital and the Royal College of Surgeons. The Fund has continued in association with the Nuffield Provincial Hospitals Trust to the present day.

So when the Nuffield Trust for Special Areas, one of the most original and inspired of his benefactions to industry reached its allotted span, at the end of 1943, the King Edward Fund was made the residual legatee and received more than £2 million to add to its funds.

REGIONAL GRANTS

There was a tendency to give particular support to projects arising in Oxfordshire, partly owing to local interest and partly because hospital coordination had been in existence longer and so was more advanced at this stage of the Trust work than elsewhere. Nevertheless, in 1944 the Yorkshire Regional Hospital Council produced a report in which they had looked at the needs of each of some sixteen different specialist branches of medicine and studied how these could be integrated. This was a stimulating exercise and attracted considerable interest. Then, in a slightly different way, the Essex Joint Hospital Advisory Council prepared a detailed study of a cancer service for the area.

In 1945 the Trust provided grants for the maternity hospital at Glasgow and also to assist the development of neurology in Manchester, but in that year there was also considerable and significant grant, not to Oxford University, but to the Radcliffe Infirmary to enable the appointment of a neurologist, Dr Ritchie Russell, not only to consolidate neurology in the region, but also to study and help members of the Armed Forces suffering from the late effects of head injuries. A number of these patients had been gathered together at the Military Hospital at Wheatley, which had evolved from the famous military head injuries hospital at St Hugh's College. Dr Ritchie Russell was already attached to the Ministry of Pensions Hospital at Stoke Mandeville, but when he was appointed to the Radcliffe Infirmary, as usual there were no beds allotted to him and his office was a corridor outside the Department of Neurosurgery and his desk the top of a filing cabinet. Within 20 years Professor Ritchie Russell had created the largest academic department of neurology in the country. A large staff of consultants, numerous assistants, ample beds, and a laboratory providing excellent postgraduate facilities, while the publications and research achievements of the department were all of a high order.

NYE BEVAN AND THE NATIONAL HEALTH ACT

In 1945 it looked as though the creative days of the Trust were numbered. For in that year Sir Farquhar Buzzard and Alderman Hyde, who had masterminded the details fo the regionalization activities of the Nuffield Provincial Trust, both died, and Prime Minister Atlee appointed that maverick politician Aneurin Bevan to be Minister of Health and Housing. The next year saw the publication of the National Health Act, the principles of which had gradually been developed by Sir Wilson Jameson and the Permanent Secretary, Sir William Douglas. Though Bevan's 'lower than vermin' onslaught on the Tories, which did him the more harm, occurred 2 years later, he had made it quite clear that he had no wish for anything like the Nuffield Provincial Trust to assist him in his plans for a national health service. Nuffield had been at loggerheads with government departments before but this was rather different, for the Chief Medical Officer, Sir Wilson Jameson, and his Deputy, Sir John Charles, who was to succeed him, were in no doubt of the valuable assistance they had received from the Nuffield Trust and hoped that this would continue in the future. So when Bevan left the Ministry of Health for the Ministry of Labour in 1951, it was possible to renew the close relationship which had existed for the past 10 years and would continue in the future.

CHANGES IN THE TRUST'S POLICY, TRUSTEES AND STAFF

However, the Trust had to examine its own position and future. The Trust had been established to facilitate the coordination of hospital services on a regional basis, and to provide funds in support of this and also for ancillary services related to that of the hospitals. Now the Government had accepted responsibility for organizing and financing a regional coordination of hospital services and, though there were considerable differences between the Government outlook and that of the Trust, there was no doubt that the basic function of the Trust had been acquired by the Government.

On the other hand, it was clear that there were many unresolved problems of the hospital services which must be settled in the near future. There was also the problem of linkage between the National Health Service and those ancillary services which were not covered by the National Health Act. Here again the Trust could very well operate to the advantage of the health of the public as a whole. So the trustees concluded that they still had a role and a very important one to perform, broadly in accord with the terms of the Trust Deed and that it could be summed up in three words 'Study, Experiment and Demonstrate'. This was to be the future philosophy of the Trust.

When Alderman Hyde resigned from the Trust's secretaryship owing to ill-health in 1943, he was succeeded by Mr Leslie Farrer-Brown who was already secretary to the Nuffield Foundation. He was a barrister who had studied economics at the London School of Economics and then held administrative posts in university departments, often with a medical bias. From 1942–44 he was secretary to the Goodenough Committee (interdepartmental committee on medical schools) and it was from that post that Sir William Goodenough suggested that he should come to the Nuffield charities. He was secretary to both bodies from 1944 until 1955 when he became Director of the Foundation and, with Lord Nuffield's approval, a trustee of the Nuffield Provincial Trust. So it was that Mr Farrer-Brown was administrative advisor to the trustees during three critical periods. First, that leading up to the development of the National Health Service; secondly, the rearrangements after the National Health Service Act came into operation on 5 July 1948; and, thirdly, the start of the present period when, to some extent, the Trust had changed its functions.

THE ROCK CARLING ERA

In 1945, at the age of sixty-eight, Sir Ernest Rock Carling, who for some time had been a member of Buzzard's Medical Advisory Council, succeeded him as chairman of what was now the Medical Advisory Panel and so became a trustee. It was during the next twelve or so years, that Rock Carling greatly influenced the outlook and activities of the Nuffield Provincial Trust. An able but adventurous surgeon and an excellent teacher of the rather didactic type, Rock Carling had devoted five years to the detailed planning and supervision of the building of his Westminster Hospital Medical School and Nurses Home, so that he knew more about the problems and successes than did the architect. Forward thinking and enthusiastic, he had earlier recognized the importance of radium and X-rays in the treatment of cancer and so played an important part in the development of this type of therapy. He was also in considerable demand as chairman of many medical charitable organizations.

As a consequence of his experience in hospital planning, he encouraged the trustees to take a critical interest in the design of hospital buildings and their influence on the efficiency and satisfaction of those that worked in them. But before this approach could be pursued there were still, awaiting completion, some of Buzzard's plans to introduce new subjects into the clinical schools.

There was the establishment in March 1948 of the Chair and Department of Child Life and Health, at the Queen's University Belfast; and the first part of the Slough Industrial Health Centre was opened on 1 May 1947, although its planning went back a long way.

THE SLOUGH INDUSTRIAL HEALTH CENTRE

In the 1920s the Slough Trading Company, of which Noel Mobbs was the Managing Director, purchased 700 acres of land at Slough from the Government, which had used it as a transport repair depot, though locally it was known as the 'dump'. The Trading Company soon established a number of small industries on the estate, which has now evolved into the important industrial area of Slough. By the middle of the 1930s there were about one hundred firms on the estate, employing some 8,000 workers, and the increased population together with the number of accidents at work, made a hospital very desirable. So in 1938 Mr Mobbs launched an appeal which raised some £20,000 but the onset of the war put an end to any such plans.

However, Mr Mobbs realized that there might be a long delay before a hospital could be built at Slough and wondered whether it might be possible to establish in the area a health centre, which at that time was much talked about, although its actual nature was far from clear. So in 1945 Mobbs discussed this idea with his fellow Nuffield Provincial Hospitals Trustees. It is opportune at this stage to mention the character of the trustees. A few were medical men and hospital teachers, but the majority were men and women of insight and ability with a sympathetic interest in the welfare of their fellows. Some were humane leaders of industry, commerce, or finance with the gift of recognizing the potentialities of a proposal or the capabilities of the proposer. It was an Oxford professor of moral philosophy, John Smith, who maintained that the main, if not the sole, purpose of education was that it 'enabled one to detect when a man was talking rot'.

To return to Slough – from his discussions, Noel Mobbs learnt that the Nuffield Foundation was interested in industrial health and it seemed likely that an industrial health centre could meet the needs of the town and the industrial estate, better than an 'ordinary' health centre, and that it was quite likely that the Nuffield Health and Hospital Services Fund, which was associated with the Provincial Trust would give some financial support. From the Trust's point of view it was an attractive experiment as the estate embraced a large number of small firms with differing activities and differing health hazards. Indeed, within a three mile radius there were some 300 firms employing about 30,000 workers. So Nuffield funds provided £25,000 and £15,000, while the industrial estate purchased 50 acres of Farnham Park for £25,000 to serve as a rehabilitiation centre.

When the scheme was announced it was welcomed very strongly by the Medical Officer of Health and some of the firms were quite enthusiastic. But the majority, like the representative of the workers and the general practitioners, were sympathetic or at the most showed modified rapture.

It was felt that there was sufficient support and no overt opposition to the scheme and so the plans went ahead. The first Medical Director, Dr Austin Eagger, was a west-country physician who had part-time responsibility for industrial concerns; he has also been a regimental medical officer and from 1941 was responsible for organizing, and then commanding, the airborne medical services.

Part of the community centre was converted into a central clinic, and there were two subsidiary clinics as well as a mobile dressing station. Farnham Park was adapted to provide a rehabilitation centre, accommodating sixty in-patients and thirty out-patients. The clinic was opened on 1 May 1947 and Farnham Park in October of the same year. Almost immediately the practical success of the service and its value as a research centre was apparent, and the opposition rapidly melted away.

Now, over 40 years later, the Slough Occupational Health Service is a non-profit-making organization under the chairmanship of Sir Nigel Mobbs, son of Sir Noel, who continued as a Nuffield Trustee until he resigned in 1955, though he remained as Chairman of the Nuffield Health and Social Services Fund until his death a few years later. The service has its main clinic at Slough, with excellent physiotherapy facilities and clinical and industrail research laboratories, while there are subsidiary clinics at Hillingdon and High Wycombe. It has a staff of four medical officers, nurses and physiotherapists, and several visiting consultants. It has a membership of 25,000 employees from 650 firms, who contribute £25 per annum for each employee. The service provides pre-employment examinations, immediate treatment of injuries or illnesses sustained at work, and continuing treatment after consultation with the general practitioner; this also applies to physiotherapy. There are special examinations for those involved in hazardous industrial activities and general counselling. The service also provides regular examination of executives, a 'well woman screening programme', and educational discussions on health matters. Not only has the Slough service proved both popular and beneficial for management and employees but it has set an example throughout the world for an organization of this type.

Venture in Industry (1965) is an account of the philosophy and achievements of the service by its first medical director, Dr Austin Eagger. The success of the Slough Industrial Health Service has resulted in the setting up of six analagous industrial health services, although each differs in some respect from the original Slough model; all have received financial support either from the Trust or the Foundation, or both.

In 1955 an Industrial Health Service was established in the new town of Harlow. Lord Taylor was, for a short time, its part-time director. It now looks after 150,000 employees from 150 companies with a medical director, three assistant medical officers, nurses, physiotherapists, etc., and continues to provide an excellent service. In 1959, in association with the Nuffield Department of Industrial Medicine of the University of Newcastle upon Tyne, a North of England Industrial Health Advisory Service was established. In 1962 other centres were set up in Rochdale. Dundee, Bromwich, and Smethwick. The Mobbs family have a right to be proud of the influence that Sir Noel's inspiration has had on this valuable link between industry and health care.

In the 1940's when Noel Mobbs was wondering whether a health centre would meet the needs of the growing population of his Slough Industrial Estate, there was considerable enthusiasm for the idea, nebulous though it often was, of a health centre. In the Health Service Act it had been suggested that health centres would form a link joining the general practitioners, the local authority health services, and the hospitals. But when these failed to materialize there were other ideas of what a health centre was, or could be. The Pioneer Peckham Health Centre, opened in 1925 was of a very special type, and in its early and later days enjoyed gifts from Lord Nuffield of some £25,000. It closed during the war, was opened again after the war, but collapsed through lack of funds in 1950. For Sir Farquhar Buzzard in 1936 the health centre was a joint endeavour between hospital and general practitioner orientated towards 'positive health'.

EXPERIMENTAL HEALTH CENTRES

In view of the Trust's change in policy and its intention to experiment in the field of the ancillary medical services, it was decided to establish three types of health centre in 1949. The first was Derbyshire House, a teaching health centre in collaboration with the University of Manchester, in which there would be a group of general practitioners looking after a fairly densely populated area, with easy access to consultant's advice, and which would also provide the opportunity for medical students to see exactly how general practice was conducted. This centre was financed jointly by the Rockefeller Foundation and the Trust. Ten years later the Trust stated that there was to be an investigation as to how the centre had functioned, but as yet no report has been published.

The second experiment was at Corby in Northamptonshire, a town that had expanded rapidly in recent years due to a large industrial centre. It had no hospital in the immediate vicinity, so it was decided that it would be useful to establish a diagnostic centre which could provide facilities, such as X-rays and laboratories, while consultants from the hospitals would visit there and discuss patients with the general practitioners, who retained their own consulting rooms and surgeries. The local authorities would hold their clinics at the centre.

The centre was opened by Lord Nuffield on 23 April 1954. Today, the centre is meeting the needs of the people of Corby to a standard far higher than was envisaged originally. Some 25,000 patients attend each year for diagnostic services, apart from those attending for rehabilitation. Attached to the centre was a twenty-bed general practitioner maternity unit, which served the town until 1976 when a district maternity department was opened at Kettering. In 1972 the Willowbrook Health Centre was built adjacent to the Nuffield Diagnostic Centre and this provides accommodation for eight general practices with about twenty-five partners and has ancillary facilities such as community dental care. Arrangements are in progress to provide accommodation for adult mentally handicapped patients and terminal care in additional buildings.

The third experiemental health centre was at the new town of Harlow, where three centres – Nuffield, Sydenman, and Osler – were opened in 1955 in different parts of the town; the major difference here was that, as a new town, there was no existing accommodation for general practices. The centres also accommodated dental practioners and local authority clinics.

Since then three further health centres have been opened, named Addision, Lister, and Keats. Addison House, completed in December 1957, was the first stage in the evolution of the Harlow Medical Centre, leading to the building of Princess Alexandra's Hospital. Before the hospital was built there was a development of specialist clinics served from St. Margaret's Hospital Epping, and local authority clinics. With the development of these specialist services at the hospital medical centre, the health centres are becoming largely restricted to general practitioner services and ancillary staff. One of the difficulties has been inadequate car parking. It was anticipated originally that the majority of Harlow patients would walk to the health centre but now there is nowhere to put their cars and such car parks that there are, are used by the staff of the centre itself.

The Trust had invested about £250,000 in the medical services of Harlow. At first Harlow Development Corporation acted as the Trust's agent, but now that the lease has come to an end the health centres are administered by a local charitable trust.

The family doctor centre, which was opened in Edinburgh in 1959, had some functional affinities with the Corby diagnostic centre. But here the centre is serving some 100 general practitioners in a part of Edinburgh not far from the University.

THE WITNEY HEALTH CENTRE

The Nuffield Health Centre at Witney opened in 1965, was one of the latest supported by the Trust, and is of particular interest as it is the first centre to conform closely to the ideals laid down by Sir Farquhar Buzzard in 1936. Its achievement was due to the inspiration and enthusiasm of the late Dr Slee, the senior partner in the Witney practice.

Witney is a rapidly expanding Oxfordshire market town which was looked after by a single group practice of six partners, who were also responsible for some 80 square miles of surrounding countryside and small villages, with a total population of 20,000. The nearest hospitals were in Oxford some 12 miles away, though for a long time certain consultants had held clinics in Witney, often in church halls and the like.

In the 1960s an area of reclaimed marshland in the centre of Witney was being developed as a municipal centre, with police station, fire station, library, etc. It occurred to Dr Slee, realizing that the practice's surgery and clinics were far from satisfactory, that it would be an excellent plan to create a health centre in this area, combining general practitioner, hospital, and local authority needs. The idea met with approval of the Trust who made a grant of £100,000 and it was agreed that the rent should be shared between the three interested parties. The centre was opened in 1965, providing consulting rooms for the general practitioners and the visiting consultants, surgeries, examination rooms, rooms for clinics, a dental department, X-rays and laboratories, and a large physiotherapy department. There were regular visits from consultants representing some dozen specialties, mostly attending every fortnight, and following an arrangement instituted by Dr Warin, the city Medical Officer of Health, local authority nurses and health visitors were attached to the general practitioners, another great advance.

In spite of ministerial vagueries in general practitioner policy, the Witney centre continued to prosper just as the town and surroundings continued to enlarge.

In 1973 the Oxford Regional Health Authority decided to create a community hospital and a second health centre to accomodate the enlarging general practice on land immediately adjacent to the Nuffield Centre, but changes in governmental policy resulted in the buildings not being completed until 1979, although the Windrush Health Centre was not opened until 1980 and only part of the community hospital could be opened a year later.

By now four of the general practitioners were working in the original

Nuffield Health Centre and four in the new Windrush Health Centre, and although relations were entirely amicable, it was decided it would be better to divide the practice functionally into two parts. This took place in April 1985. The following year the Nuffield Hospital Trust offered to sell the Health Centre to the general practitioners as the 21-year lease had been reached, but, owing to the uncertain condition of the building, this offer was rejected and the building was purchased by the Oxford District Health Authority, who became the new landlords on 1 January 1987.

The evolution and success of the Witney Nuffield Health Centre, which was recorded in a film in 1970, has become widely known and widely copied, and more than confirms that the way of developing an attitude of positive health was to integrate on a regional basis the hospital, general practitioner, and preventative services in a health centre occupied by the general practitioners, 'the fingers of the profession' as Buzzard called them.

LORD TAYLOR AND 'GOOD GENERAL PRACTICE'

The Trust's interest in general practice was not limited to health centres, but also in the function of general practice itself. In 1949 the Trust appointed a Dr J.S. Collings to make a survey of general practice, which was published in the *Lancet* in 1950, entitled 'General Practice in England Today, a Reconnaissance'. It was extremely critical of the whole general practice pattern and caused considerable concern and resentment. The Trust set up a Committee under Sir Wilson Jameson to consider how a more objective study could be obtained. Dr Stephen Taylor (created Lord Taylor of Harlow in 1958 as one of the first life peers) was invited to undertake this. He had served as a neuropsychiatrist in the RNVR and joined the Ministry of Information as Director of Home Intelligence; he instituted social surveys which, in one form or another, have continued ever since. As Vice-Chairman of the Harlow Corporation he was largely responsible for instituting the health centres, though at that time his socialist beliefs coloured his medical views. Adopting the principles he had used in his social surveys, his study was essentially a non-statistical, detailed, descriptive social review of the work of ninety-four doctors in thirty practices distributed throughout England and Wales. Half were in industrial areas, six in residential areas, and nine in the countryside. There was no attempt at a random sample but a selection of what were believed to be sound general practices. The outcome was his *Good General Practice 1954,* which was one of the most important contributions that he made to British medicine. It came at a time when general practice, depressed and under attack, was much in need of encouragement for the future.

Since then, the Trust has made many and various studies of all aspects of general practice but perhaps one of the most important, in addition to the general postgraduate scheme, has been the support given to the Royal College of General Practitioners on the vocational training of general practitioners.

THE FUNCTION AND DESIGN OF HOSPITALS

The Trust's dozen Rock Carling years were characterized by the investigation into the function and design of hospitals and the job-analysis studies, typical of Sir Ernest's practical and clear-minded approach to a problem.

The grand design for the functional creation of a hospital was directed by Mr Richard Llewelyn Davies, supported by a small team which included a physician and a nurse, aided by a whole range of consultants of various specialties from this country and abroad. After much exploratory work, it was decided to build an experimental ward at Larkfield Hospital, Greenock, and at Musgrave Park Hospital, Belfast, while the experimental out-patient unit was established in the Corby Diagnostic Centre; in addition, an operating suite being built at a Belfast Hospital was based on the studies of the team.

Studies in the Function and Design of Hospitals published in 1955 summarizes the 5 years of the experiment and became the standard work of reference for hospital architects. When the Trust's experimental unit came to an end in 1954, Mr Llewelyn Davies became Director of the Division for Architectural Studies of the Nuffield Foundation until it was disbanded in 1960 owing to Mr Davies being elected Professor of Architecture in the University of London.

THE JOB ANALYSIS OF NURSES

The Trust's interest in the 'job analysis' of nurses' work goes back to their support, in 1941, of the King Edward Hospital Fund's recruitment centre and that of the Department of Health for Scotland. The report of the Ministry of Health's working party on recruitment and training of nurses

(1947) showed that they had insufficient information as to exactly how a nurse's day was spent. So the Trust decided to make a practical investigation or 'job analysis' of both the hospital and the public health nurse. This, of course, required the building-up of a job description. A complete analysis of the work content in twenty-six wards in thirteen hospitals was made and an analogous method was used for the various types of public health nurse. What the survey provided was the essential factual information, which up to that time was lacking, of the work being performed by nurses in various fields, and provided a reasonably reliable basis on which any alterations in training or practice might be made. The report with its recommendations appeared in 1953 as *The Work of Nurses in Hospital Wards*. It was probably one of the most influential investigations that the Trust carried out. The report was translated into several languages and formed the basis of discussions, at the World Health Organization, the College of Nursing, and the Ministry; it had a profound effect on the training and practice of nursing in hospitals.

These two studies were far from being all that was achieved during the Rock Carling era and it would be sufficient to mention some of the areas of interest that were initiated during this period. But reference should first be made to the £27,000 grant given in 1954 to build a new Mignot Memorial Hospital on the island of Alderney. The entire population was evacuated during the Nazi occupation and when they returned they found that their little hospital, once a public house, with the bar converted to the operating theatre and delivery room, was in a poor state. They turned to the Trust for help, which was sympathetically received; it was also an opportunity to design a hospital and health centre in a unique situation. The Foundation's division of architectural studies, after consulting with the local practitioners, the matron, and the President of the States, designed a six-bedded hospital with out-patient and other facilities, built in local stone. The foundation stone was laid by Her Majesty the Queen on 27 June 1957.

THREE NEW INTERESTS – THE AGED, THE HANDICAPPED, AND AUDIT

In 1952 the final report on the functions and design of hospitals was published, and the Trust then turned its attention to three subjects which would continue to be of interest up to the present day – geriatrics, the handicapped, and audit. Mary Sargaison's *Getting Old in Common Lodgings* (1954) raised a corner of the curtain on one aspect of old age. For she was the almoner to the geriatric unit of the Belfast City Hospital. She well knew the problems and the independent pride of these old people and soon there were reports not only from Aberdeen, Glasgow, and Sheffield, but also from Guildford and Oxford. 'Successful rehabilation of the aged after injury' was the keynote of a seminar at the Slough Industrial Health Centre, and others followed its example.

It was also recognized that help was needed for the handicapped, and one of the earliest grants in this field was to assist in providing a mobile meal service in a part of Essex where the meals were cooked in hospital kitchens and often were specially prescribed for the handicapped confined to their homes. This was followed by a whole range of grants to assist the handicapped in many and various ways. Today, aiding the handicapped is one of the main concerns of the Trust.

It is doubtful whether the Trustees realized that when, in 1952, they approved a grant to allow a study of the value of laboratory investigations, they were supporting one of the earliest instances of medical audit; this was followed by studies of anaesthestic deaths. But it is probably better to delay this matter until CEPOD (confidential enquiry into peri-operative deaths) is being discussed.

In 1944 the Trust established a Chair of Psychiatry at Leeds University, but 10 years were to elapse before any further grants were made in relation to mental care. However, since 1954 there has been much active support in this field, with an average of four new grants each year. Many of these were investigational but, in addition, the Trust provided grants for the building and equipping of day centres, community mental health centres, sheltered workshops, and schools for mentally disturbed children. Very often successfully bridging the gaps between the responsibilities of hospitals, local authorities, and education.

ALTERATIONS IN OUTLOOK

During the Rock Carling era both the internal arrangements and the outlook of the Trust began to alter once again; the death of Sir William Goodenough on 25 May 1951 had a profound effect.

Quite apart from his financial genius, Goodenough and Buzzard had influenced Lord Nuffield's philanthropic designs for more than a quarter of a century. It was Goodenough who proposed and achieved the setting up of the Provincial Trust and the Foundation so that the decisions on how the benefactor's millions should be spent were largely in the hands of trustees rather than Nuffield himself.

Lord Nuffield appointed as chairman, both of the Foundation and the Trust, the Hon. Sir Geoffrey Gibbs KCMG. He was also a banker, having been chairman of Barclays Overseas Development Corporation, but he was also chairman of the National Corporation for the Care of the Aged and other charitable enterprises.

In July 1957 Lord Nuffield welcomed as new trustees Lord Cohen of Birkenhead CH, who had been a member of Buzzard's medical advisory council from the Trust's early days, and Dr John Fry OBE, a very knowledgeable general practitioner.

In 1958, Sir Ernest Rock Carling retired from the Trust; he died two years later.

There were also administrative changes, Leslie Farrer-Brown, who had been secretary of both the Trust and the Foundation since 1943, became Director of the Foundation in 1955, but at Lord Nuffield's suggestion became a hospital trustee until he retired in 1968.

Gordon McLachlan, who had joined the Trust in 1953, became its secretary in 1956, an office that he held for more than 30 years. An Edinburgh graduate, McLachlan served as a gunnery specialist in the RNVR; then training as an accountant, he worked in Edinburgh for a while and then became the first deputy treasurer of the newly formed North West Regional Hospital Board and, in 1953, succeeded Miss Livock as accountant to the Trust. He was also secretary to the National Corporation for the Care of the Aged, whose chairman was Sir Geoffrey Gibbs. The latter shared with Goodenough not only his banking ability but also that of recognizing the qualities of junior members of his staff, an ability which Gordon's subsequent career fully endorsed. Generous in outlook, McLachlan was always ready to encourage promise in young people. The number of important lectures that he was invited to deliver all over the world is a confirmation of his excellence in exposition, though sometimes his approach was idiosyncratic. On occasions there was a lack of concurrence of viewpoint between the trustees and their secretary. Nevertheless, by the mid-1970s Gordon had become something of an *éminence grise* in the world of hospital administration, for he knew his ways about the corridors of power on both sides of the Atlantic, enjoyed his perlustrations there, and was always welcomed by those in authority, for not only were many of his ideas stimulative, but he never sought or expected that they would be acknowledged. So it was very appropriate that he should hold the Rock Carling Fellowship during the Trust's Jubilee Year.

The third, and probably least important, change during this period was that, in 1955, the Trust gave up their offices in Mecklenburgh Square and joined the Foundation for about 10 years at Nuffield Lodge before moving to their own offices in nearby Prince Albert Road.

In Sir Farquhar Buzzard's day the Medical Advisory Council was a carefully selected group of forward-thinking medical men who knew one another well and could meet comfortably in a college senior common room. In those days there were no specialist sub-committees or working parties but there were the regional hospital councils, many of which had their own medical advisory committees. Projects would develop from the discussions in the advisory council or there might be applications which the council would consider from the regional committees or from indviduals seeking financial support for a project. The trustees, after considering the views of the advisory council, would come to their own decisions.

When Sir Ernest Rock Carling was chairman of the Medical Advisory Panel it had swollen to thirty members with a general purposes committee. Each of the main projects in which the Trust was interested had its own advisory panel. The regional committee had largely been disbanded but there were still advisory committees for Northern Ireland and Scotland.

THE FELLOWSHIPS AND PROJECT PREPARATIONS

When Sir George Pickering became chairman of the Medical Advisory Panel he preferred to work with a small group and so reduced the membership to five; thus it remained. The number of sub-committees and working parties was greatly reduced. A consequence of these changes was that the trustees themselves initiated new approaches, and one of these was the appointment of fellowships. The first of these, founded in 1961 was the Rock Carling Fellowship, in memory of their distinguished fellow trustee. It was to be awarded annually to a person of proven ability, chosen by a selection committee. The fellow would be required to deliver a lecture, subsequently to be published, which would crystallize contemporary thinking on one of those subjects in which Sir Ernest took a special interest, such as medical education, ethics, hospital services, radiation, etc.

The lectures delivered by the first fellows – Sir John Charles, 'The Social Context of Medicine' (1962); Sir Robert Platt, 'Doctor and Patient, Ethics, Morale, Government' (1963); Professor W.V. Mayneord, 'Radiation and Health' (1964) – set the high tone which has been maintained to the present day, as much a tribute to the ability of the panel of selectors as to that of the fellows themselves.

Initially it had been the trustees' intention that the fellowships should only be offered for a period of 5 years, but they proved so popular that it was decided to continue them and double the stipend. It might seem invidious to select from this galaxy individual lectures for remark, but there were two or three in which the subject chosen was particularly apposite at the time of its delivery, such as Professor Butterfield, 'Priorities in Medicine' (1968); Professor Archie Cochrane, 'Effectiveness and Efficiency, Random Reflections on Health Services' (1973); Professor Tom McKeown, 'The Role of Medicine; Dream, Mirage or Nemesis?' (1976); Sir Raymond Hoffenberg, 'Clinical Freedom in Today's Society' (1986).

A year after the trustees founded these fellowships, they established a very different, but also important, visiting fellowship arising from the friendly relations that existed between Gordon McLachlan and Dr Edwin Crosby of Johns Hopkins Hospital, who was chairman of the American Hospital Association. Each year at Ithaca, New York, the Cornell University Graduate School of Business and Public Administration organizes a four-week development programme for hospital administrators. The Trust was invited to nominate a senior administrative officer from Great Britain to attend the course free of charge, although the travelling expenses would be met jointly by the Trust and the employing authority. This arrangement proved highly successful, for not only were the fellows able to attend the course, but also to visit American hospitals and discuss mutual problems. The Lycett Green enquiry into the recruitment, training, and promotion of administrative and clerical staff in the hospital service (HMSO 1963) recommended that there should be training in management subjects. The Trust had already achived this, not only by these fellowships but also by giving financial support to the Nuffield Centre on Hospital and Health Service Studies at the University of Leeds.

A little later the Trust, in association with King Edward's Fund, established an American visiting fellowship, later known as the Crosby Fellowship, enabling senior American administrators to spend 6 months discussing their mutual interests with their opposite numbers in this country.

In the early 1960s another policy change was suggested to the trustees by McLachlan, in that from time to time he would present a series of projects which it seemed might well be suitable for investigation by the Trust. The range of subjects suggested was often very broad, but once it was decided which project should be studied an informal seminar would usually be held to work out details, sometimes inviting experts to illuminate the discussion or even appoint a research fellowship, as occurred in Professor Ashford's department at Exeter when the Trust was interested in information management. Sometimes the subject selected by a Rock Carling Fellow or the new Queen Elizabeth the Queen Mother Fellowships might prove relevant. This arose when Dr Russell Nelson, former president of Johns Hopkins Hospital, came over as a Crosby Fellow in 1973, and his stimulating observations were published in the *Lancet.*

In 1984 Professor Alain Enthoven, Professor of Public and Private Medicine at Stanford University, was invited on a special fellowship, as the Trust was interested in the possibility of the interrelationship of public and private medicine in the health service.

An advantage of this careful planning was that it gave an opportunity of encouraging junior staff members in some of the provincial hospitals to undertake *ad hoc* surveys in relation to the main problem, and so reveal their capabilities.

When all the information had been gathered together there would be a symposium with a general discussion, and then the study would be prepared for publication, which was the basic object of the exercise. Naturally this procedure was only adopted in major projects and grants were still being given for many smaller investigations.

In the Fifth Report (1958–61) is, I believe, the first mention of a private conference organized by the Trust. This took place in December 1960 with a discussion on operational research; a rather nebulous wartime concept of which the Trust had its own unit, under the direction of Brigadier J.D. Welch from 1949 until his death in 1963. This unit made two useful studies, first on a central syringe service and the second on central sterilization. But the conclusions of the conference were, as far as I know, never published. Sir George Schuster, the chairman of the Oxford Regional Hospital Board, was very enthusiastic about operational research, although it was never very clear what its merits were. It was a wartime applied science technique to solve problems in the field. Operational research has given way to Oxon's applications. There may be a useful role for this form of enquiry for planning in the National Health Service of the future.

'MEDICINE, A LIFELONG STUDY'

The Trust's second private conference, held at Oxford a year later, on 16 and 17 December 1961, had a very different impact. After nearly 20 years, the chairman of the Trust's Medical Consultative Committee was again the

Regius Professor of Medicine at the University of Oxford. Sir George Pickering was a sound physician, and had made some valuable contributions in clinical research following in the traditions of Sir Thomas Lewis, but he was outstanding as a stimulating and provocative thinker, enlivened with a delightful whimsical personality. 'Medicine a Lifelong Study' was the theme of Sir George's Christ Church Conference. Supported by the Trust he had gathered together the key representatives of the universities, the University Grants Committee, the Ministry of Health, the Royal Colleges, the British Postgraduate Medical Federation, and the Regional Boards.

He opened the conference by asking three consecutive questions. Is postgraduate education important? If so, is it adequate? If it is not adequate, what can be done to improve it immediately and in the future?

The Regius Professor could not be gainsaid. Obviously there were organized postgraduate courses at London, Edinburgh, etc., and many of the university hospitals, available to the young doctors working there and to the general practitioners in the vicinity. This would not only be a stimulus to enliven what was often a heavy load to bear, while an awareness of modern advances would enhance the care of their patients. To achieve this in each regional hospital there should be a senior doctor who would be the clinical tutor. A seminar room and a library and perhaps a lunch room for informal discussion would be needed. It would also depend on the willingness of the senior medical staff to provide the teaching, aided perhaps by colleagues from other hospitals.

There was an immediate response at the conference, a sense of urgency, and an outline was prepared as to how this regional postgraduate education could be achieved. Although this was a completely new venture for the Trust, the trustees set aside £250,000 to finance these regional schemes, partly by interest-free loans, partly by grants for staff or equipment. The Ministry gave the scheme its support and the pharmaceutical industry also gave financial support.

When news of the outcome of Sir George's Christ Church Conference appeared in the medical journals in February 1962, the *Lancet* spoke of the trustees offer as a splendid financial catalyst 'can we really be content with medical education until every hospital in the land is in some sense a teaching hospital'. Innumerable schemes from all over the country were submitted to the Trust for financial support. In 1967 an overall review *Postgraduate Medical Education – A Retrospect and Prospect* resulted in the formation of a Central Council of Postgraduate Medical Education.

It is certain that the Trust's support for Sir George Pickering's concept of regional continuous postgraduate medical education had a greater direct impact on the medical profession as a whole than anything else that the Trust has initiated, and this benefit was extended to the whole population, well and not so well.

Lord Nuffield, though ailing, was heartened to learn that the Trust was supporting this project, for he had always preferred that his gifts should have an immediate or near immediate impact. Furthermore, so many of his gifts had been for postgraduate education; the first Oxford Regius Professor that he had known, Sir William Osler, had talked to him of the importance of what he called the 'five yearly brain dusting'. Nuffield's first major gift to medicine in 1929, was for a postgraduate medical school at Oxford, which came to full fruition 7 years later, and one of his last personal gifts in 1948 was the establishment of the Postgraduate Nuffield College at the Royal College of Surgeons.

Until the Christ Church Conference, there had been a tendency for the Trust's interest and grants to move away from practical medical services with improvement of patient care and to concentrate more on the administration and organization of hospital services, and this would continue for a while. This may have been influenced by the enforced change in the Trust's policy, but a better balance is beginning to appear.

POLICY IMPLEMENTATION UNDER A NEW CHAIRMAN

Early in 1966 Sir Geoffrey Gibbs resigned from the chairmanship of the governing trustees and was succeeded by Sir Edgar Williams CB, CBE, DSO, who had been a trustee since 1963. Sir Edgar, a historian and fellow of Balliol College Oxford, had played a key role in intelligence in the desert campaign with the 8th Army and later with other Army Groups. After the war he returned to Oxford as Warden of Rhodes House, but in addition was a member both of the Board of Governors of the United Oxford Hospitals and the university's Nuffield Committee, which in addition to administering the funds of the Nuffield Postgraduate Scheme, endeavoured to satisfy the rival demands of the Nuffield clinical professors. So he was familiar with the ways of medical men and hospital administrators when he took over the chairmanship of the Nuffield Trust, where his critical incisive approach rendered him so valuable in the trustees' deliberations.

The medical trustees who had been appointed before Sir Edgar joined the Trust, were Lord Cohen of Birkenhead, a superb clinician, a masterly medical administrator with great powers of clarity in discussions; Dr John Fry, a general practitioner who played a large part in the development of the Royal College of General Practitioners; and Sir Norrie Robson, another physician administrator but very different from the suave Lord Cohen. It was his sincerity of purpose combined with a humourous touch which enabled him to bring opposing colleagues together. Intolerant of the machinery of administration, he accepted with some equanimity the time he had to waste in unravelling unnecessary complexities.

Norrie joined the Trust in 1967, having had an exciting war in the Navy, created the first full-time academic clinical department in Australia, and having just been appointed Vice-Chancellor of Sheffield University, carrying the University through the turbulence of student unrest and the stresses of changes in medical policy. His chairmanship of the Central Committee for Postgraduate Medical Education made it clear which aspect of the Trust's policies interested him; he had little enthusiasm for hospital administrators or empire builders, but he believed strongly that the Trust should remain an independent, critical, but positive force.

The lay trustees at this time, were Leslie Farrer-Brown, the director of the Foundation and one-time secretary of the Trust, two financiers, a banker, and a lady deeply interested in a range of charitable endeavours closely related to the Trust's interests.

In 1972 Sir Edgar addressed the American Hospital Association on the 'Trust'. He first outlined the qualities which he believed were necessary for the chairman and secretary of a charitable Trust, and then considered the functions of the Nuffield Provincial Hospitals Trust itself. The Trust must be receptive of the ideas of others, never hesitating to be a plagiarist or an intellectual broker, ready to search out significant gaps in the health service, where public money cannot in the first instance be applied. Having decided on a particular project the Trust must spend time, expertise and money to see whether it was truly worthwhile. If the outcome was unsatisfactory, this might result in a considerable saving of public funds. The outlook should essentially be an independent one. It could only carry out an investigation for the Government if the trustees themselves felt that it was warranted. They would always be helpers, but inevitably critical helpers.

Sir Edgar, perhaps purposely, did not give any examples of how the Trust policy was working. However the Eighth Annual Report contained a summary of projects supported by the Trust up to 1970, and this could be extended to 1980. From this it seemed possible to gain an impression, perhaps erroneous, of the Trust's changing policy, which could be summarized as books rather than buildings.

Table 22.1.
Nuffield Provincial Hospitals Trust 1939–80; ratio of creative to enlightening grants (in percentages)

	Creative	Enlightening
Pre-1950	65	35
1951–60	16	84
1961–70	14	86
1970–80	5	95

The projects were classed as creative (buildings or posts) or enlightening (educational or investigational). The table shows in each decade the percentage ratio of the two types of grants. Grants in relation to the postgraduate education scheme have been purposely omitted.

Although the number of creative grants for each decade has remained fairly constant over the half century, the number of enlightening grants has increased thirtyfold, and this increase has been particularly marked recently, when the Trust's policy moved towards the gathering of strategic intelligence.

During the period up to 1961 the Trust published some 18 volumes embracing nine subjects: the regionalization philosophy, hospital costing, the work of nurses in hospital, a study in the function and design of hospitals, good general practice, child health, accident and casualty services, and the care of the aged and the handicapped. All these reports had a profound influence on health care, not only in the country but throughout the world. In the period between 1970 and 1985 the Trust published 80 volumes dealing with some 350 subjects. It will be interesting to know which of these volumes has influenced government policy on the health service.

A copy of 'Counsels and Ideals' from the writings of William Osler in Lord Nuffield's library has a mark against 'it is much simpler to buy books than to read them and easier to read them than to absorb their contents'. It has been suggested that some of the recommendations of the recent White Paper, though perhaps influenced by the Trust's studies failed fully to appreciate their import.

It was also Osler, reviewing the history of an eponymous lecture, who wrote, 'a majority of the men come into that great group of the silent ones, the voiceless, mere vowels and consenants to us, without association or traditions and who are today as though they have never been'. Now there is so much talk of audit, Domabedian models and evaluation – we just used to talk about follow-up – it might be informative and perhaps salutary if a peer review of the impact of the various grants made by the Trust were carried out.

The current enthusiasm for audit has, at least in part, been generated by the Trust's investigation into quality of care. As was mentioned earlier, back in 1952 the Trust gave a grant for one of the earliest instances of medical audit, and in that same year the report of the confidential maternal mortality enquiry was published, which inspired the CEPOD studies, supported by the Trust and the King Edward's Fund.

CEPOD

Personal experience caused Lord Nuffield to insist, in spite of academic protests, that Robert Macintosh should be his first Nuffield Professor of Anaesthesia. At Oxford, Macintosh, deeply concerned about anaesthetic deaths, though few other people seemed to be, learnt from his colleague Professor Moir, the Nuffield Professor of Obstetrics, of the existence of the confidential enquiry into maternal deaths and felt that something of the sort might be valuable in determining the causes of anaesthetic deaths. He felt that the coroner's inquest on 'death on the table' was unsatisfactory, as the proceedings were too public and it was too easy to 'cover up' incidences, while it was unlikely that the pertinent information would be obtained, either because it was not recognized or because it was not available from the witnesses; procurator fiscal proceedings were no better. So, in 1944, he wrote to the president of the Association of Anaesthetists that an enquiry about anaesthetic deaths, along the lines of the confidential maternity enquiry, should be instituted.

He received an official reply that the Council, after long discussion, decided that no action should be taken in the matter. Baulked in this direction, Macintosh, with his colleague Dr Mushin, continued to collect information on these cases and, in May 1948, gave a paper 'Death Under Anaesthetics' at the Royal Society of Medicine which was intended to shock, and succeeded. From the data that he and Mushin had collected, he concluded that the commonest cause of post-anaesthetic death was asphyxia, consequent on the unconscious patient being placed in the ward in a potentially dangerous posture and without adequate nursing supervision. The second commonest cause was that the anaesthetist gave the wrong drug, or the right drug in the wrong dose. The first hazard could be minimized by education and closer attention to unconscious patients. The second was more difficult because the double-check system used by the pharmacists was time consuming and often, in an emergency, speed was essential. He ended his talk by suggesting that there should be small, sensitive professional committees to enquire into these deaths. The object should be prevention rather than attributing blame, and it might be useful to include a psychologist or a sympathetic general practitioner 'to whom the anaesthetist is more likely to open himself'. Macintosh's persistence won through and, in November 1949, the Council of the Association of Anaesthetists agreed to set up a committee to look into the matter; from this, and with grants from the Trust, important information was gathered and analysed.

However, there was a weakness, in that surgeons were not involved in these enquiries. This was overcome when the Association of Anaesthetists and the Association of Surgeons established a joint committee with the creation of CEPOD (Confidential Enquiry into Peri-operative Deaths), which resulted in a pilot study in three regions, supported by the Trust and the King Edward's Fund; this became the National CEPOD study, supported in part by the DHSS.

Excellent and necessary as are these investigations, they represent a particular type of critical follow-up, while the Royal College of Physicians in their paper 'Medical Audit, The First Report, What, Why and How?' discusses the subject in the broadest terms. One should not forget the words of the president, Sir Raymond Hoffenberg, 'While costs and the use of resources should be taken into account in these projects, these factors should not be allowed to influence choices adversely, where clear benefit to patients can be demonstrated.'

'. . . LOOKING FORWARD'

In 1977 the Trust suffered the grievous loss of two of their medical trustees, Lord Cohen and Sir Hugh Robson, whose experience and advice had on many occasions proved invaluable. They were succeeded by two former Rock Carling Fellows whose lectures had been memorable. Professor Sir Andrew Watt Kay, Regius Professor of Surgery in the University of Glasgow and Lord Butterfield, Regius Professor of Physic in the University of Cambridge, and they were joined a few years later by Professor John Ledingham, an Oxford physician and clinical scientist, who had formerly been Director of Clinical Studies in the University Medical School.

When Sir Edgar Williams retired from the chairmanship of the trustees, he was succeeded by Sir Maurice Shock, Rector of Lincoln College, Oxford and formerly Vice-Chancellor of the University of Leicester, who had been a governing trustee since 1980. When Mr Gordon McLachlan retired from the secretaryship of the Trust he was succeeded by Dr Michael Ashley-Miller, an Oxford graduate with considerable experience in community medicine in many parts of Great Britain and an enthusiast for its more practical aspects.

It is inevitable that there will be alterations in the Trust's policy. The broad lines have remained unchanged but recently there has been an increase in grants directed towards assisting the health needs of the people of Scotland and Wales. An address entitled 'Disablement, Problems and Prospects in the United Kingdom', was given by the Rt Hon Lord Campbell of Croy, BC, MC, the first of Queen Elizabeth, the Queen Mother's Fellows, in 1981, the International Year of the Disabled, and the White Paper on Community Care was also published in that year. This has been associated with an intensified interest by the Trust in the aged, and the physically and mentally handicapped, which has been reflected in over £1 million in grants.

ENVOI

Some may feel, and they may well be right, that the balance and emphasis in this essay is imperfect. Other historians may see the vast achievements of the Trust in a very different light. Yet it is hard to believe that anyone could deny that during its 50 years the Trust has established an effective collaboration within a circumscribed area of the curative and preventative aspects of health care; the linking between the hospital and general practitioners through diagnostic or health centres of varying types; the development of the industrial health centre, with its emphasis on rehabilitation; the student health service; the need for surveys and analysis of jobs before entering or considering building or staffing; and the care of the aged and the physically and mentally handicapped, not in the custodian sense but in an endeavour to enable them to achieve the maximum contentment within their limitations. The Trust has brought into the academic world, to their mutual advantage, practical aspects of medicine such as plastic or accident surgery, child health, and community health. It has provided fellowships so that the thoughtful and experienced can set out their ideas that others can consider and appreciate, and finally, has created a style of postgraduate education readily available to those engaged in their ordinary tasks, which will stimulate them towards major achievements.

One might conclude this essay with the title that Sir Farquhar Buzzard gave to the address which heralded the birth of the Nuffield Provincial Hospitals Trust, 'And the Future'.

Chapter 23

When trustees first met

Dame Janet Vaughan[1]

In 1943 Lord Nuffield established what has become known as the Nuffield Foundation, with a basic value of £10 million and with the following objects:

1. The advancement of health and prevention and relief of sickness by such means as the ordinary trustees shall, in their absolute discretion, think fit, and in particular, but without prejudice, to the generality of that discretion, by medical research and teaching and by organization and development of medical and health services.

2. The advancement of social well-being, in particular by scientific research and the organization, development, and improvement of technical and commercial education, including the training of teachers and the provision of scholarships and prizes.

3. The comfort and care of the aged poor.

4. Such other charitable purposes as shall be declared in writing by (a) Lord Nuffield in his lifetime, and (b) after his death by the ordinary trustees and managing trustees.

   In the first formal document about the Foundation, Sir William Goodenough, then Chairman of Barclays Bank, and at that time Chairman of the Interdepartmental Committee on Medical Education was named by Lord Nuffield as Chairman of the New Foundation, and five other trustees, of whom I was asked to be one, were also named. I was already working with Sir William Goodenough as a member of the Interdepartmental Committee on Medical Education, as was Sir John Stopford, Vice-Chancellor of Manchester University. Also chosen as trustees were Sir Frank Engledow, Professor of Agriculture at Cambridge, Sir Hector

Lord Nuffield signing the deeds of the Nuffield Foundation in the company of Janet Vaughan and William Goodenough.
[F.J. Minns]

Nuffield was not by nature a 'committee man'. A solitary thinker and planner, his offices reflected this. The Longwall St. office.

251

Hetherington, Vice-Chancellor of Glasgow University, and Alderman William Hyde of Oxford City Council. William Hyde was a close friend of Lord Nuffield and also well known to William Goodenough. The three men had for many years collaborated in connection with the organization of medical services in the Oxford region. I remained a trustee until 1967, serving under the chairmanship first of Sir William Goodenough and then of Sir Geoffrey Gibbs.

The work of the Foundation since its inauguration is recorded in the published reports, 1946–82. Lord Nuffield himself played little part in the day-to-day work of the Foundation, and as trustees we had little contact with him. When I met him, as I did from time to time, he was particularly interested in the scientific investigations that were being carried out at his insistence on the biological and physiological problems of the ageing process. He was inclined to think that the trustees were not sufficiently interested in the problem, though we supported such investigations with generous funds.

In formulating and deciding policy, the trustees depended on the cooperation of a group of expert advisors, in particular members and officers of the Research Councils and government departments, but they were prepared after such discussions to initiate new developments which they thought important. Their first act, initiated by Sir William Goodenough, was to appoint a committee under the chairmanship of Seebohm Rowntree to investigate the problems of ageing and the proper care of old people. A report, *Old People,* was published in 1947 and aroused considerable interest and action. It was welcomed by the Minister of Health and the Assistance Board, and stimulated much further work, both by the Foundation and other organizations.

Our work as trustees involved much discussion not only among ourselves, but also with the applicants for grants and with people whose advice we sought. This meant that over the years we learnt a great deal about the needs of universities, of the hospital services, and of the Commonwealth. For instance, we became concerned in 1944 about the lack of teaching and research associated with industrial medicine. After appropriate discussion and enquiry, finance was offered to three universities, Manchester, Durham, and Glasgow, to enable them to establish departments. Such departments have since developed in different ways to make use of the different opportunities the universities could make available.

I have some personal memories that will not appear in any formal records and which are perhaps worth preserving since they give a picture of how the Foundation did its day-to-day work. First of all, what fun we had in the early days of the Foundation. Our meetings were held in the Savoy Hotel which, even in wartime, provided splendid entertainment. One of the things that Will Goodenough believed was that people worked better together if they also dined and gossiped together. When we abandoned the Savoy and moved to Nuffield Lodge we still held our monthly meetings in association at least with lunch, and often dinner. For our first meeting during the Second World War I stayed the night at the Savoy. An elderly waitress in cap and apron brought me my breakfast in bed. She wheeled in an immense silver trolley with a domed lid to carry my weak coffee and meagre slices of toast, yet all set out with the splendour befitting the hotel used by crowned heads and visiting celebrities. 'Rough night we have had Madam, but the Savoy is still standing' she said, and began the usual tale of bomb damage.

One of our earliest projects as the war was ending was a scheme to bring young medical men from the Commonwealth over here on fellowships. This idea was first discussed very late one night, in the old Café Royal grill room, when the secretary of the Foundation, Leslie Farrer-Brown and I dined with an extremely senior officer of the Australian Forces in Britain.

He was enthusiastic about the fellowship plan but agreed with me that one must bring the wives as well. As he so rightly said, 'These men have been fighting in foreign lands for three or four years. Their one idea when they get home is to marry their girls, and they won't want to be separated immediately. The girls must come too.' I was anxious that the girls should come for another reason. They were in the future to be important people as the wives of senior academic and professional men and it was essential that they should be educated as well as their husbands. Among my own friends I knew too many cases where the men had been to America on a scholarship or fellowship and the girl had stayed behind. The fact that they had missed a shared experience did no good to their marriage and often left the girl less well educated than her husband. When the scheme to bring both men and women came to the trustees at a formal meeting, in spite of the warm support of the commanding officer, I had a tough battle on my hands. Both Sir John Stopford and Hector Hetherington opposed the wives. 'It will prevent them working' was their firm belief. However in the end I had my way. Foundation House in Leinster Gardens took in Nuffield Fellows, their wives and babies until 1972. Today Nuffield Fellows and large families are housed in much more splendid accommodation.

One day, around1945, Sir John Stopford described to the trustees over lunch how he had been taken out by an enthusiastic young lecturer in Professor Blacket's department of Physics at Manchester to some fields owned by the University to show him a new sort of telescope he was constructing, 'a radiotelescope' as, he called it, quite different in principle from the ordinary optical telescope. Sir John had been made to climb up and down ladders in the wind and rain, over ploughed fields and down muddy lanes, but he thought the project exciting and that the Foundation should support it. The trustees agreed after lunch to the establishment of an experimental station at Jodrell Bank under the care of Bernard Lovell and the general direction of Professor Blacket. They gave an initial grant of £10,000 over 5 years which was doubled in 1946. In 1948 the Department of Scientific and Industrial Research began to meet half the running cost of the new telescope. The problems, both financial and engineering, involved in the final achievements of Jodrell Bank dominated meetings of the trustees for many years.

Today 'business studies' are extremely fashionable but I well remember the Foundation's early interest in the Administrative Staff College at Henley, which was just being set up in 1948. The trustees all went down to stay at the college for the weekend and spent Sunday morning rowing on the river at the end of the lawn with mixed efficiency. No one fell in.

Note

1. Dame Janet Vaughan, FRS, FRCP, DM was an original trustee of the Nuffield Foundation. She died in 1992.

Chapter 24

The Nuffield Foundation

J. W. McAnuff

Men may establish charitable foundations from a variety of motives. Lord Nuffield's predominant concern, certainly, was to further a number of important causes he had in mind in medicine, science, and social welfare. An alternative he appears to have considered was to create separate new organizations for each of those aims. This would have been less effective and, as is now well seen, it would drastically have limited action on future needs and opportunities. His foundation, which he endowed with Morris Motors stock to the value of £10 million, was formed as a charitable trust in 1943, when he was aged 65. In those dark days of war, when government too was starting to plan for peacetime reconstruction, it was a courageous act of faith.

The widely drawn terms of trust were, in essence: the advancement of health and the prevention and relief of sickness; the advancement of social well-being, with special reference to the role of scientific research; the care and comfort of the aged poor. There was provision for Lord Nuffield, and for the trustees after his death, to extend the charitable purposes. In 1951 the advancement of education was so added, but that no further additions have since been found necessary is a tribute to the original vision.

The deed of trust made pointed reference to Lord Nuffield's belief that the fruits of private enterprise are vital in the growth of commonwealth. The wording of the relevant clause has, in practice, restricted the Foundation's territorial range to the British Commonwealth. A second, explicit, restriction, on the sale of the original stock, intended to assure continuity of both the Foundation and Morris Motors, was seriously to imperil the first of those intentions a quarter of a century later.

Nuffield invited two business associates to join him as 'ordinary' trustees (custodians of the capital), and appointed Sir William Goodenough, his banker and close confidant, to be chairman of the managing trustees – a group selected largely by the powerful Goodenough. It was composed of one other banker, four leading scientists and physicians, and a university vice-chancellor. The managing trustees had full responsibility for the income, and for a strategy, under the constraints of the ordinary trustees' power of veto and of a formidable list of the founder's own priorities. The list included Nuffield College, Oxford, health services, social medicine, Commonwealth scholarships, rheumatism, catarrh, homes for the aged, and dentistry. Most of Nuffield's 'special items' – the causes which, collectively, had motivated the greatest of all his benefactions – were in due course faithfully pursued; and his influence was to remain, and be felt. It is a duty of charitable trusteeship to consider how best to give effect to the donor's intentions. There were the makings therefore of some conflict between the wishes of a living donor (Lord Nuffield lived for 20 years after the birth of the Foundation) and equally strongly held ideas of the very eminent and knowledgeable trustees. Such conflicts were, happily, fairly rare, and never disastrous, but ever since, especially when their course was not clear (Nuffield himself had said that to spend money wisely was much harder than to make it), the trustees have always sought to picture what in the circumstances the founder would have wanted.

The new foundation was able to set up house with its elder sister, the Nuffield Provincial Hospitals Trust. Until 1962, when their paths diverged, the two bodies collaborated in several schemes of common concern, notably laying the groundwork for the advance of hospital and academic rheumatology, and of the then equally backward speciality of occupational medicine. Foundation grants provided the first UK university chairs in both subjects; and brought occupational health care and rehabilitation within the reach of thousands of small firms.

In all matters connected with its objects which involve major issues of public policy the Foundation is required, by its trust deed, to consult with appropriate departments of government. These consultations have invariably been mutually helpful – not least in facilitating the takeover by official agencies of Foundation initiatives which had proved their worth (although lately such consummations have been much harder to achieve) – and out of them came, in the 1960s, proposals for practical experiments in widening industry's own provisions for the health of people at work. Heartened by the success of earlier pioneer Nuffield schemes in Slough and Harlow, where groups of small firms subscribe to run cooperative health services for their employees, three new services were launched with the aid of starting capital and tapering recurrent grants, to see if the same concept was viable in areas of older industry, typified by Dundee, Rochdale, and West Bromwich. Results were encouraging, and since then a handful of other areas of concentration of small-scale industry have found the resources to start up their own group services. But progress around the country has been slow, comparing unfavourably with that by Britain's partners in the EEC. Raising the starting capital, for premises and equipment, is clearly a problem. Some employers used to object that they had no need to pay for additional medical facilities for their employees when the National Health Service provided all that was necessary. It is now increasingly recognized that the group services make an important contribution to preventive medicine, and that they are therefore, to that extent, complementary rather than supplementary to the NHS. Members of these services find their employees have less time off work through sickness and are more quickly rehabilitated after injury. They declare that their membership is good value for money, and that it is quite simply good business. On the strength of that, the Foundation need not despair of the full fruition of its programme, though it will have some while longer to wait for it.

In the beginning the trustees worked to a 5-year plan, determining on a firm balance between appropriations for their own initiatives and a smaller share for opportunistic grants. They resolved to be pioneers not settlers, giving primary stimulus to worthwhile people, projects, and institutions, and willing to take the kind of risks which would be improper for agencies handling public funds. At the end of the Second World War the trustees were ready with commitments to fellowships and scholarships, dentistry, industrial medicine, child health, and the needs of old people.

The aim of the fellowships and scholarships was very much as Lord Nuffield had conceived them – to generate a two-way traffic between the UK and Commonwealth countries, to realize their full potential for training. The first target groups were those pursuing academic careers in teaching or research, but schemes of awards were also introduced to encourage the growth of specific fields of study, for example rheumatology, child health, and dentistry. It was said of Nuffield dental fellowships and scholarships that they helped 'breed a whole race of more scientifically orientated dentists'. Away from the academic scene there were awards directed at other walks of life, such as administration in industry and government. One of the most popular schemes enabled young farmers to spend three months or so studying agricultural systems at home or abroad.

Fellowships and scholarships were, for many years, the principal instrument for Foundation assistance to Commonwealth countries. Gradually the balance changed, as more opportunities for project and programme work were discovered, and as other provision for fellowships and scholarships expanded dramatically throughout the world. For much of that expansion the Foundation was both pathfinder and pacemaker.

The benefits to many thousands of Foundation award holders, and through them to countless others by way of teaching and example, have been immeasurably great. Perhaps, too, this has been the most cost-effective of all Foundation activities. Benefits for Nuffield Fellows visiting the UK were, moreover, enhanced from the beginning by a decision enabling wives and families to accompany them. Dame Janet Vaughan, has recalled that this proposal was the occasion for a tough battle with her colleagues, in which she had to deploy every argument for the best interests of the married state and for what nowadays we call 'equal opportunity'. As many as possible of the London-based fellows, and families, were housed in a small colony of foundation-owned furnished flats, wherein a multi-cultural community could enjoy much added social and educational advantage.

At the peak of this important branch of Foundation activity there were no fewer than 30 award schemes in operation. In a typical year, such as 1969, awards were made to 245 individual men and women whose interests ranged as diversely as medicine, dentistry, biology, social science, government service, agriculture, teaching, social work, trade unions, law, broadcasting, and many more.

Inherent in the problems looming on the post-war social scene was a dearth of data and of understanding. In facing up to one of their most pressing obligations, the care of old people, the trustees therefore commissioned a searching survey, the result of which, the Rowntree Report, was to arrest public opinion and to guide a £1 million programme of action over the following 10 years. Half that sum was earmarked for the new National Corporation for the Care of Old People, which now operates as the Centre for Policy on Ageing (CPA) and continues to be the main channel for Foundation support in that field.

The Centre has a lower public profile than those of its distinguished contemporaries Age Concern and Help the Aged, whose roles are much concerned with publicizing the issues, fundraising and direct action. The CPA works rather at the political and professional levels, serving primarily those responsible for planning and implementing policy, and furnishing them with information and advice. In the words of the Rowntree Report, the Corporation (CPA) 'shall be used as an information centre, a clearing house for all matters connected with the elderly'.

The centre's funds, now over £5 million a year, are used in part to support demonstration and pioneering projects, among which have been short-stay homes, day centres, chiropody schemes, employment schemes for older people, laundry services for the incontinent, and large-print book services. Britain's first sheltered housing association, the Hanover Housing Association, was established by the Centre in 1963, and since 1974 over £4 million has been administered, on behalf of the Hayward Foundation, for improvements to voluntary residential care homes.

Over the 40-odd years of the CPA's existence the challenge of the problems of old age, like the size of the ageing population itself, has not, of course, lessened. The Centre will continue to define the nature and the causes of disadvantage in old age; to promote studies designed to afford relief and improvement; and to make known these findings and have them fully discussed and tested, if necessary with the aid of field experiments.

As well as providing about one-third of the CPA's income, the Foundation assists much other promising work lying outside the scope of the Centre and equally dedicated to the increase of well-being in old age. The broad aim is to add to the understanding of medical and biological problems in that stage of life. What, for example, are the underlying processes involved in the ageing of human tissues and even of individual cells? There have been many grants for specific research projects in this science of gerontology, and for stimulating research interest in what is still a neglected area of biology. Some Foundation-supported work has shown that in experimental animals maintained on severely restricted diets there is a slowing down of biological ageing and an appreciable increase in longevity. Implications for the human condition seem obvious.

In medical matters generally the trustees were directing most of their attention to the promotion of positive health and to the solution of basic problems in human biology. This approach overrode, one might say it transcended, the temptation to put a lot of research effort into the causes and cure of specific diseases. The exception of rheumatism, because of the founder's interest, attracted in 1948 a gift of £0.45 million by Captain Oliver Bird, later increased by his widow to £0.75 million. Under the guidance of expert committees the income has been used mainly to support research on the aetiology and fundamental biological aspect of rheumatoid arthritis, osteo-arthritis, and other disorders of joints and connective tissue.

The trustees did what they could to help repair the badly weakened post-war state of so many centres of learning and research. There were large grants to revive the work of the National Institute for Economic and Social Research, the Population Investigation Committee, and several UK university departments of physics. It was not otherwise easy to discern the real needs of the social sciences: their time was to come. The physical sciences did not stay long in the forefront, however, giving way to rising claims of biology, but in the early 1950s there came a proposal of far-reaching consequence. This required, in effect, a £0.3 million rescue operation, involving a personal contribution from Lord Nuffield, to help build the Jodrell Bank radiotelescope, which was to promote historic advances in cosmology and space technology. Sir Bernard Lovell, who came to personify in the public mind the new subject of radio-astronomy, has given the following account:[1]

Early in 1952 the Nuffield Foundation agreed to share with the Department of Scientific and Industrial Research (DSIR) the cost of a 250 ft steerable radio telescope at Jodrell Bank. This unique instrument took 5 years to construct and when it came into use in the autumn of 1957 it was burdened with debt and the subject of investigation by the Public Accounts Committee. However, the telescope's ability to detect the launching rocket (an ICBM) of the Soviet Sputnik in October 1957 and the vital part it played in the Soviet and American space programmes created the atmosphere in which a solution was found. The DSIR agreed to pay half of the outstanding debt provided the University (of Manchester) raised the balance. Eventually, after the success of the telescope in controlling the American Pioneer V space probe in 1960, Lord Nuffield and the Foundation generously offered to make a further grant to the University to clear the balance of the debt.

The telescope acquired wide publicity early on because of its engagement with space programmes but its primary purpose was to study the universe in the radio wave region of the spectrum: in this way scientists have been able to make important advances in the exploration of the universe. The great adaptability of the telescope is revealed by the remarkable situation that today the objects of study – radio galaxies, quasars, pulsars, for example – were unknown in 1957. In studying some of these objects the telescope penetrates many billions of light years into space and thereby into the past history of the universe.

Originally expected to have an engineering and scientific life of 15 years the telescope remains, after 32 years of continuous day and night use, one of the most important astronomical instruments in the world, and it is widely used by the international community.

By the end of its first decade the Foundation had spent £4.2 million of an aggregate £5.2 million. Social research – the trustees took a practical approach in their consideration of social problems, favouring experimental and applied work – education, and Commonwealth development were now assuming greater prominence. The Foundation played a significant part in the private sector of growing international aid activity in this period, illustrated by many grants for innovations in higher education, health care, and agricultural systems, and the study and optimum use of natural resources, particularly in Africa. Among important home-based undertakings were the Overseas Visual Aids Centre and the (in-house) Centre for Educational Television Overseas.

The best known work of the Foundation is its school curriculum development programme. 'Nuffield Science' became a household word; and to teachers across the world the name Nuffield is synonymous with the enlightened teaching of experimental enquiry-based science in schools. The programme extended to modernizing the material and presentation of many other subjects, especially mathematics and modern languages. About £1 million was committed to these purposes in the 1960s.

It was in the mid 1950s that the Foundation first put its toe into school science waters, by funding at the Royal Institution in London a series of experimental demonstrations illustrating sixth form course work. The popularity among schools and students of this departure chimed in with a growing professional awareness of the deficiencies of traditional science teaching. The stage was being set for a thorough review of what needed to be taught (putting in much new material from the rapid advance of science itself, and making room for it by judicious 'dead-heading' within the existing syllabus), using more relevant and exciting methods of presentation, with an accent on learning by doing, all to achieve greater understanding of science – and a greater enthusiasm for it.

This massive task, the Science Teaching Project, was put in hand with the aid of an initial Foundation grant of £0.25 million. The project, spanning all school stages from primary to advanced level, was manned by teams of teachers of outstanding quality, with help from the country's foremost scientists and from many other experts. Government had given its blessing, and as the work proceeded so the interests were engaged of educational publishers, laboratory suppliers, local education authorities, universities, and examining boards. The Foundation shouldered a heavy burden of responsibility for coordinating all this effort. The consequences of the project were by no means confined to the UK, and soon there was a lively export market for its ideas and active advice, which led to the joint funding by the Foundation and by Government of the Council for Curriculum Development Overseas.

The Foundation's schools curriculum programme was never intended as an end in itself, to manufacture, as it were, a range of finished products. The purpose was to institute a lasting process of renewal of teaching materials and methods: and to encourage others to join in the quest for continuing improvement of resources available to teachers. In this it undoubtedly succeeded beyond all expectation.

Annual income rose above £2 million, then £3 million, and grants, too, got bigger. An official report on social work training led the trustees, in partnership with the Joseph Rowntree Memorial Trust, to start a national institute for that purpose in 1961, with support of over £0.4 million. Other big grants of the time inlcuded those to found the Nuffield Unit of Medical Genetics in Liverpool, to help re-house The Royal Society of London, and to provide novel facilities for each of seven new English universities of a kind outside the scope of their normal budgets. Financial well-being also gave rein to much longer-term commitments, such as a £1 million 10-year programme for training and research in food safety: and it encouraged a more adventurous outlook. The founder might have been at least surprised by the trustees' favourable responses to proposals for a Nuffield Library at the Shakespeare Birthplace, a theatre for Southampton University, and a George Orwell memorial archive fund in London.

The food safety programme has a topical ring to it, with the recent run of national alarms and excursions in mind, but ideas for this Foundation initiative were taking shape as far back as 1960. The prime mover was the late Sir Frank Engledow who, until his death at the age of 95, had served the foundation as trustee and consultant for 42 years. Sir Frank's distinction in plant science led to his appointment to the Chair of Agriculture at Cambridge and into a wide range of advisory work in food and farming matters. He perceived that rapid changes in eating habits and in food technology were opening up large new areas of concern about nutritive values and possible toxicity. An article in the scientific journal, *Nature,* a quarter of a century ago had said: 'More and more food is artificially treated with preservatives, flavourings, colourings and other agents: the calculated results of labour saving and added (consumer) appeal may, therefore, be accompanied by increasing and not so readily ascertained toxic risks. There is no doubt that understanding of the long-term biological effects of these practices is not keeping pace.'

The plan of action which came from the deliberations of Sir Frank and a group of experts drawn from industry and the universities was twofold: first, to encourage training in disciplines relevant to food safety and testing (e.g. the biochemistry of food metabolism, comparative toxicology and pathology); secondly, to stimulate and to support research into appropriate problems of food science. In practice, the Foundation offered training scholarships to attract into the field young specialists in physical, biological, medical, or veterinary science; and grants were made for a number of basic studies of toxic risks associated with food additives and with food processing, such as meat curing. Notably, a Nuffield Unit of Laboratory Animal Pathology was established in Edinburgh to develop that subject as a discipline in its own right and to act as a training centre for food safety research and testing.

It has to be said that, in terms of other interested parties taking up the Foundation's lead, the broader results of the food safety programme were disappointing. In 1968 it was noted that 'the food industry itself, with a few praiseworthy exceptions, seems not yet willing to accept its own due share of responsibility for promotion of relevant research'. How does it look today, one wonders.

The origins of the Nuffield Unit of Medical Genetics offer another example of an individual trustee seizing on an idea whose time had come. From the early 1950s the Foundation had been supporting in Oxford the work of the late Professor E.B. Ford, who had a special interest in the evolution and genetics of wild populations. One of his associates, the late Professor P.M. Sheppard, on moving to Liverpool in 1957, continued some of this work in collaboration with Dr C.A. Clarke (later director of the

Nuffield Unit and now Emeritus Professor Sir Cyril Clarke). The tactics of their collaboration were to try to understand the inheritance of wing patterns in mimetic butterflies: the strategy was to apply this understanding to problems in the genetics of human disease, e.g. the problem of differences in the incidence of disease between people of different blood-groups. Clarke and Sheppard did indeed find that the butterfly mimicry was controlled by a set of genes, as are the human Rhesus blood-groups.

Dame Janet Vaughan saw that this was the time, and Liverpool the place, for a major thrust in medical genetics. She encouraged Ford, Clarke, and Sheppard to work out a scheme, which she and her fellow-trustees subsequently backed with their largest ever single grant of £0.35 million. An early, direct, result was a method of preventing haemolytic disease of the newborn – the so-called 'Rhesus' or 'yellow' baby – thus saving many hundred lives each year in the UK alone. This disease is caused by genetic differences between the mother and the fetus, and the creation of the Unit's new facilities in Liverpool, in close association with existing scientific and clinical resources there, made possible the development and rigorous testing of a prophylaxis now administered routinely to 'Rh-negative' mothers throughout the world.

Medical genetics in Liverpool went on to prosper in many directions. Apart from scientific and medical advances made within the Unit it has been steadily nurturing and exporting talented people: six of its geneticists are now holding professorial posts in other universities. Sir Cyril Clarke has noted that none of all these achievements of the Unit might have happened if modern notions about 'medical audit' had been applied to vetting the original butterfly research proposals. It is good to be able to record therefore that the butterfly work continues, under Sir Cyril's direction; and that it is still being supported by the Foundation.

In the late 1960s, having concern for the existence of serious gaps and imperfections in the working of law in society, the trustees began to open up a wide field of socio-legal inquiry and action. With an initial allocation of £0.15 million they established in 1970 their legal advice and assistance programme. An in-house programme of research resulted in five volumes, published by Routledge and Kegan Paul in 1978.

Two of the more enduring of the programme's early innovations are the Legal Action Group and the Newham Rights Centre. The Legal Action

Group is a flourishing organization for the improvement of legal services. It publishes a regular bulletin and organizes courses. There are ten local groups as well as headquarters in London. Newham Rights Centre, set up in 1973, was by no means the first law centre. It was, however, one of the few to rely on charitable funds and, some would say, it derived freedom in its early days from being independent of central or local government funds. At the end of the experimental period financed by the Foundation, Newham Rights obtained funding from the Lord Chancellor's Department.

The earmarked £0.15 million was soon exhausted but the trustees readily continued to make *ad hoc* grants in this area. In 1978 they funded the first service for conciliation in divorce, the Bristol Courts Family Conciliation Service. The conciliation movement proved to be powerful, and the Foundation has since then made several more related grants but for research and development schemes. Government recognizes that conciliation is now established as an option for divorcing couples and some courts are now able to offer conciliation services.

A less radical but equally successful experiment was the introduction of a Citizens's Advice Bureau in the Royal Courts of Justice in 1977. Although Government was initially sceptical about the need for such an office it now occupies a permanent and important place in improving access to the law at the Royal Courts of Justice.

The trustees have spent about £1 million on research and experiment in legal advice and assistance since their original allocation ran out. Although other support for socio-legal research is available, the Foundation's programme has been unique.

Excursions of a unique kind have also been made into the contrasting field of aquaculture, with the primary aim of building up academic resources for training and research. A conspicuous outcome of this interest is the pre-eminent Institute of Aquaculture at Stirling University. Like most successful organizations the Institute sprang from small beginnings. Twenty years ago a young veterinary pathologist in Glasgow was pleading the case for academic studies of diseases in fish, neglect of which was held to be impeding the development of fish culture worldwide. The Foundation was already pursuing a long-term interest in scientific aspects of fish farming, and it responded to Dr Roberts by establishing him in a unit of aquatic pathobiology at Stirling with a staff of two and a budget of £76,000 over 6 years. Today Professor Roberts has a staff of over 90 and an annual budget approaching £2 million.

It was a dramatic illustration of the Foundation's essential role of 'priming the pump'. A modest amount of initial help – not so small as to hinder early progress nor so large as to induce a comfortable complacency – was here sufficient to confirm quickly the unit's scientific worth and authority. Soon the embryo Institute was able to widen its study and teaching horizons to take in most matters of importance to fish farming in temperate regions and in the tropics as well. Now there are Institute research programmes operating in a dozen countries abroad and its training courses have benefited students from over 50 countries.

Support for all this activity has been attracted increasingly from university and research council sources, but to an even greater extent from the Overseas Development Administration and a variety of other public and private agencies. Those looking for 'relevance' in the conduct of our universities, and for their greater financial emancipation, will find gratification in the Institute of Aquaculture's substantial earnings from fees for services to fish farmers, and from the production of its own fish farms.

The Institute's growth over nearly 20 years matches equally impressive growth in the size and prosperity of fish farming in the UK. Most of the industry is located in Scotland, where production of salmon rose from 4,000 tonnes in 1983 to 20,000 in 1988 and is expected to exceed 50,000 in the 1990s. The present annual turnover of nearly £100 million is said to be more than that of the entire Scottish sea-fishing industry. The least that can be concluded about the connection between these two success stories is that each is much indebted to the other, and will remain so.

The Foundation's fortunes were still highly geared to those of the British motor industry; and dire events there sadly brought near-ruin in the early 1970s. The commercial failure of British Leyland destroyed most of the value of the original endowment, and this calamity was aggravated by the ravages of high inflation and by a stockmarket slump. The ordinary trustees eventually became empowered to diversify investment of the funds in their sole charge, but their strong ties of loyalty to the founder delayed the necessary moves beyond the eleventh hour. The shrunken proceeds of sale were, however, greatly augmented by reserves prudently built up over the years by the managing trustees, whose subsequent exercise of their own, unfettered, investment powers restored the income levels – albeit in drastically reduced real terms. Meanwhile, there were the consequences not only of an abrupt loss of over half the income but also of having to plough back much of what was left in order to rebuild the sorely depleted capital values. Moreover, it was imperative to adapt to other, external, changes, viz. rapid expansion of the universities, enormously greater government provision in most of the Foundation's fields of long-standing interest, and effects of the wind of change in the Commonwealth. Severe strains were being imposed, too, by periodic shortfalls in government funding of its research councils, provoking insupportable demands upon private sources.

In such a different world the Foundation had to become much more selective, and specialized; as well as leaner. The trustees sharpened the hitherto hazy distinction between their own functions and those of the official research councils, finally moving away from council preserves and from that style of support altogether. Impelled by a none the less high sense of duty towards the academic community, they perceived great benefit to science and social science from the introduction of many hundreds a year of quite small grants (less than £3,000). These are for innovative or experimental work, specialist conferences and working parties, and often for preparing research ground for larger proposals to be submitted elsewhere. It is a popular, efficient, and very productive form of support, fully exploiting the Foundation's advantages of swift and flexible action. Research is indirectly but effectively nourished also through schemes of personal awards to allow academic staff to spread their wings. Aside from research, there is specific encouragement for monitored experiments for the improvement of systems of health and social care.

Arrangements were made to secure continued, independent, life for the school curriculum projects (by setting up, for example, the Nuffield Chelsea Curriculum Trust, for science and mathematics); and attention turned to higher education. Support was given for inter-university collaboration on new course materials and methods to raise teaching and learning performance at undergraduate level; and for many other improvement schemes in this sector. The Foundation moved on again, as always it must, to new areas of need and promise, now including further and informal education and applications of high technology to education of the handicapped. Two important educational ventures, of quite different kinds, are the funding at Bristol of Britain's first 'Exploratory' (cf. the American Exploratorium and Science Centres) and of a major programme for non-sectarian education in Northern Ireland. The Exploratory – a place where children and adults can learn about science and technology by 'interacting' with working exhibits – has proved an excellent model for other similar science centres now springing up all over the country. The trustees have been taking a keen interest in this cause of enlarging public understanding of science and are developing a number of other initiatives to the same end. Not unconnected with that interest are their plans to help shape the courses and methods required for the Government's current policy of the teaching of technology in all schools – a matter which would certainly have been dear to the heart of Lord Nuffield.

Foundation action is not necessarily, nor all that easily, directed into fields at the centre of public debate. There are good reasons for this, but the opportunity to try to help overcome the basic weakness of the Northern Ireland schools system is one that not only bears on a tragic, persistent ill in our society but also gives direct impression to two of the Foundation's principal objects – the advancement of education and of social well-being. Over the years 1986–88 about £0.7 million was devoted to the support of integrated schools in Northern Ireland – by far the largest commitment the trustees have undertaken for some time.

From as long ago as 1830 some words of Bishop James Boyle powerfully sum up the predicament, and the ideal, then as now:

> I do not see how any man, wishing well of the public peace, and who looks to Ireland as his country, can think the peace can ever be permanently established, or the prosperity of the country ever well secured, if children are separated, at the commencement of life, on account of their religious opinions. I do not know of any measures which would prepare the way for a better feeling in Ireland (more) than uniting children at an early age, and bringing them up in the same school, leading them to commune with one another and to form those little intimacies and friendships which often subsist through life.

For all practical purposes the education system in Northern Ireland is still divided along religious lines. Many feel that, as it stands, the system contributes to the continuing divisions between the two communities. None will claim that integrated education of itself can resolve the whole of that problem, yet without it there must be less prospect of lasting improvement.

It is in that hopeful spirit that, in 1981, a group of parents started their own all-ability secondary school, Lagan College, for Catholic and Protestant children to be educated together as a matter of deliberate policy. Other schools, both primary and secondary, have followed, under the stimulus of the Lagan success and to meet growing demand. The 'demand' factor is crucial to attracting government support, which so far is forthcoming only after a school has completed a proving period. Meanwhile there is total dependence on private individual and corporate finance for the school buildings and for running and equipment costs; and it is to assist with these heavy burdens that the Foundation has been making substantial grants and loans in selected cases. Further sums of £0.25 million have been allocated for these purposes in each of the years 1989 and 1990. The Foundation is, moreover, taking the lead in coordinating the activities of other trusts working in this field. It is fairly confidently expected that these combined efforts will give the integrated schooling movement sufficient credibility and momentum to secure full government support for it in the foreseeable future.

Cost inflation, and the rise of other provision, led to replacing Commonwealth academic fellowships and scholarships by shorter-term awards for visits to the UK for training and career development in a variety of professions. Grants for research projects overseas declined in favour of strong support for appropriate technology and education in less-developed areas: and new ways of fostering scientific endeavour in those areas are now being tested.

Their progressive reassessment of scope and aims enabled the trustees to define more special interests, and to identify more openings for initiative. Significantly, they have mobilized the Foundation's strengths for mounting independent studies of issues of contemporary public importance. In 1975 the Centre for Agricultural Strategy was started at Reading University, whose remit was to formulate rational principles for the better conduct of British agricultural policy. Coordinated grant programmes have effected critical reviews also of housing policy, and of the social consequences of national transport policy (or lack of it). Perhaps the most successful of such policy studies, in terms of their influence on official thinking and on public opinion, is one that has demonstrated the balance of advantage of permanently moving our clocks forward one extra hour (maintaining British Summer Time in winter and introducing Double British Summer Time in summer). Since 1977 committees of inquiry have been commissioned to study dental education, the profession of pharmacy, town and country planning, and learning of modern languages after the age of 16: and to recommend and report publicly.

The independent inquiry is probably one of the things the Foundation does best; and for which it is best placed. Subjects of inquiry are, in practice, restricted to those where the Foundation has experience, and good access to people and organizations most able to help. Committees of inquiry make heavy demands on the sponsoring body – in setting them up, providing services and house-room, helping the preparation and publication of reports and, of course, funding (for what is nearly always a longer period than anyone first thought). Such ventures are not therefore to be undertaken lightly, nor on the cheap. In the last analysis their feasibility, and success, depend on finding eminent experts who will make time to meet together frequently over two, three, or even more years and give the matter a lot of other attention in between.

Nevertheless, Nuffield inquiries have increased in number and in diversity in recent years. This suggests both a natural and an acquired aptitude for the task. It acknowledges, too, the Foundation's authoritative standing and its constitutional impartiality. It can safely be assumed that Nuffield Reports, and their recommendations, will never be subject to pressures from any paymaster or lobby: they will be based as much as ever possible on matters of fact rather than opinion and, so far as human sensibilities are concerned, they will aim to be just rather than strive to be scrupulously 'fair'.

The very first of the kind was the Rowntree Report, mentioned earlier, which was published in 1947. This classic description of living conditions and particular needs of old people was a sure cornerstone for the edifice of all future relevant study and action. Another cornerstone, for developments of a very different nature, was the late Professor Hilde Himmelweit's *Television and the Child*, a book based on an investigation financed by the Foundation, which became a standard work of reference in what continues to be a very live subject.

There also appeared about that time, in 1960, the report of a Nuffield committee, chaired by Sir Frank Engledow, on 'Principles for British Agricultural Policy'. That report was used for a long time as a university teaching text, but it is also of interest for having been the starting point for discussions which led to the Foundation setting up the Centre for Agricultural Strategy. The Centre's *modus operandi* is based upon the committee of inquiry concept: a small staff conducts critical studies of British agricultural policy issues, guided by specialist working parties and advisory groups. That some of its reports have met with hostility here and there does not so much affirm the rightness or wrongness of their conclusions as warrant the power of the fearlessly independent inquiry method to, at the very least, stir informed debate.

The genesis of proposals for Nuffield inquiries follows no set pattern. The initial suggestion can come from within or without; and in the course of preliminary discussions the subject, or its boundaries, might be modified substantially. Thus, the dental education inquiry, which reviewed the whole matter of education and training for dentistry in the UK, started from an approach concerned only with postgraduate education. Again, for some time the trustees and staff had been considering problems arising from ever more intensive use of land under increasing agricultural, industrial, and social pressures. Faced with an impressive number of proposals for piecemeal research and experiment, the trustees concluded their most useful and timely contribution, instead, to be to organize a committee of inquiry into the system of town and country planning – the main agent of control of competing demands for land.

It could be asked why any or all of these recent inquiries – into dentistry, pharmacy, and land use planning – should not have been the business of government, using an instrument like a Royal Commission; and paid for out of public and not private charitable funds. (Royal Commissions seem nowadays to be out of fashion, or out of favour; and have sometimes been caricatured as devices for delaying or even preventing action.) All three subjects are certainly fraught with public policy issues, and all are associated with more or less conspicuous amounts of public spending. However, with the best will in the world, a government-sponsored-and-funded inquiry cannot place itself entirely beyond reach of the political process. To set up a government inquiry is in itself a political act, after all.

Nuffield reports have usually attracted widespread notice. Although dealing essentially with affairs in the UK, they also arouse much interest abroad: the pharmacy report, for example, has had to be translated into Japanese. Major recommendations in the planning report turned out to be anything but welcome in some quarters but, again, this can be taken as a vindication of the exercise; and in this case as a hint that reforms proposed by the report must await a favourable turn of the wheel of political fortune (meanwhile languishing as victims of 'the principle of unripe time'). The Foundation has itself followed up the report by making grants for a small number of projects relating to the findings. Similarly, the pharmacy report has pointed the way towards a new programme for the study of pharmacy practice and of the role of the pharmacist, which the trustees are supporting.

Encouraged as they are by their growing experience of committees of inquiry, the trustees are now planning such an incursion into the difficult subject of medical ethics: they have already been grant-aiding projects to improve understanding and teaching about the very challenging moral issues being thrown up by the rapid advance of medicine and biology.

In its 50 years the Foundation has made grants totalling more than £63 million – in support of what one observer declares to be almost every aspect of British intellectual and charitable activity. Capital assets today are about £92 million and the annual budget is over £4 million of which, approximately, £800,000 goes to science and medicine, £1.2 million to social research and experiment, £900,000 to education, £250,000 to Commonwealth awards, and £200,000 to care of the old. The Oliver Bird rheumatism fund accounts for £250,000. Smaller sums are disbursed from three other endowments:

(1) the Commonwealth Relations Trust, originating from an anonymous donation to Mr Baldwin when Prime Minister, for exchange visits by professional people from the UK and Commonwealth;

(2) the Elizabeth Nuffield Educational Fund set up by Lady Nuffield in 1956 to help women and girls complete educational and training courses; and

(3) the Viscount Nuffield Auxiliary Fund for the blind, and the profoundly deaf, and handicapped children.

The Foundation's widely respected persona was born of the aspirations of the founder and the provisions of the Trust Deed, and moulded by trustees and officers – not least by Leslie Farrer-Brown, the first secretary (later director) who held office for 21 years. Sir William Goodenough, the first chairman, was succeeded by his fellow-banker Sir Geoffrey Gibbs; Lord Todd (a Nobel Laureate in chemistry); Lord Trend (sometime Secretary of the Cabinet); and currently Lord Flowers (Vice-Chancellor of London University). The present director is Robert Hazell, a barrister, who heads a staff of 15. The seven managing trustees meet every three months but are otherwise much involved individually with Foundation business, in its advisory and selection committees, and in regular contact with the staff. To a constant ferment of ideas from these activities is added the gratefully appreciated help of a host of advisers and referees – the sum of all has worked to win and to hold Nuffield's prominent place in the ranks of creative foundations.

For 33 years, until 1986, the foundation enjoyed the use of a gracious villa and 4½ acre garden in Regent's Park. Such surroundings were highly conducive to the meeting of minds, and to good fellowship, at formal and informal gatherings, as well as to the effective conduct of day-to-day business, conferences, and the work of committees. The trustees recognized a duty, beyond that of the good husbandry of Lord Nuffield's benefaction, to care equally for this legacy from Regency times. The house was one of Decimus Burton's minor masterpieces, dating from 1823, and is one of only five villas left of 40 and more which ornamented Regent's Park at that period. Calling on the best advice available, the trustees had the interior restored as nearly as possible to the original style. The pleasure garden, as it would have been called in those days, was also given back something of a Regency character, under the guidance of garden historians. The cost of tending so large an area would have been an embarrassing charge on charitable funds, and the garden was in fact underleased to University College London,who used a good part of it for productive research into cytogenetics, plant and tree ecology, and plant physiology. However, the dictates of economy and of practical convenience led the Foundation to move to its present, more central, address at 28, Bedford Square, London WC1B 3EG. Here a Georgian architectural ambiance contrasts favourably, if a little less grandly, with that of the Prince Regent.

This review of what, so far, has been achieved by Lord Nuffield's largest benefaction is necessarily selective: others might want to make a different selection, from so large a horn of plenty. Only the perspective of posterity will truly show where there have been the most benefits to mankind from all those people and projects the Foundation has from time to time supported. By then the horn of plenty will be that much larger. Perhaps, who knows, the best is yet to be.

Notes

1. A full account will be found in B. Lovell, *The Story of Jodrell Bank* (OUP and Harper & Row, 1968).
2. Details of all the Foundation's grants and activities can be found in its annual reports (triennial since 1983), obtainable from the office address above. An informal history, *A Biography of the Nuffield Foundation*, has been written by Ronald W. Clark (Longman, 1972). Other relevant information and discussion is contained in: P.W.S. Andrews and E. Brunner, *The Life of Lord Nuffield* (Basil Blackwell, Oxford, 1955); P. Thomas, *The Aims and Outcomes of Social Policy Research* (Croom Helm, 1985); B. Whitaker, *The Foundations* (Penguin Books, 1979).

Chapter 25

Lord Nuffield and BUPA

E.F. Webb

BUPA, the British United Provident Association Limited, is now a household word. But today not many people realize that without Lord Nuffield's backing it might never have come into being.

When the National Health Service was created to provide free medical treatment 'from the cradle to the grave' for one and all, arrangements were made to allow people who so wished to make their own independent private arrangements on payment of the full cost. Hitherto, such people had been able to shield themselves against such expenses, which even then were considerable, by joining one of the many provident associations, which in return for an annual contribution provided insurance. These bodies were, however, mostly small; it was uncertain how many of their subscribers would wish to continue under the regime, and it was evident that most of them would not be able to continue. A conference was held in London in 1946 under the chairmanship of Sir William Goodenough, who with Alderman William Hyde, was Lord Nuffield's adviser on his benefactions, particularly to the medical world. The conference decided it would be unfair to leave members who might wish to maintain their contributions to their medical insurance provident funds without cover, and, in addition, that the valuable freedom to choose a specialist should be fostered as long as a demand existed. It was felt that these objects could best be achieved by the foundation of a national organization, open to all, which would be strong enough to stand on its own feet provided sufficient initial financial backing was forthcoming.

It was at this juncture that Lord Nuffield offered his financial guarantee of £250,000 – in those days a considerable sum, which enabled the founders to go forward with confidence. In recognition of the importance of his support, at its first General Meeting on 30 June 1947 members elected Lord Nuffield as joint President of BUPA, together with the Earl of Harewood – the late king's brother-in-law.

So far from withering away, the fledgling BUPA soon began to grow, slowly at first and then increasingly rapidly, so that by the end of 1989 the original 30,000 registrations had increased to 1,900,000, covering well over 3,000,000 persons. The early expectations that the NHS would meet all of most peoples' needs had given way to the realization that inevitably there were limits to its resources, especially as both medical science and demand were ever growing.

By the middle of the 1950s the demand for private accommodation was exceeding the supply. Many of the existing beds were in old-fashioned nursing homes, not equipped to deal with modern medicare; the remainder were pay-beds in NHS hospitals, and it was Government policy gradually to reduce their number. So in mid-1957 BUPA took the initiative by foundng a nursing homes trust organization with the initial object of rescuing and developing such existing institutions where this was practicable. BUPA provided a financial base, to support fund-raising locally. This conception of encouraging local support accorded with Lord Nuffield's ideas, and he agreed to allow his name to be embodied in the new organization's title – the Nuffield Nursing Homes Trust. There are currently 32 Nuffield Hospitals (as they are now known) located throughout the United Kingdom.

More recently, to meet the still growing demand, BUPA has formed its own hospital subsidiary company, which presently owns and operates 30 acute care hospitals, also spread throughout the United Kingdom.

So an astonishing transformation has taken place. Forty years ago it was only with reluctance that private medicine was allowed to continue alongside the NHS, and for many years afterwards the independent sector was despised and criticized as being anti-social and elitist. Only just over a decade-and-a-half ago, with the planned phasing-out of private beds, the independent sector was once again threatened with extinction. But with the change of Government in 1979, the atmosphere altered completely, and today the independent sector is increasingly recognized as an ally in the provision of a whole range of hospital and other specialist treatments. Its additional facilities are already helping to reduce queues and waiting lists.

Throughout these years BUPA has taken the lead in developing provident insurance, in providing the type of warm and human service so necessary in helping people threatened with illness, in keeping the supply of beds in line with demand, and in sponsoring preventive and other therapeutic services.

It would be an exaggeration to attribute all these developments to Lord

Nuffield's initiative. Yet it can be stated with conviction that without the support of his financial guarantee and prestige, BUPA could not have developed into today's well-respected and wide-reaching organization, with its growing role in the healthcare field.

Note

The author of this chapter, Teddy Webb, with typical modesty has not referred to his own huge and unique contribution to BUPA from 1947 to date, as General Manager, Chairman, and now President.

Lord Wigoder, Chairman of BUPA

PART FOUR

The Consequences of Wealth

Chapter 26

The kidnapping attempt

Carolyn Rutherford

During the 1930s Lord Nuffield's accumulation of great wealth, coupled with continuing and diverse philanthropy, made him the target for an endless stream of personal requests for financial assistance. As a well-known public figure he could also attract the attention of people with less savoury motives in mind, and in 1938 the bizarre story of an attempt to kidnap and hold him to ransom was revealed.

The whole episode, reported in the *Oxford Mail* as 'more like a "thriller" than real life', was planned to involve the almost theatrical use of disguise, an abduction at gunpoint, and a forced race to a yacht chartered under an assumed name. It was only forestalled by one more twist in the tale – an accomplice who secretly switched sides to collaborate with the police.

It had all begun in April 1938, when a man calling himself John Bruce Thornton renewed his former friendship with a Major Ramsden by advertising for him in a London newspaper. Thornton had for some time considered that it would be relatively easy to kidnap Lord Nuffield, simply because such an idea was totally unexpected. But, he needed an accomplice.

As Thornton and Ramsden got to know each other again Ramsden revealed that he was in need of money and Thornton jumped at the chance. He immediately suggested kidnapping Lord Nuffield, making it clear that he had had the idea for a long time, possibly since travelling on the same boat to Australia, back in 1930.

From this point on things happened quickly and Ramsden was drawn further and further into Thornton's schemes. The plan was to kidnap Nuffield from his Cowley office – at gunpoint, if necessary – and drive him to a yacht where he would be forced to write three letters: one to his secretary covering his absence, one to a bank authorizing payment of £100,000 to a Dr Webb, and a third introducing Thornton as this same Dr Webb. A Ford car was bought, trading Ramsden's in part-exchange but keeping the old licence for future use. Thornton also gave some thought to disguising his own appearance during the kidnap and bought false gold caps to fit over his own teeth, a wig, and even corsets to alter his body shape.

The next step, on 20 April, was to charter a yacht where Lord Nuffield could be held until the letter of credit had been successfully negotiated on the Continent. Eventually the *Pierrette* was hired from West Mersea in Essex, which was to be sailed round to Pin Mill near Ipswich. Ramsden's role was to stay with Nuffield while Thornton masqueraded as Dr Webb. Nuffield was then to be released, blindfolded, on shore while the two men got away.

Thornton then told Ramsden to get hold of false number plates for the car and, more ominously, to buy padlocks and chains that would keep Lord Nuffield helpless on the drive from Oxford to the yacht. It was at this point that Ramsden started feel uneasy about the whole idea and soon after reported it to the police, who informed Lord Nuffield. However, since there was so far only the intention to kidnap it was decided that Ramsden should stay in Thornton's confidence but at the same time report back to the police.

The main problem, now, for Thornton, was exactly how to request a meeting with Lord Nuffield in a way that was both plausible and certain to be granted – it must not arouse suspicion or run the risk of being rejected unseen by office staff, particularly by Wilfred Hobbs, Nuffield's private secretary who, as Thornton told Ramsden, was 'always with' Lord Nuffield. In the end, Thornton decided to pose as a journalist, R.C. Wilson, writing a series of articles on prominent businessmen for publication in the United States. On 20 May he hired a typewriter under the name of A.G. Wilson and, in the car near Colchester, typed the following letter:

> Queen's Hotel
> Birmingham
> 21st May 1938

My dear Lord Nuffield,

I am writing a series of articles on outstanding and prominent businessmen in England and Europe for publication in America.

From what I have heard of yourself and your work I am extremely desirous of including you in this series as being the outstanding personality in England today.

As the background of these articles is a personality and character sketch of the individual I would be extremely grateful if you would grant me an interview to suit your convenience.

I am not interested in seeking financial assistance in any shape or form for either business or charitable purposes.

A draft of the article concerning yourself would, of course, be submitted to you for your approval before publication.

I am visiting various business centres in England and will be in the vicinity of London and Oxford during the week beginning 23 May, and will then take the liberty of 'phoning you asking when you can grant me an interview.

Yours truly,

(Signed) R.C. Wilson

The next day Ramsden took the yacht round to Pin Mill and on the night of the 23rd both men stayed at the Spread Eagle Hotel at Thame: a telephone call was made to confirm an appointment with Lord Nuffield for the 24th at 6 pm, and the kidnapping was all ready to put into action.

Contingency plans were also made by Thornton: a threatening document ironically called a 'Letter of Introduction'. This was a strange mixture of gangland brutality and fussy attention to detail, and although Thornton later claimed it was merely part of scenario for a film plot, it got straight to the point with menacing directness:

To Viscount Nuffield
Read this carefully before passing any remark and do not show it to any other person:
(1) I am packing two Automatic Pistols of large calibre and will immediately shoot you through the guts if you attempt to raise alarm or suspicion: Any help will be too late to help you.
(2) You will ask me to come and see your Children's Hospital.
(3) Cancel any appointments which you may have today.
(4) Walk out with me to my car and the Chauffeur will do the rest. Do not on your way out attempt to make a run for it – it means instant death to you and anyone who attempts to interfere.
(5) Smile chat and be cheery even if it hurts – Do not raise suspicion anywhere or –
(6) I am a quick and accurate shot with a gun but do exactly what you have been told and you have nothing to fear.
(7) Place this letter on your desk with the remark 'The writer of this letter is a close personal friend of mine.'
(8) Dismiss anyone who may be in your office.
(9) Do not attempt to leave me under any pretext whatsoever
(10) Offer me a cigarette before the car starts and light one yourself.
(11) Make sure that we are not followed by any one of your folk – It's fatal for you.
(12) Jump to it I'm in a hurry.

But, in an extraordinary last-minute change of plan, the attempt to kidnap Lord Nuffield never actually took place. Inexplicably, Thornton withdrew from the scheme only half an hour before the meeting. One theory is that he had been drinking heavily the night before and felt too ill to go through with it. But, whatever the reason, when Ramsden, wearing his chauffeur's hat and in the car with false number plates, met Thornton at the Clarendon Hotel as arranged at 5.30 pm Thornton said that he was calling the whole thing off, that they couldn't do it that day, and told Ramsden to drive him to the country. Accordingly Ramsden drove on with him nearer to Cowley where he stopped and secretly phoned the police, who decided in any case to move in and surround the car. Thornton, however, was found with a Browning automatic strapped under his arm and another pistol and more ammunition in the car. The 'props' for his disguise and the letters to be sent from the yacht were also there. Clearly, Thornton had only decided to pull out right at the last moment.

At the trial, when he was sentenced to seven years in prison, it emerged that 'Thornton' was only one of many aliases. Thornton's real name was Patrick Boyle Tuellman, a man with a long history of criminal activity: over 18 years he had obtained £82,000 through blackmail and extortion, and his record perhaps added to the grim reality of the whole scheme to kidnap Lord Nuffield, even if it had resembled a fictional 'thriller'. Quite apart from the written threats, the chains, pistols, and blindfolds, there was also the question of how Lord Nuffield would have been forced to sign the letters of credit against his will: police searching *Pierette* found a collection of implements including hypodermic needles and surgical instruments which might have been intended to 'persuade' him. Lord Nuffield was apparently annoyed not to have been allowed by the police to go through with the kidnapping – he would have liked the opportunity to deal with the kidnappers himself. Fortunately, such a deadly confrontation never, in the end, took place.

Chapter 27
More bullets were effective

F. John Minns

General Stanislas Sochaczewski of the Polish Army was one of many hopeful visitors to Oxford during 1939 and 1940 who was convinced that the famous Lord Nuffield would help him, even though the British War Office had given him scant encouragement. He had brought with him an invention for the rapid indoor training of raw recruits in the efficient use of a service rifle. Unfortunately his plea for an interview with his Lordship was refused, as were so many others, for various reasons, in those very troubled times. Lord Nuffield was under tremendous pressure at the time for a number of reasons and the post bag each morning often took an hour to clear, telephone calls being severly screened.

His particular reason for seeking Lord Nuffield's help, however, was considered so compelling by an Oxford banker, Mr E.W. Robertson that I was asked to examine the facts of the matter, possibly then to act as an advocate. My meeting with the General and his English-speaking advisor, Zygmunt de L. Bakanowski PMC, quickly revealed the surprising information that the General had achieved total success in convincing the French Army authorities, but had then been utterly foiled by the military collapse of their country.

The General had been very fortunate to have escaped from France in June 1940 with the retreating British forces. He went immediately to the War Office in London but was fobbed off by extremely preoccupied busy officers, rather understandably at that time. He was then advised to try to see Lord Nuffield, but was no more successful.

I was handed the most impressively signed and massively sealed document which stated that the French Government had recently contracted to use General Sochaczewski's invention. But alas, it was signed and dated only a few days before France was overrun by the German Army. I was then shown the rather crude drawings of the invention and told that he desperately needed a prototype to be made in order to convince the cautious War Office of its value. The point was made that my small factory

*Lord Nuffield testing the Swift Training Rifle. With him (L. to R.) Z. de L. Bakanowski,
F.J. Minns, Lord Donegal, Wing Cmdr. A.J. Brown, Flt.-Lieut. P.G.H. Fender and Flt.-Lieut.
H. Young.*
[F.J. Minns]

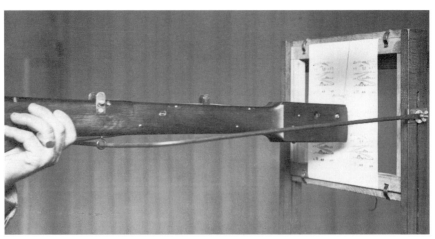

Close-up of the Swift Training Rifle target.
[F.J. Minns]

was a more suitable place to make a British prototype of his device than the mass production Nuffield factories at Cowley or elsewhere.

A prototype, when made, indicated the need for design improvements and, in due course, led to orders from the Home Guard. Given the name of the Swift Training Rifle, the invention was used by Captain Jacklin, a musketry training instructor, who quickly trained *indoors* ten teenage recruits who then competed outdoors, using service rifles and live ammunition, against ten Home Guard men who had served in the 1914–18 War. The teenagers won so very easily that the contest was stopped.

Interest by the Royal Air Force, then responsible for the weapon training of the RAF Regiment, charged with the ground defence of aerodromes, resulted in an order for 8,000 units from the Ministry of Aircraft Production. This order was classed as extremely urgent. More orders followed from Allied Forces.

The reason given to me for the Royal Air Force taking such a quick interest in a fast indoor method of weapon training was that in 1940 they were being starved of ammunition so were lacking in musketry training and consequently failing to defend airfields in Europe from ground attack by enemy land forces.

For such large orders to be supplied so quickly I had to ask Lord Nuffield for the help of the buying staff of his Cowley Works in order to purchase the metal parts required from various engineering firms having spare capacity. He called his local director, Alfred Keen to his office and agreed to undertake this limited but crucial function. Most of the Swift Training Rifle was machined at Botley in Oxford from imported hardwoods. Assembly and despatch was done at requisitioned premises and the order was fulfilled. Members of the RAF Regiment trained by the British invented machine gun trainer (which logically followed the Swift Training Rifle) would remember using the severely vibrating synthetic trainer which also fired small electric sparks into a paper target burning small holes as the device was traversed across the portrayed 'field of fire'.

The astonishing success of the Sochaczewski method of indoor weapon training *without the use of live ammunition* also led to British-designed electrically operated devices for the training of recruits to use machine guns, again without wasting live ammunition.

A task force, said to have been Canadian, was reported to have used the Swift Training Rifle for last minute training on board their sea transport while crossing the English Channel at night prior to D-Day on a very hazardous dawn raid to test the German coastal defence at Dieppe.

The photograph reproduced of Lord Nuffield using the Swift Training

Rifle at the Randolph Hotel Oxford was published in the *Sunday Despatch* and aroused comment when it was seen that he was holding the synthetic rifle incorrectly. He was known to be ambidextrous but may have had better vision in his left eye. Flight Lieutenant P.G.H. Fender, seen standing on the right, will be remembered as a cricketing stalwart of former years.

The Swift Training Rifle is on display at the Royal Air Force Museum at Hendon.

THE 1942 HOUSE OF LORDS DEBATE

The military success of the Sochaczewski-invented Swift Training Rifle musketry training method was historically confirmed when Lord Mottistone rose on 29 September 1942 in the House of Lords to ask HM Government (I quote from *Hansard,* HMSO Vol 124 No 82):

... whether in view of the present war situation they will arrange immediately for the training to arms of the whole male population on the lines successfully adopted by the Royal Air Force for the protection of their establishments.

He later said:

I think it was Lord Donegal who wrote an article pointing out the importance of the matter and Lord Nuffield who said it ... had got to be done ... Shortly afterwards I saw an article in *The Rifleman* giving a description of this particular method, which is one of the many means which the Royal Air Force has adopted in order to save time.

He went on to say:

I sought the opinion of ... a man who is very keen about this thing ... that is Lord Nuffield ... and he said I hope you will tell members of the House that I would have attended the House (debate) myself but I have to preside over a most important meeting concerning all the hospitals in Great Britain and I cannot possibly get away, otherwise I would have been in my place.

Summing up at the end of a lengthy debate Lord Mottistone said:

... as we are Enemy Number One to the Germans, it seems reasonable that we should follow the example of other countries who are not Number One. I have also pointed out that the Royal Air Force had found that what was supposed to be very difficult is very easy. I may remark that there is no optimism about Lord Nuffield because it is quite clear that he has gone into the matter with great care and so have others.

If the noble Lords had been informed of the simplicity and relative ease of manufacture of the Swift Training Rifle it is quite possible that the motion would have been carried – but they were not the House of Commons, and men often react against things that seem too simple and are not fully explained.

Lord Nuffield knew both aspects of the matter.

He knew that without disrupting the war effort at all during the past two years enough Swift Training Rifles had actually been made in Oxford to successfully train thousands of service men in the Royal Air Force and Allied Forces.

He knew that this new invention, having been proven for production could easily be assembled in greater quantities using the same unskilled workforce.

He knew that men in his large factories would welcome the opportunity to become 'crack shots', so – if the need did arise – be able to defend their homes rather that remain helpless in the face of an invading enemy as so many Continentals had done recently.

He knew that as little as six hours indoor training of each factory worker would produce remarkable musketry skills.

But, he also knew that, with all resources under Government control, he, Nuffield, could do nothing but praise the invention.

Chapter 28

His million-pound disappointment

F. John Minns

Second only to having no son to succeed him, the greatest disappointment of Lord Nuffield's life was that, for two very strong reasons, he had to give way substantially when offering a million pounds for a purpose of the utmost importance to him.[1]

It was his most ardent desire in 1936 to found a college, essentially in Oxford, for a specific purpose. He therefore asked the University of Oxford if it would accept such a gift to establish a College of Engineering on a fine site he already owned. He envisaged well-designed new buildings having the very best workshop and laboratories fully equipped with the latest available instruments and machines so that his scholarly-trained engineers should rise to the forefront of British Industry. He wished such a college to also educate its students in modern business management and accountancy to bring together the practical and theoretical advancement of British industry. He was a staunch loyalist. He expressed the hope that his new college would 'produce a flow of recruits to industry'. He expected these students would attain an Oxford degree in such subjects to raise their status to a parity with the other professions and thus attract more school leavers to enter industry.

Such was his ambition. It was, however, very unfortunate that he, who had been so outstandingly successful in a severly practical world, should find that the then Vice-Chancellor of the University of Oxford, the austere Dr A.D. Lindsay, held very different views on the subject of educational priorities.

Lord Nuffield, the practical man, a native of the Oxford he so greatly loved, had already bought the ideal site for an Oxford College. It was a derelict tract of land situated between the railway station and the centre of Oxford, known as the canal wharf, long disused and an eyesore to residents and visitors. It would complete a ring of colleges around the ancient city on the west, between Worcester and Pembroke Colleges with a long frontage to New Road.

Having secured this unique site it could only be Oxford University, no less, that should administer and give the status necessary to a college to be so well funded. He expressed his ideas with great fervour and enthusiasm but to no avail. It is almost certain that at any other university Lord Nuffield's fervent wishes, as well as his money, would have been keenly and gratefully accepted. Not so at the academically traditional ancient University of Oxford.

Land being immovable, and its use for other purposes in this prime location being unacceptable, capitulation was virtually forced upon him. The derelict site had to be used to enhance the beauty of his beloved Oxford. Decisive as always he gave way, perhaps too quickly. It was a very hard decision and one that he always bitterly regretted having to make: his great disappointment being the use made of the college bearing his name, not the location, upon which he was adamant.

That the use to which the college on completion was put did not, to his mind, even remotely conform to that first proposed to him by the Vice-Chancellor, Dr Lindsay, in 1936 was evident to those to whom he often spoke so sadly of his college. He did, however, relent sufficiently from his annoyance to attend the opening ceremony of Nuffield College and in later years much enjoyed the friendship of the College Warden, Sir Norman Chester, who softened his unhappiness considerably. However, he never withdrew from his conviction that the benefit to the country would have been far, far greater if his money had been used for the higher training of engineers.

Not all senior members of Oxford University it seems had agreed in 1936 with the Vice-Chancellor's diversion of Lord Nuffield's benefaction to advance political and social studies, as recorded quite forcefully by Dr A.L. Rowse the leading historian, a Fellow of All Souls College, Oxford and the British Academy, who, in his book *Oxford in the History of the Nation* wrote:

In 1936 Nuffield . . . wished to found a college for the study of engineering, but was over-persuaded by the sanguine (and socialist) master of Balliol, Dr Lindsay, who favoured philosophy, politics and economics – already well enough provided for. When the war came there was an acute shortage of engineers: the intuition of the man of genius had been right after all. Whether there is much value to be attached to the academic study of politics, or the academic study of economics, for these are practical activities to be learned in the field of action, is open to question.

THE HORN OF PLENTY

"SAY WHEN!"

[With Mr. Punch's congratulations to Lord NUFFIELD, who has increased his enormous gift to Oxford University for Medical Research by another £750,000.]

Cartoon. Punch, *2 December 1936.*

Turning for professional confirmation from industry of the acute shortage of engineers observed by Dr Rowse, I looked first to the heartland of British engineering, the industrial Midlands, and I am most grateful to the Chancellor of Birmingham University, Sir Alex Jarratt, Chairman of Smith's Industries plc who kindly responded as follows:

> I refer to your letter about the benefactions made by Lord Nuffield and especially the missed opportunity to establish a College or similar institution devoted to the study of engineering.
>
> As you will know, Lord Nuffield made more than one bequest to the University of Birmingham and was a member of the University's Appeal Committee in 1954. His very welcome generosity did not, however extend to engineering.
>
> I find it hard to answer your question as to whether a well-endowed engineering institution under the aegis of Birmingham University would of itself have been of great benefit to this country during the last 50 years or so. Certainly I am of the view, shared by many others, that we have not devoted sufficient attention and funds to the training of engineers in this country and our economic performance has probably suffered in consequence.
>
> Even today when there is far more support for engineering and undoubtedly a continuing need, it remains difficult to encourage sufficient young people to come in to the profession. I think this has much to do with social attitudes and the career preferences promoted by schools (and by parents) as any other factor.

Lord Nuffield was particularly anxious to place university-trained engineers into his motor industry so the views of the Chairman of the Ford Motor Company of Britain (1980–86), Mr Sam Toy, are most significant to this industry. Mr Toy very kindly answered my question most thoroughly in the following way:

> Time spent on 'if only' exercises is frequently misspent, but perhaps something can be learned on this occasion – and if the lesson is properly applied, the future of our Industry may benefit.
>
> What I have to say of course, stems mainly from experiences within my own company, but I don't doubt that other Industrial Companies could probably tell similar stories.
>
> From 1949 onwards Ford Motor Company Ltd embarked on a Graduate Trainee recruitment programme, that rapidly became its practically exclusive source of management material. In fact the annual intake of graduates of all disciplines was generally in the order of one hundred and fifty to two hundred.

During the late sixties, our then Chairman, Sir William Batty, introduced an ongoing programme of quarterly reviews of management development convering all aspects of the subject. During the mid seventies his successor, Mr Terry Beckett, later Sir Terence Beckett of the CBI, and I, at one of these meetings, took time making one our regular analysis of the then recent intake of Graduate Trainees; which Universities they had come from; what they had read; their progress in the Company etc., only to be astounded to note that during the whole of the proceeding five years, only one Oxbridge man had joined the marketing organisation of Ford of Britain. Urgent action to correct this situation was taken, but stimulating interest in the Universities in joining Industry and in particular the Motor Industry was an uphill battle of very considerable difficulty – having in mind the high incidence of graduates going on to something defined as 'further education'; the then attractions of 'the City' etc.

In particular, when we took a look at the supply of 'Production Engineers' it was practically non-existent, and so we funded for the next ten years a lectureship in the subject at Sidney Sussex College in the hope that perhaps a few of our budding engineers might be induced to at least take an appraising look at our Industry, when deciding on career prospects.

Finally, as a Cambridge man, may I suggest that what I would call the 'Ivory Tower' mentality is not confined to 'the other place'. I quote from a recent address from a very senior person at Cambridge:

'In short, universities are to be treated more and more like businesses and the market approach is the order of the day. Little of this is either palatable or appropriate to the academic community of our size and complexity.'

I hasten to acknowledge, by the way, that I have quoted out of context, but the words seemed to me to be so appropriate and indicative of what I believe to be the attitude of far too many 'academics', that I couldn't resist the quotation. Of course our Universities, must be given academic freedom, and of course there is much more to a cultured society than 'core-sand and smoke', but some of the managements of our Universities would, in my opinion, do well to remember that their very existence depends on the support of regular Industry in its broadest sense – and that among other demands, a regular supply of well educated and well trained industrialists of the future is a must from our Universities if they are to play a proper part in our society.

Now how does this relate to Nuffield's proposal of the thirties? Well I happen to believe that the knock-on effect of an engineering College in the thirties would have effected Britain's competitive position all down the years – who knows, our engineers and industrialists of today might have been as highly regarded by our society as those of Germany or Japan are today!

From the above authoritative judgements it is clear that British industry could have attracted more highly-trained recruits had a specialist college at Oxford University given prestige to engineering and allied subjects prior to and since the Second World War.

Lord Nuffield's foresight sadly led him into a bitter and expensive disappointment. But I am sure he would not wish this chapter to end on a despondent note, out of tune with the rest of this commemorative book, so I conclude with a story concerning one of his more modest benefactions that would have gladdened his quiet nature.

Towards to end of the last war, a young Royal Air Force officer, who had survived the Battle of Britain and had been in action for 48 hours without sleep, was suddenly recalled for duty at 4 am next morning. He was in London and had spent ages looking for a place to sleep. Every hotel was full so, in desperation, he went to a police station and begged for the use of a cell for a few hours rest. He guessed that some very special flying operation must be planned for the morrow and knew that he would be useless without sleep. The police officer told him that they could do better than a cell and directed him to a nearby Nuffield hostel for Serving Officers that had been recently opened by HM the Queen. At the hostel he was welcomed, given a comfortable bed, called in time for a very early breakfast and found that transport had been arranged for what was his immediate participation in the D-Day operation.

He said that he was sure that he owed his life to that hostel and the generosity of Lord Nuffield. He told this story a few years ago to B. Huntley, Curator-Hostess at Nuffield Place, Lord Nuffield's home, having seen there a decorative plate that reminded him of his meal at the hostel. It was a piece of the china chosen by the Queen for the hostel she had opened, the sample of which Lady Nuffield had kept.

Note

1. The University does not consider that this chapter represents a full picture of this particular piece of history; for another account the reader is referred to chapter 6 (and in particular pp. 63–70) of *Economics, Politics and Social Studies in Oxford, 1900–1985* by Sir Norman Chester (Macmillan, 1986).

Chapter 29

Life in a millionaire's household

Bronwen Huntley

In the autumn of 1964 I was asked by Nuffield College if I would take over the running of Nuffield Place near Henley, the last home of Lord Nuffield who had died in 1963. In my first interview with Norman Chester, the Warden of Nuffield College, which now owned Nuffield Place, I was shown a picture of a most attractive country house. I was given the bare outline of the situation. It was Norman Chester to whom Lord Nuffield voiced his last bequest. He offered the balance of his fortune on his death to keep and maintain his house, Nuffield Place, and the gardens in perpetuity. He envisaged a place that should be kept as a home to provide a retreat for members of Nuffield College to find peace for special study, and leisure and pleasure for a limited stay. It was not to be used as a lodging house. There were other reservations: the house was not to change in character or the furnishings, except for some renovations as would be necessary.

The members of his domestic staff at the date of his death were to be allowed to continue there, and those in cottages were to remain in them until death. At the time there were two indoor staff, a housekeeper named Kathleen Francis and Mrs Mitchell, the wife of a gardener, her assistant. There were two full-time gardeners, Widdows and Mitchell. Finally, Nuffield told the Warden that he was not going to die a millionaire.

It was an offer the Warden could not refuse but he told me he had many misgivings about it. It was too far away from Oxford and it would cost thousands a year to keep it as intended, but when the will was read there seemed to be plenty of money to do all Lord Nuffield had wanted.

I was asked if I would take over the full responsibility of the house and gardens. A house would be built for me attached to the main house and I could live my own life as I wished and be able to engage more staff if needed. It seemed a challenge I could not refuse.

It was bitterly cold day on my first introduction to the house. Everywhere looked calm and beautiful. A neat hedge on the right with trees and lawn beyond and, on the left, shrubberies. There was still a smattering of snow and the silence that always accompanies it. It should have been a good omen but as we turned to the main door at the bend in the drive my heart sank.

It was not because of my first glimpse of the house itself, as it has a very pleasant appearance. It is not old, having been enlarged in 1915 by Sir John Wimble and used by his family as a country cottage. It had then been called Merrons Mount. The walls of the house are in red brick inset with bricks of slate blue. Friends had told me it was a grim, forbidding house full of gloomy furniture and without one vestige of interest. The depression I felt was a total lack of welcome as from a house unused. The main door was studded with iron bolts in mock Tudor design and pale for want of a coat of varnish. It had one of those bell pulls that clang like a toll of doom throughout the house.

After what seemed ages we heard the sounds of bolts being drawn and the door was opened by Mr Keith Lucas, the Domestic Bursar of Nuffield College. There were several people inside, including the Warden and his wife, Mr and Mrs Chester (later Sir Norman and Lady Chester).

Mrs Chester accompanied me around the house. First, the drawing room. My first impression was of opulent gloom. The floor was covered with oriental rugs. There was a handsome long sofa upholstered in tapestry and several walnut chairs, also in tapestry. They were good reproductions, Queen Anne style. In an alcove stood a large HMV gramophone cabinet. I had been told that the staff had kept meticulous care of the house since Lady Nuffied died. By now she had been dead five years and Lord Nuffield one. There was a lovely chest of drawers in walnut. The dining room, with its stippled walls, presented a perfect period picture of the 1930s. A large refectory table in oak ran the length of the room. At the far end was a large oak armoir made up of old wood with a curious look of old iron. On the floor was a beautiful sapphire carpet with a brightly coloured flower border. Along the left wall as one entered was an oak sideboard and on the wall above, a tapestry panel. There were six high-backed chairs around the table, each upholstered in hand-worked tapestry.

Facing us as we walked into the dining room hung a portrait of Lord Nuffield. The only time I had spoken to him was at a Red Cross bazaar in the Town Hall at Oxford. He was introduced to me in the company of another man, General de Gaulle, also destined to be world famous, but the kindliest of these two now looked down at me with the twinkling blue eyes I remembered from that time, and his picture seemed to give me a welcome.

Next to the dining room is a small sitting room. The walls here were in the same dingy yellow, stained by tobacco smoke. A fine carpet almost covered the floor, it looked to be a Wilton. On the right as one entered was a glass-fronted cabinet in mahogany. Behind the door on the right was a walnut glass-fronted cabinet filled with lovely pieces of blue and white china. This had been in the boardroom of the Wolseley works when taken over by Lord Nuffield, who had it and its contents sent to his home, much to the delight of Lady Nuffield.

Lady Nuffield seemed to have been very fond of the sapphire blue carpets covering the main staircase and landing of the first floor. In all the bedrooms the carpets were a rich deep pile called Liner carpet, as used in the state room and suites on luxury liners. At the top of the main staircase was a walnut chest.

Lady Nuffield's bedroom was separated from Lord Nuffield's by an enclosed sun-porch. Her bedroom, like the rest of the rooms on that floor, was luxuriously furnished. Soft, thick carpet on the floor, a walnut bedroom suite, a tapestry stool, Persian rugs on the floor and a screen embroidered in silk, an antique fire-screen piece. From there we passed through the sun-room to Lord Nuffield's bedroom. Here were photographs of many famous people and a clock that was said to have come from Buckingham Palace. The bed lay straight across the middle of the room with its head against the disused fireplace. It was an ordinary divan bed with a shabby gold rayon coverlet. Over the bed and hanging from the mantle-piece above was a tattered electric light shade with a small bulb inside. Lord Nuffield had fixed this up himself.

On the far right-hand side of his bedroom a large cupboard had been built in. This I heard later had been installed by Lord Nuffield on a day when Lady Nuffield had been out. Kathleen, the housekeeper, told me that it had all been a secret from her because she always complained of the muddles in his room. Here he kept his personal hand tools he had used as a cycle repairer, and a shoemaker's last from the days when he had to mend his own and his wife's shoes and boots. On the right on the middle shelf was a small mahogany box and in this was a bottle in which was his appendix. This had been given to him by the surgeon who had performed the operation. Lady Nuffield was quite pleased when she returned from Oxford, and from then on referred to the cupboard as his toy cupboard. In it he kept several broken items, mostly clocks he was going to repair one day.

In the main kitchen was an Esse cooker unit and by its side, leaning against a table, was a small middle-aged woman who was introduced to me as Kathleen the housekeeper. Between Kathleen and Lady Nuffield there had been a love-hate relationship. Whatever love Lady Nuffield had left from her love of her husband was centred on Kathleen. In spite of the terrible rows that often occurred between them causing Kathleen to run home to her mother, it was Lady Nuffield who would beg her to come back. But her loyalty to both Lord and Lady Nuffield was paramount.

When all the details of my appointment were settled I went to Nuffield Place to see the architect and look through his plans. I met the gardeners, Mitchell and Tony Morris. I liked them both and my first impression was not misplaced as they both proved the towers of strength I needed in the years to come.

Not having an inventory, I asked Kathleen to give me a list of all the linen. The real linen cupboard was full of old picture frames while the linen was tucked away in all kinds of unusual places. I met Mrs Mitchell the same day, and what a breath of fresh air she brought with her. She was helping Kathleen sort out the linen as the workmen were expected the next day. It was a race against time to clear the rooms before they started to build my residence. She told me that wherever they looked they found linen sheets, pillow cases, table linen, all in mint condition, and most had never been used. There were towels of soft, rich pile, pretty bedspreads, loads of new dusters and cleaning materials, all hidden in different cupboards. Pulled out from another cupboard were the sheets and pillow cases that had been in regular use. I could hardly believe what I saw. Sheets had been turned top to bottom and even the quarters had been patched and darned. Looking at one of these Mrs Mitchell exclaimed, 'to think that dear old man slept and died on one of these sheets. I know, because I washed them all after, and all this lovely linen he never enjoyed.'

Kathleen told me that Lady Nuffield had insisted on strict economy as she had known what it was to be poor. There had been a time in her early married life when her husband had verged on bankruptcy. Some friends came to his rescue and she had given all she had, except her wedding ring.

In the Spring Kathleen and I walked in the garden to get away from the workmen banging about in the house. As we were returning to the house Kathleen said, 'I wonder what the daffodil walk is doing.' I followed her to a green sward the far side of the tennis court, suddenly the most beautiful sight lay before us. For the whole length of the paddock a carpet of spring flowers swayed before us in the gentle breeze. I could understand the poet's urge. A path divided the area and for at least fifteen feet on each side of this were daffodils of every colour and shape, such as one only sees at horticultural shows. I gasped at each rare specimen I touched. Kathleen smiled at my pleasure and said, 'wait until the rhododendrons and azaleas come out and the magnolias and all the blossom trees.' She was silent as we returned to the house. Once again she kept turning as though someone was following us. Then she said, 'I knew his Lordship would never leave this place.' 'Did he ever think of doing so?' I asked. 'Well, there was a time when her Ladyship came back from America after the war and found that a Borstal was right next door. They did look for a place then but it never came to anything.' I had heard this from several people. At some time Lord Nuffield had given a large sum of money for the use of Borstal Institutions. It could never have occurred to him that the Home Office would use his money so near to his home. When Lady Nuffield returned from America where she had lived for most of the war years she was horrified, and never enjoyed a moment of peace from that time until her death. From then on she became a recluse and wanted to live elsewhere. They did look at houses but they were all too big or too far away from Oxford to suit Lord Nuffield.

Lady Nuffield was of a very nervous disposition. The main gate was kept closed, also the main door. Old sacks covered the hedges bordering the drive that also led to the Borstal. She lived in dread of any escapees entering the gardens. The thought of bombs had frightened her enough but this was a constant fear.

One of the stipulations I had made was that I should be allowed to pick flowers for the house. We also sent flowers to Lord Nuffield's grave every Friday but this ceased when I left Nuffield Place.

One day Kathleen and I were taking stock in Lord Nuffield's bedroom. She explained to me the circumstances of most of the articles and the associations of the different photographs in the room. She opened the two doors that separated his room from Lady Nuffield's. She said they were always kept open so that they could talk to each other. Lady Nuffield used to have first look at the morning newspapers. She would call from her bedroom, 'William, I have pencilled in something you should help.' On this occasion it was a boys' club that needed help to form a football club as they were all too poor to provide anything for themselves. That same day Lord Nuffield sent someone to this northern town to find out the details and, hearing their need was genuine, he bought a field for them, provided enough money to fit them out with football clothes and, said Kathleen as an afterthought, he had even given them the goal posts.

Mrs Mitchell knew all about the food that was eaten at Nuffield Place. When there was to be a real slap-up dinner party the caterers were called in and all the best table linen was brought out and the silver and the lovely blue and crystal glasses. The silver candelabra was given a special rub-up and Widdows was ordered to pick flowers. Lady Nuffield laid the table herself and once she let Mrs Mitchell and Kathleen look at the table when it was ready. 'You should have seen it', Mrs Mitchell said, 'it looked so lovely, that was the time the Emperor of Ethiopia came and some of his staff. However, we were not allowed to go in again. The caterers just brought the food and we had to warm it up in the kitchen. Lady Nuffield came running in and out with dirty dishes for us to wash-up while she took in the next course. I often wondered what the Emperor must have thought of her popping in and out like that. After all, he only had to clap his hands for dozens of servants to come to him.'

I did see how it may have looked when I gave dinner parties there and invited some of the members of Nuffield College, but I had to use my own candelabra and silver condiments, as all the valuables had been taken to the College.

They both loved their garden – Lady Nuffield for the flowers and Lord Nuffield in order to don old clothes and potter about doing odd jobs, particularly on days when the gardeners were off duty. Kathleen said, 'One day he was trimming the hedge at the end of the drive when a stranger drew up at the garden gate and spoke to him. He asked his Lordship if it was the house where that chap Nuffield lived. When his Lordship said it was, he asked him what sort of a chap Lord Nuffield was. His Lordship replied "Oh, he was not so bad when you go to know him." Then the man said he didn't expect he paid him much and his Lordship replied "It was enough, and there was a bit left over for others." Then the man took out half-a-crown and gave it to him – and wasn't his Lordship pleased! He came in and told us all about it and showed us the half-crown and then put it back in his pocket. He told everyone about this – he thought it was so very funny.'

Note

1. Nuffield Place, near Henley, is open to visitors on the second and fourth Sunday afternoons of each month from May until September. See press announcements.

Chapter 30

The loneliness of success

F. John Minns

Although thousands had worked with and for Nuffield, and millions knew of him, few had been allowed to get to know him really well. The anecdote with which the previous chapter concludes, shows that Nuffield realized this. Moreover, his great amusement at the incident provides a glimpse of his concealed good nature. Truly, 'he was not so bad when you got to know him'. He was almost an introvert, much preferring to meet and converse with others on a one-to-one basis; good at extracting by pertinent questions what he wanted to know but disinclined to expose his own thoughts to another until he was ready to express as a directive his decision which would finalize the discussion. His paramount authority had enabled him to become quite autocratic in his dealings with people. His executives were summoned to his office, as were virtually all others to whom he granted appointments. He rarely granted interviews to press reporters and was not a clubbable man, even while President of the Bullnosed Morris Car Club which Egerton Ferguson and I founded in 1952. He was a figurehead in the MG and other car clubs. His membership of the Royal Automobile Club foundered due to some early difference of opinion but he did, many decades later, accept an official invitation of the Club Council to a celebratory luncheon to commemorate his eightieth birthday at which his portrait was presented to the club. Amongst those attending were many famous in the world of motoring.

The first chapters of this book portray the manner in which he rose from a modest start in life to show great enterprise, to build an industrial empire, and then to become Britain's best known charitable benefactor, giving away during his lifetime more than any previous Englishman. It now only remains to take a final look at the impact these accomplishments had upon the man himself. How did his quiet character, his modest working environment, and his dedication to the careful distribution of his great wealth affect the closing years of his life?

First, it was clear that he had learnt, both from his youthful

The presentation of the portrait by F.J. Minns at the RAC luncheon.
[F.J. Minns]

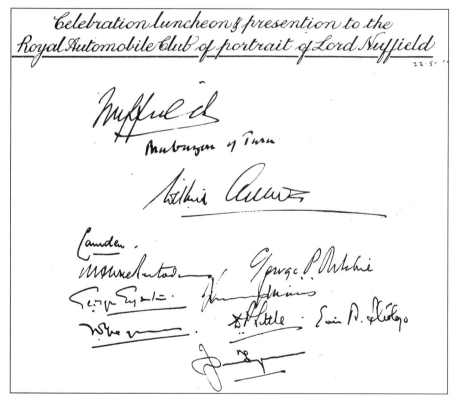

A signed menu commemorating the RAC presentation luncheon. Signatures include those of Lord Nuffield, the Marquis Camden, Lord Brabazon of Tara, Wilfred Andrews, M.A.W. de Bertodano, George Eyston, J.D. Fergus, W.P. Little, F.J. Minns, George Ritchie, Eric Strologo.

determination to train for and win long-distance cycle races – a lonely sport – and from his early business experience, to depend entirely upon himself; indeed it was in his very nature to be firmly independent. This was often shown in personal business deals but quite significantly when each of his chief executive co-directors, Leonard Lord and Sir Miles Thomas, took their leave of him in 1936 and 1947. On the first occasion, some wit at Cowley Works said 'there just wasn't enough room in the Board Room for two Lords'. He could quietly face any such serious and preventable loss to remain in supreme control rather than be pressurized by an understandably ambitious assistant, however eminent and competent. The following quotation and his consequential resistance to such pressure illustrate the strength of will he exercised.

> With the end of the war an increasing amount of Sir Miles Thomas's time became taken up with service on outside public boards. Since the Vice-Chairmanship involved complete responsibility under Nuffield for the management of the whole organisation, it was anomalous that it should be a part-time office.[1]

Lord Nuffield had become increasingly annoyed that his popular chief executive, Sir Miles Thomas, was continuing ambitiously to foster such a serious division of his time and loyalty to outside interests. It is hardly surprising that Nuffield, as chairman, could not accept the assumption by his vice-chairman, Sir Miles, who had considered himself to be 'in double harness' with him,[2] while at the same time increasingly becoming a part-timer in the huge business.

Total loyalty had always been demanded by his Lordship of his staff and even at seventy when he was becoming a tired man, his strength of purpose did not allow him to be overridden, even by the outstanding Sir Miles. Many years of total control had given him no thought of sharing his authority and such an ill-matched alliance between two such strong characters would not have been good for the business.

Such independence of character had increased his manner of some aloofness but significantly the loss of competent chief executives did not cause any downturn in the profitability of the vast business that he had always controlled. But it must have added to his self-imposed solitude.

Having become a multi-millionaire, he had not retired grandly to live on the fruits of this success as Morris, the great car manufacturer.

When he once said to me 'it is more difficult to give money than to make it' I must admit that I, then a young man in my own business, was

Morris on two wheels: at the Iffley Road track, Oxford.
[F.J. Minns]

Morris on four wheels: taking well-wrapped companions for a spin.
[Courtesy of Oxfordshire County Libraries]

temporarily unable to believe him but, as he continued to dwell earnestly upon his sincere concern as a donor that unearned money could do great harm to the weaker-minded recipient, I could not but accept his viewpoint – he should know, being very experienced in both earning and giving! He always monitored with great interest and sometimes sadness, the results from his giving.

As a success story, his extraordinary life must seem close to the ultimate when compared with ordinary human achievement. His attainment of objectives, however, was self-effacing and never aimed at personal financial gain. He was always so deeply absorbed in the practical achievement of whatever he was making at the time, whether it was just one bicycle or a million cars, that wealth came to him almost as a surprise.

One consequence of his individuality was that he worked so much alone, first with his hands at a bench and later by imposing his firm decisions rather than by collaborating with others at a meeting – a trait that caused more than one misfortune. Always courageously relying upon his own judgement he was sometimes too enterprising and, consequently, he did make mistakes, yet still prospered because they were few and affordable. His commercial judgement was acute, but his faith in the unproven ability of others, who were perhaps overstretched by the sudden task allotted to them, was unwise – for example, his attempts to manufacture cars in France and to run a coal mine in Wales – was, it seems, ill-planned for such distant and difficult ventures.

Very few people got to know him at all closely; he became more withdrawn as he advanced in age, public stature, and wealth: fewer still were admitted to his increasingly withdrawn private life. Entertaining visitors at his home was not favoured except upon special occasions. It may be that he inherited this trait from his mother – a contented recluse; a widow who lived alone for the last 18 years of her long life in her small house, refusing her son's offers of companionship or better accommodation. She extremely rarely ventured outside her home with its small garden during all those years.

As a man who never had the slightest interest in wealth as a personal advantage and who never bought yachts, mansions, Rolls-Royces or racehorses, like most other millionaires, his unostentatious lifestyle left him free and without distraction to pursue his chosen objectives, which were often huge in concept and which he alone conceived and acted upon after scant, if any, discussion with others.

He was an ardent patriot, and probably the most appreciated pleasures of his life were the occasions when he was publicly honoured, first in 1917, when he was awarded an OBE, followed by a baronetcy in 1929. In 1934 he was created a Baron to become Lord Nuffield and in 1941 was made a GBE. In 1938 he was again greatly honoured by being raised to be a Viscount. Many academic, civil, colonial, and medical honours were also bestowed upon him. He had it all; but the lifestyle of a wealthy Viscount was not sought by him.

Alone, he had started at his workshop bench; alone for so many years he made weighty decisions in his small office at Cowley; and, finally, as privately as possible he lived quietly in retirement at Nuffield Place.

His fame as *Morris*, who first made cars affordable, so becoming Britain's largest manufacturer, reached its peak when aged about sixty; his new-found fame as *Nuffield*, benefactor extraordinary, began to be greater than his former popularity.

It is known that, when so dispirited by his abortive attempt to found a college of Engineering in Oxford, he saw the wisdom of appointing eminent trustees charged with very specific powers to administer the large charitable trusts to be funded by the rest of his fortune. The Nuffield Foundation and many other Nuffield Trusts, most of which have been reviewed in previous chapters, will have now completed 50 years charitable service under investment skill and trustee care. They are still granting annually financial aid to those chosen causes within the parameters which, as founder, Lord Nuffield had carefully stipulated in each Trust Deed. Beneficiaries, in particular, doubtless appreciate the good work of the past and present trustees.

Many thousands of purchasers of Morris, MG, Wolseley, and Riley cars during Lord Nuffield's lifetime realized that they were thereby contributing to funds which were placed into these trusts by the wise generosity of the man who always saw better uses for his millions than personal grandeur.

Finale

In the Introduction, the question was posed, 'how did it all happen?' Hopefully, the chapters by various informed hands, together, have shown how. I believe they also answer a still more searching question, 'was Lord

Nuffield just the greatest and most effective industrialist of his time, or was his achievement an enduring, perhaps perpetual, one? The answer to be gained from these pages accords with the truly informed verdict of Sir Miles Thomas[3] in giving the first Nuffield Memorial address to the Institution of Production Engineers. Sir Miles concluded his address[4] with the following words:

> . . . it is fitting to pay tribute to one of the greatest figures of our age. Without the spur of his vibrant determination to build up a motor car manufacturing business that would hold off competition from America, France, Italy and any other motor manufacturing countries, this United Kingdom of ours would have been far worse off and we owe him a great debt of gratitude. Not only did his precept and example bring about a situation that protected us from competition but laid a base and a springboard from which we could export our products to all over the world.
>
> I salute my old chief, as do millions of others, with the dedicated respect that a really great man deserves for all time.

On 22 August 1963 a life of inestimable worth ended. Sorrow was expressed, and tribute was paid worldwide.

Her Majesty the Queen sent a telegram from Balmoral reading:

> I am deeply distressed to learn of the death of Lord Nuffield whose many generous benefactions will long be remembered especially in Oxford.
>
> Elizabeth R

Her Majesty Queen Elizabeth the Queen Mother sent a telegram from Buckingham Palace reading:

> I was deeply grieved to learn of the death of Lord Nuffield of whose Foundation and Provincial Trusts I have been most proud to be the Patron. By his generousity and foresight Lord Nuffield has brought benefit to countless people and his contribution to the welfare of our country will always be remembered with gratitude.
>
> Elizabeth R Queen Mother

At the simultaneous Memorial Services on 10 October, 1963, which were held at St Paul's Cathedral in London and at the University Church of St Mary's in Oxford, representatives of Her Majesty the Queen, Her Majesty the Queen Mother, of the Princess Royal and of the Prime Minister, together with many notables in large congregations, attended to pay a last tribute to William Richard Morris, Viscount Nuffield, 10 October 1877 – 23 August 1963.

Notes

1. P.W.S. Andrews and E. Brunner *The Life of Lord Nuffield* (Oxford, 1955), p. 251.
2. M. Thomas, *Out on a Wing. The Autobiography of Sir Miles Thomas* (1963).
3. Later Chairman of various bodies, including the British Overseas Airways Corporation, the British Productivity Council, and Monsanto Chemicals.
4. Given at the Royal Institution, London on 18 November 1964.

Lord Nuffield at the sitting room window, Nuffield Place, 1962.
[Courtesy Oxfordshire County Libraries]

List of
Major Benefactions

Compiled by Dorothy Silberston

Date	Beneficiary	Sum donated
1926	Borstal visitors	£10,000
1926	Chair of Spanish Studies, Oxford University	£70,000
1930	Observatory site, Radcliffe Infirmary, Oxford	£100,000
1932	Maternity Home, Radcliffe Infirmary, Oxford	£40,000
1933	Wingfield-Morris Hospital, Oxford	£31,380
1935	New wards, Radcliffe Infirmary, Oxford	£8,000

Massive increase 1935–43, after Morris Public share offer (aged 58–66, Viscount 1938)

Date	Beneficiary	Sum donated
1935–41	Nuffield Institute of Medical Research, Oxford	£16,000
	Nuffield Fund for research in opthalmology, Oxford	£25,000
	Acland Nursing Home, Oxford	£30,000
	Endowment for Oxford & District Joint Hospitals Board	£300,000
	Horton General Hospital, Banbury, Oxford	£20,000
	Medical School Trust, Oxford	£2,000,000
	Medical School: buildings, Oxford	£200,000
	Medical School Trust: Dominion Scholarship Fund, Oxford	£168,000
	Nuffield College, Oxford	£1,000,000
	Higher Studies Fund, Oxford	£100,000
	Worcester College Endowment Fund, Oxford	£50,000
	Pembroke College Endowment Fund, Oxford	£50,000
	Physical Chemistry Laboratory, Oxford	£100,000
	St Luke's Church, Cowley, Oxford	£36,600
	Nuffield College, Oxford, addition to site	£40,000

cont.

1935–47	National Hospital for Nervous Diseases, London	£29,000
1935–49	Pioneer Health Clinic, Peckham, London	£35,000
1935–37	Nuffield Fund for Cripples	£275,000
1935–45	Nuffield Fund for Orthopaedic Services in Australia New Zealand and South Africa	£321,800
1936	Nuffield Trust for Special Areas	£2,000,000
	Guy's Hospital, London, Nurses' Home, other donations	£94,740
	Albert Dock Hospital, London, fracture clinic	£10,000
	Papworth Village Settlement for disabled, Cambs.	£25,000
1936–47	Queen's Institute of District Nursing	£15,000
1937	Nuffield Benefaction for Employees	£2,125,000
	Great Ormond St. Hospital for Sick Children, London	£50,000
	Princess Elizabeth Orthopaedic Hospital, Exeter	£25,000
	Enham Village Centre for Disabled, Hants.	£10,000
1937	Bishop of Coventry's Church & Hall Appeal	£10,000
	Y.W.C.A. Central Club, Gt. Russell St., London	£50,000
	Kipling Memorial Fund	£25,000
1937-40	Royal Berks. Hospital, Reading, Berks.	£34,000
	Physical Department, Birmingham University	£60,000
	Students Union, London University	£50,000
	Bicentenary Appeal, London University	£10,000
	Elderly Nurses' National Home, Bournmouth	£10,000
	Air League, Cadet Corps	£10,000
	Boy Scouts Fund	£50,000
	Children's Safety First Campaign	£10,000
	Territorial Sports Board	£50,000
1938–44	Iron Lungs for Hospital in UK and Empire	£62,620
1939	Nuffield Trust for the Forces of the Crown	£1,650,000
	King George's Fund for Sailors	£25,000
	Red Cross & St John Organization	£100,000
	Nuffield Provincial Hospitals Trust	£1,200,000
	Institute of Production Engineers Research Fund	£25,000
	2.5 million cigarettes for troops on active duty	£2,500
1940	RAF Benevolent Fund	£250,000
1942–54	Anaesthetising apparatus & vaporizers - given to Service Hospitals (developed in Oxford)	£46,640
1943	Nuffield Foundation	£10,000,000

cont.

It is not possible to disentangle which benfactions were made personally, and which by his Trustees nor to give exact figures. He was Trustee of the Provincial Hospitals and Forces Trusts, and the Nuffield Foundation, not of others. Gifts where he was directly involved include –

1943	Master Mariners' Fund	£43,000
1943–54	Repayments to Special Areas Trust transferred to King Edward's Hospital Fund, London	£1,600,000
1944	Rebuilding, Guy's Hospital, London	£250,000
1944–51	Nuffield Orthopaedic Centre, Oxford	£70,000
	Medical Scholarships at Worcester & Pembroke Colleges, Oxford	£20,000
	Medical Scholarships at 4 Women's Colleges, Oxford	£14,900
	Endowment of 3 Research Fellowships, Lincoln College, Oxford	£50,000
	Nuffield Dept. of Clinical Medicine, Oxford, extensions and equipment	£50,000
1948–51	Residential College, Royal College of Surgeons, London	£250,000
	Faculty of Anaesthetics, Royal College of Surgeons, London	£11,000
1952	Royal Alexandra & Albert Schools, Reigate Surrey	£20,000
1955	Royal College of Obstetricians & Gynaecologists, towards new buildings	£125,000
1956	Endowment of Chair of Dental Research, Faculty of Dental Surgery, Royal College of Surgeons, London	£100,000
1960	Jodrell Bank telescope (other money from Nuffield Foundation)	£25,000

Total Donations   **£25,770,180**

1943–1990 Since 1943 the Nuffield Foundation alone has given
      away more than –   **£52,000,000**

Index